THE AWFUL KILLING
OF SARAH WATTS

THE AWFUL KILLING

OF SARAH WATTS

A STORY OF CONFESSIONS, ACQUITTALS AND JAILBREAKS

MICK DAVIS
&
DAVID LASSMAN

PEN & SWORD
TRUE CRIME

First published in Great Britain in 2018 by
Pen & Sword True Crime
an imprint of
Pen & Sword Books Ltd
47 Church Street
Barnsley
South Yorkshire
S70 2AS

ISBN 978 1 52670 730 7

A CIP catalogue record for this book is
available from the British Library.

Printed and bound in England by TJ International Ltd, Padstow,
Cornwall

Pen & Sword Books Ltd incorporates the Imprints of Pen & Sword
Archaeology, Atlas, Aviation, Battleground, Discovery,
Family History, History, Maritime, Military, Naval, Politics,
Railways, Select, Transport, True Crime, Fiction, Frontline Books,
Leo Cooper, Praetorian Press, Seaforth Publishing, Wharncliffe and
White Owl.

For a complete list of Pen & Sword titles please contact
PEN & SWORD BOOKS LIMITED
47 Church Street, Barnsley, South Yorkshire, S70 2AS, England
E-mail: enquiries@pen-and-sword.co.uk
Website: www.pen and sword.co.uk

*To our respective wives, Lorraine and Claire, for all their
support during the research and writing of this book.*

Contents

Acknowledgements

The authors would like to thank the following: Brian Marshall of the Frome Museum for all his help in the initial stages (and who turned out to be a distant relative of the victim, Sarah Watts); Lyndon Thomas, also a descendant of the Watts family, for all his initial research and encouragement, as well as writing the introduction and reading the manuscript in draft form; Helen Leadbeater for reading the manuscript in draft form and her comments; Elaine Callaghan, a descendent of the Maggs family for her help with that family via the Ancestry website; Colin Perry for his prodigious work tracing the Hurd family history; Dr David Robinson for his help and support regarding the research of Detective Sergeant Henry Smith and the Metropolitan Detective Branch, and C. John Cotton of the Historic Shipping website for his help and knowledge on all things nautical; The staff at Frome Library for all their help; Frome Society for Local Studies; and finally, Frome Community Education for running the Local History course which facilitated the meeting of the two authors and gave the impetus for this collaboration.

Foreword

Many years ago I was tracing my family tree, looking at the Watts family from Frome. I kept coming across the story of Sarah Watts, the subject of this book, but dismissed it as not being part of my ancestry. It seemed to me that if she were related, I would have heard about it. But it was a story that wouldn't go away, and eventually I discovered that Sarah was the sister of my great, great grandfather. The more I read about Sarah, the more I wanted to make sure that she was somehow remembered. So I wrote up my research and deposited a copy with Frome Library.

I am absolutely delighted that Mick Davis and David Lassman decided to do the job properly. They have added immeasurably to my account. They have put the flesh on all the characters involved and brought them back to life in a way that I didn't know was possible. They have managed to research and organise a mass of historical detail so that a very complex story with lots of different threads results in a 'whodunit' which still fascinates today.

Lyndon Thomas
May 2017

Introduction

The murder of Sarah Watts at Battle Farm, West Woodlands, in September 1851, was originally going to be just one article in an anthology of crime and murder within Frome and the surrounding areas, but it quickly became apparent that this story warranted a whole book to itself.

The brutality of the crime itself, along with the national interest in it, certainly brought it into the league of the Francis Saville Kent murder, only a few miles away at Road, nine years later. It also involved an investigation by a member of the Metropolitan's Detective Branch – a colleague of Inspector Jack Whicher who would be sent down to investigate the Road Hill House murder – along with several other similarities, but there was so much more that is unique to this case.

Many of the characters involved in this story could almost warrant books of their own, and the town itself is of an extraordinary character; one not given to idle boasts, yet can claim numerous feats and achievements belying its meagre population. For example, at one time, due to the textile industry that flourished in the town, it was 'bigger than Bath' in terms of wealth and prestige, and it has more listed buildings than anywhere else in Somerset, including Bath.

The main source material relating to this story comes from the transcripts of the inquests, magisterial proceedings, Quarter Sessions and assizes courts. Although it seems the originals of all these no longer survive, due to the huge amount of interest there was in the case – locally and nationally – proceedings were widely reported in the press. Each newspaper would publish slightly different versions – although the main facts would be the same – dependent on the individual traits of the court reporter or publication involved. What the authors have done is to take all this reportage and combined it into what is probably the fullest and most accurate account there is likely to be without the original transcripts to work from.

As for the evidence itself, as given by witnesses during all these proceedings, there is naturally a lot of overlap between the testimonies given before the local magistrates and later, before the circulating judges at the assize courts, but there are enough differences in several cases to make each of value and warrant their inclusion. And, of course, not all witnesses gave evidence in both courts, while some accounts were more detailed than others, along with changes in emphasis or added detail. Grammar and punctuation have been rationalised in some cases to make the proceedings easier to understand and the names of witnesses, places and events have been corrected – using the 1851 census returns – where conflicts have arisen between accounts.

The court reporters often gave a list of replies to questions without printing the questions themselves, which saved space but made some accounts rather stilted; again, punctuation and grammar has been changed to make some passages more comprehensible, along with the addition, in several instances, of the supposed question. That said, pains have been taken to keep the transcripts as close to the originals as possible, and key facts of the case have been reproduced verbatim.

For those coming to the case for the first time, we do not want to give too much of the story away, suffice to say that at the end of the book we outline our beliefs regarding the resolution of this most intriguing crime. For now, despite the awfulness of the killing of Sarah Watts, the innocent 14-year-old girl at the centre of this story, we hope you will find this case as fascinating as we did (and still do) and that it will stay with you for a long time after the final page of this book has been read.

Mick Davis & David Lassman
March 2017

PART ONE

(24 September 1851 – 6 October 1851)

The Murder

On Wednesday 24 September 1851, a little before 9 o'clock in the morning, Leah Watts left her home in West Woodlands and began the three-mile walk towards the nearby town of Frome. It was market day and she was going to sell cheese produced on the farm where she lived with her husband and youngest daughter. She would spend all day at the market and by the time she walked back home it would be around four in the afternoon. On her return, she would discover her life changed forever.

Leah Watts had been born Leah Lydbury, fifty-three years earlier, in the village of Nunney, which lay three miles north-west of Frome. She was still in her teens when she fell pregnant, but by the time she gave birth in June 1817, the father of the baby had done the respectable thing and married her; the ceremony took place at All Saint's Church in her home village. Seven further children were to follow over the next twenty years, although the fourth – a boy named Thomas – died when only 2 years old. The rest of the children had reached adulthood and left the family home; all except the youngest, Sarah, who had turned 14 earlier that year.

A few minutes after Leah had left the farm, her husband John also set out for the market. He had been born in the Wiltshire village of Corsley, in September 1789, to David and Elizabeth Watts. At the time Corsley was in the grip of expansion, in terms of industry and population; with the latter standing at between 1,500 and 2,000 people at its height. If the Watts family had stayed where they were, John may never have met his future wife, but in 1802, when he was 13, his father was appointed pastor of Trudoxhill Congregational Chapel and the family moved across the border to neighbouring Somerset. David Watts remained in his position at the small hamlet of Trudoxhill for the next twenty years. By the time of his death, in 1822, John had met and married Leah Lydbury and the couple had given him two grandchildren – the first of which they named David – with a third on the way.

The early years of John and Leah's marriage had seen the couple living at Trudoxhill, but between the birth and death of their fourth child, 1824 and 1827 respectively, they moved to nearby Marston Gate. Rural life in the 1820s and 1830s was tough for agricultural labourers like John, especially bringing up a family; the men who worked on the land saw their jobs and skills increasingly supplanted by the new machinery that heralded the great industrial revolution. This led to the period known as the 'hungry forties', although, near decade's end, the Watts' fortunes seemingly changed when Leah inherited a substantial amount of money from her recently deceased half-sister, Martha.

Martha Lydbury was married to Henry 'Harry' Cornish, a farmer at Hassage Hill in Wellow; when he died in 1845 she inherited his estate. Two years later, in 1847, Martha also died and in her will the sum of £50 was bequeathed to Leah. With this money, the family could move from their rented cottage at Marston Gate to nearby West Woodlands and a small farm owned by the Battle family; where they took on the tenancy of the farm that was now their home.

Battle Farm was an eighteen-acre dairy farmstead located near the junction of two roads. The main one was the turnpike road that linked Frome with the village of Maiden Bradley and in fact one of the toll houses that served it – Weighbridge Cottage – was a mere stone's throw from the front door of the Watts' farm. The other, a smaller highway running north-west from the first, made its way over a small bridge and on between fields and pastures, towards the tiny hamlet of Tytherington. Beyond this, it eventually joined the main route that linked Nunney and Marston Gate. The Watts kept a small herd of cows on their farm and during the spring and summer months, cheese would be made from the animals' milk for the family's consumption. If any excess was produced, it would be taken to the market to be sold.

After John Watts had left the farm on that Wednesday morning it was not long before he caught up with his wife and they walked the remainder of the route into Frome together. This was one of the rare occurrences when they were both attending the market, as it was usually Leah who went, with her husband undertaking the excursion only occasionally. They reached the outskirts of the town and descended a steep gradient known as Culver Hill, located within an area known as Lower Keyford; once a separate settlement from Frome, but more recently amalgamated with its larger neighbour. Here was the Woolpack Inn and as the couple went by, they passed a small group of men, standing opposite the hostelry, observing the activities and movements of those around them.

The route into the town centre was busy with farmers, many in aggregated groups, driving their livestock along the outlying roads and lanes, then down the wide, sweeping thoroughfare of Bath Street – the main route into the town from the south – and on into

et place. There had been a market in Frome since before
nsday book, with this regular Wednesday one having been
a royal charter towards the end of the fifteenth century.

Halfway down Bath Street, near the entrance to the church of
St John the Baptist, the Watts stopped. Outside the entrance to the
church grounds was a stone screen or gateway, a roofed structure
marking the entrance, where various tables with straw on them had
been set up. It was from one of these that the couple would aim to
sell their wares. The church, in whose shadow they stood, was said
to have been erected on the remains of an original Saxon one.

Despite the Watts' change in circumstances, farming was still
a hard life and everyone, including young Sarah left back at the
farm, had to pull their weight. Today was no different and before
John had left, he reminded his daughter of several things he wanted
completed by his return. After saying goodbye, he had walked out
of the front door and began his journey to market. It would be the
last time he would see her alive.

Sarah Watts was born on the 2 May 1837, a little over a month
before Queen Victoria ascended the throne. With both her parents
at market and being in sole charge at home, there was a lengthy list
of chores to be done throughout the day. She kept her own company, except for the family dog, and didn't really have any friends
– her father would later recall – only those made during the time
she was at school. Sarah had left there two summers previously,
when the family had moved to the farm, and she had been helping
her parents full time ever since. It was laborious work, especially
for someone so small for their age, but she did not complain. She
worked diligently throughout the morning but as it was nearing
1 o'clock, she began to feel hungry. She would finish one more
chore and then prepare her lunch. As Sarah made her way from
the pigsty towards a dung hill, she thought she saw someone out of
the corner of her eye on the road, about 30ft away. It looked like
Alfred Allard, a neighbouring boy of about her own age who lived
on nearby Tuckmarsh farm, but she could not be sure and so she
did not wave.

By 3 o'clock in the afternoon the Frome market was all but finished and many of the farmers and stall holders, depleted of their
livestock and produce, were partaking of a post-market drink in
one of the many hostelries in the town. John and Leah Watts had
neither time nor money for such indulgence and began the journey
back to their farm. John arrived home first, a few minutes ahead of
his wife, and on entering the farmhouse called out in his normal
manner: 'We're home'. He then sat down, opposite the fireplace,
ready to change his boots. He shouted to Sarah to bring his other

pair to him, but there was no answer. He called again but there was still no reply.

The farmhouse was quiet throughout, except for what John perceived to be the sound of their dog making a lapping noise. He stood up and went through into the adjacent dairy room, where he saw that some spilt whey was the object of the animal's attention. He then saw a sight which would live with him for the remainder of his life. There, on the floor in front of him, was the lifeless body of his daughter, Sarah. As he came closer he could see there was blood on her face, her lips had turned purple and her clothes were torn. His first impression was that she had had a fit. He bent over and instinctively adjusted and straightened her clothing. Her skin was cold to the touch. He then stood up and in somewhat of a daze, went to summon help. On reaching the front door he met his wife, who by now had also arrived back. 'The poor maid is dead,' he told her, and then went off towards the direction of Weighbridge Cottage – the toll house – around 70yds away, down the road, to find Mrs Court who lived there.

As her husband went to get assistance, Leah Watts entered the farmhouse. She took her shawl and laid it on the kitchen table, next to an old silk handkerchief, and went through to the dairy room. She stared at the body of her lifeless daughter in disbelief and then, in shock, she began to call out: 'She's dead, she's dead.' On hearing these distressed cries, neighbours from the surrounding farms came running and by the time John Watts returned home, accompanied by Mrs Court, a throng of people were gathered in the farmhouse.

Although devastated at his daughter's untimely death, John Watts knew there was work on the farm which still had to be completed. So, while the neighbours comforted his wife and busied themselves inside the farmhouse, he went outside to attend to the herd of cattle and lead them to pasture. He knew this time of day saw the highest sugar content in the grass and was therefore the optimum period for grazing; which in turn would produce superior milk and ultimately cheese. At this point, any thoughts of murder, regarding his daughter's death, were far from his mind.

While John was outside tending to the cows, Sarah's stiff, lifeless little body was taken upstairs by several of the gathered neighbours and laid out on her bed. At the same time, tea had been made for the devastated mother and on her husband's return some was also made for him. It was now, however, that the suspicion that their youngest child had not met a natural end was aroused. It was realised that several items – bread, cheese, and butter – were missing. On going upstairs, it was discovered that a black frock coat, a similarly coloured cloth waistcoat, and a shawl were also gone, along with a handkerchief and pair of gloves.

With this altered perspective the Watts could now see that drawers had been hurriedly opened in their room and Sarah's. Elsewhere in the house, a cupboard had been ransacked and an old teapot inside it had been emptied of its contents; a pile of old bills, put there by John Watts, now lay scattered about the floor. Also in the cupboard, six silver spoons and a pair of sugar tongs, all wrapped in paper, had, for some reason been removed, examined, and then returned to their place. Everything now seemed to point to their daughter having disturbed a burglar, who had then killed her. With this revelation, it was obvious that the authorities needed to be informed with the utmost urgency.

A grief-stricken John Watts set out for Frome for the second time that day, a little over an hour since he had discovered his daughter's body. He retraced his steps to the outskirts of the town and down Culver Hill, then up the other side into the parish of Keyford and on into Frome proper. His destination was the house of Francis Giles, situated on Christchurch Street West in an area known as 'Behind Town', which the local GP shared with a younger brother and female servant. As soon as the 31-year-old surgeon was told of what had happened, he got himself ready to make his way out to West Woodlands.

Meanwhile, John Watts headed back along the route he had just walked, as far as a grocery shop situated along Keyford Street. The shop stood next to The Crown public house and was owned by Richard Grist, who was also one of the town's petty constables. He was informed of what had happened and after hearing the gruesome news, Constable Grist set off to organise a colleague to go to Battle Farm, as swiftly as possible.

With the matter in the hands of the law, John Watts left the shop to make his way back home. As he came out he noticed a man standing outside The Crown. The stranger asked the reason for the visit to Constable Grist's shop. When told, the man gave his condolences and offered to buy the bereaved father a drink. John accepted and the two men walked together, in silence, back towards West Woodlands, but only as far as the Woolpack Inn on Culver Hill, the hostelry John and his wife had passed that morning. After entering the public house, John Watts drank the beer bought for him and returned home, not reaching the farm until after dark.

While John Watts was in the Woolpack Inn being consoled, the local constable tasked with investigating the crime, James Hoddinott, had made his way out to Battle Farm. As soon as he arrived, his attention focused on some blood on the kitchen floor and a silk handkerchief on the nearby table. When he discovered that the latter belonged to nobody presently in the house, or anyone who had been there in the aftermath of the body being found, he took possession of it as possible evidence. Constable Hoddinott then went into the dairy room and saw a 'spot of blood' on the floor, as he would later record, and a bloodied mark on the wall. It also appeared that part of the whey in the trendle had been thrown on the floor and there was blood underneath the stool upon which it stood. The body had been cold when found, or so he was informed, which indicated that the girl had been dead for a while before her parents' return. Hoddinott remained at the farm most of the evening, carrying out his investigation, and was still there when John Watts returned at around 9 o'clock.

The surgeon, Francis Giles, had reached Battle Farm around 7.30. On his arrival, he went straight upstairs to Sarah's body and began his initial examination. Although in her early teens, the body in front of him on the bed was that of a pre-pubescent girl. There was bruising on her forehead and her face was swollen. Along with this, he noted several scratches on her neck, all on the left side. It was then that he made the dreadful discovery that would bring a whole new level of depravity to the crime. Having examined her genital area, Francis Giles realised Sarah Watts had been raped before being killed. The poor creature had been subjected, if the bruised, battered, and bloodied body was any indication, to one of the most sustained, horrendous, and barbaric ordeals he had ever been called upon to examine in his career as a medical surgeon.

Meanwhile, unaware of the full and awful details of the case, people at the farmhouse and immediate vicinity, along with those in surrounding areas who had by now heard the news, were beginning to speculate as to how the murder might have been committed. As the exact circumstances of what had transpired at Battle Farm on that market-day Wednesday become known though, the whole population began to speculate about who could have perpetrated such a horrific and heinous crime on such an innocent and waif-like girl?

2

The Day After

By mid-morning on Thursday 25 September 1851, Frome and its environs were awash with the news of the Sarah Watts killing. As meagre facts mingled with hearsay, rumours and third-hand accounts, one thing became clear. The brutality of the crime – the rape and cold-blooded murder of an innocent 14-year-old girl – had shocked even the most hardened of locals; people to whom violence and death was an accepted aspect of their grim everyday lives.

From its very beginnings, Frome began to acquire a reputation for lawlessness and criminality. Indeed, it was said the reason St Aldhelm had founded the Church of St John the Baptist near the end of the seventh century, bringing the town into existence, was to 'civilise' the bands of outlaws and criminals who lived within the surrounding Selwood Forest. Although this worked to a certain degree and the settlement prospered throughout the next centuries as an important textile centre, belligerent and subversive undercurrents remained, erupting sporadically in rioting, killings, and other nefarious acts of hostility, usually committed by, and amongst, members of society's lower levels.

However, it was not just the under classes who were the victims of violent disturbance or death. In 1476, for example, Ankarette Twynhyo – lady-in-waiting to the Duchess of Clarence and a prime suspect in her fatal poisoning – was forcibly abducted from her home in Lower Keyford and taken to Warwick Castle, where she was unceremoniously tried and sent to the gallows, still protesting her innocence. Two centuries later, Thomas Thynne of Longleat and Member of Parliament for neighbouring county of Wiltshire was assassinated while riding in a carriage in London, and a riot that lasted for three days in 1832, during the election of Frome's first MP, saw the death of at least one political supporter. The successful Whig candidate, Thomas Sheppard, along with 300 of his followers, had to take refuge inside Fromefield House from an angry mob made up of opposition factions, who laid siege and were only dispersed by the arrival of the militia – a Troop of the Seventh Dragoons – deployed from nearby Trowbridge.

As for violent crimes on children, such as that perpetrated on Sarah Watts, these were rare within the county, but not unheard of.

In 1823, for example, 13-year-old Betty Trump had been 'cruelly murdered', as the newspapers reported it, on her way back home to Buckland St Mary, near Chard; her killer was never found. The year before that, 9-year-old pauper child William Bartlett, apprenticed to a chimney sweep in Bridgewater, had suffered appalling and relentlessly cruel treatment at the hands of his master and mistress. When the case came to court after the death of the unfortunate boy, accounts of whipping by an assortment of particularly brutal instruments, violent naked beatings, and regular starvation, were told in front of an increasingly disgusted public gallery. Perhaps the greatest crime of the entire episode, however, was the fact that the perpetrators were found not guilty. Only the year before, in 1850, 17-year-old Thomas George had been found with his throat cut in a barn at nearby Nunney. Although a detective had been sent down from London to investigate and a local man had stood trial, he was acquitted and once again, the perpetrator was never caught.

Much of the day-to-day violence that existed in Frome could be blamed, in part, on the economic hardship created by the decline of the town's woollen industry. From its heyday in the late seventeenth and early eighteenth centuries, when Daniel Defoe claimed it to be more prosperous than Bath and that 'if their Trade continues to increase for a few more years more, as it has done for those past, it is very likely to be one of the greatest and wealthiest inland towns in England,' it had sunk to such a point that a century later, William Cobbett, on one of his famous rural rides, observed that 'these poor creatures at Frome, have pawned all their … best clothes, their blankets and sheets, their looms; any little piece of furniture that they had'. As to the woollen industry itself, he wrote that though this 'sort of manufacture … cannot come to a complete end; still it has received a blow from which it cannot possibly recover'.

Throughout the rest of the nineteenth century, with the apathy of the town's clothiers towards mechanisation, while at the same time the northern towns embraced the new technology, Frome, along with the other main textile centres in the region, found an acceleration of this decline and the town was soon filled with the unemployed from various related occupations that the woollen industry could no longer support. In 1843, eight years earlier, Frome's population was estimated to be 11,600, with around half of these men, women and children capable of work. But of this figure, only a third were in partial employment and only a mere three per cent (equating to 172 people) had full-time work. Further evidence of this seemingly irreversible process had appeared in the *Bristol Mercury* the previous year. Reporting on a meeting of woollen manufacturers in the Gloucestershire, Somersetshire and Wiltshire areas, which had taken place at the White Hart Hotel in Bath, the newspaper reproduced a series of bleak statistics put forward by Mr Wood, a representative from Frome:

> One-sixth of the houses were now uninhabited,' Wood stated, 'while out of a total of 28 woollen mills stretching along the river Frome (the main source of power) only 15 were now employed, and even then not fully, five are void, three were being used as corn-mills and the remaining five were only half-employed. Almost fifty per cent of the broad and narrow looms in the town were now unemployed, while manufacturers had decreased their productively and quantity in the same period from 50 manufacturers making 300 pieces a week, to 14 making 150 pieces per week. Perhaps not surprisingly pawnbrokers were flourishing, while other trades were depressed.

The discouraging piece ended with the proclamation that there were neighbourhood villages which had once been in a prosperous state, but were no longer producing 'even one piece of cloth per week'.

It wasn't just urban areas feeling the effects of the industrial revolution. The countryside was being transformed and revolutionised by the mechanisation of agriculture and the rural way of life that farmers, their workers and respective families had known for centuries, was almost obliterated in decades. But despite the occasional violent uprisings and the irregular smashing of machinery, the mechanised onslaught was merciless, and year upon year the number of unemployed, both in the towns and the countryside, rose exponentially.

To counteract this unprecedented rise in joblessness and poverty, Poor Laws were introduced and organisations to help the needy sprang up everywhere. Many local people, however, decided against turning to the workhouse for survival and began to take matters into their own hands – crime. Stealing the foodstuffs and other items required to feed and clothe themselves and their families, or more violent acts, such as mugging or murder, to obtain the money to pay for the bare necessities. Of course, thieves, robbers and cutthroats had always existed in the area, as elsewhere. It was said that during the early part of the eighteenth century, groups of men carrying long poles with iron crooks at the end, would roam the streets of Frome at night, tripping up passers-by to rob them. And in case there was any resistance, these thieves often took with them large mastiff dogs, who would be set upon the victims.

The desperation which now pervaded large areas of Frome exacerbated this problem and so the newspapers became full of reports of petty crime, as well as expressions of frustration and agitation; drunkenness, rioting and vandalism.

On this Thursday morning in late September 1851 though, the town's focus was entirely on the murder out at West Woodlands and the search to find the culprit. At Battle Farm itself, the Chief Constable, his subordinates and several magistrates, were already trying to establish fact from fabrication. As one of the Watts' relatives would later recall, regarding the scene at the farmhouse:

> *I was there all day* [and] *went away at 11 at night; I was in the milk-house sometimes, but not staying there; some magistrates were there, and constables, with neighbours; I knew most of them, but perhaps not all … some went up and saw the body, and then went out … those who were allowed to go upstairs were persons connected with the family.*

Among the constables gathered at the farm was James Hoddinott, who had been the first to visit the crime scene, and Edward Newport, who owned an ironmonger's shop in the town centre. As the former had not reached the farm the previous evening until 6.30, his investigation had been hampered by impending darkness. In the morning light, however, things became clearer in many ways. The night before he had noticed a mark of blood on the milk house wall, but now in daylight he could see there were several more as well. Hoddinott also noticed blood in the whey tub, which he mentioned to his fellow constable, as well as more blood underneath the trendle that stood on a stool and was half-full with whey.

As observant as the constables were, however, the question in the mind of many locals, and perhaps uttered openly in the shops and public houses in the town and surrounding areas, was whether the law officers were up to the task of apprehending the perpetrator. It was not a criticism of the individual constables concerned, but just that the system of policing they were subject to, and which Frome maintained, along with the rest of the county, was still based on the parochial one: the centuries old tradition which saw its chief constables elected to their posts once a year at the Court Leet. This was the manorial court held by the lord of the manor for his tenants, which dealt with aspects of petty law and order and the administration of communal agriculture. In Frome this was under the manorship of the Earl of Cork and Orrery, who at that time was Edmund Boyle, whose family holdings in the area included Marston House, in nearby Marston Bigot. To assist the chief constables, there were also tithing men – or petty constables – providing voluntary, part-time assistance as and when required. In Frome, there were three of them: one for the centre and one apiece for the parishes of East and West Woodlands.

By the mid-nineteenth century, however, many in authority had come to think of these petty or parish constables as being 'unpaid, untrained and unwilling to undertake any protracted investigation' and so, for the past twenty or so years, as in the textile and agricultural industries, there had been a revolution taking place within the policing of communities and law enforcement in general. Against an historical backdrop of suspicion and resistance towards an organised police force, the government had managed to pass the Metropolitan Police Act of 1829, paving the way for the Home Secretary, Robert Peel, to introduce a Metropolitan Police Force into London. This saw parish constables replaced by more than a thousand officers on the capital's streets, patrolling a seven-mile radius around Charing Cross to 'prevent crime and pursue offenders'.

The successes enjoyed by the Metropolitan Police Force gave rise a decade later, in 1839, to the County Police Act, which allowed counties to create their own local constabularies. Wiltshire embraced this new act wholeheartedly and became the first county nationwide to establish its own force. An advertisement placed in the *Wiltshire Gazette*, in December 1839, for recruits to this new force attracted men by the droves and by the following March, twelve superintendents and 170 men (forty deployed in towns, 120 in rural areas) were in place to fight crime. The results were swift and in the first three months, numerous crimes and incidents were reported. These included a highway robbery, five burglaries, nine cattle thefts, twenty-four assaults, thirty-five drunk and disorderly, fifty-nine felonies and sixty misdemeanours.

Across the county border, in Somerset, magistrates seemed as apathetic in embracing the new realities of the situation as the clothiers, and doggedly continued to appoint their chief constables and petty constables each autumn – usually around October – in the way it had been done for centuries. Even when they had a chance to reform, rather than replace, their system through the introduction of the Parish Constables Act of 1842 – enabling the appointment of paid parish constables, or the 1850 amendment to it – they chose to ignore it and carried on regardless. But now they would have to do so in the full spotlight of the newspapers, whose reporters descended on the town. Although Frome did not have any publications of its own at the time, the brutal murder had attracted the interest of regional and national newspapers, including *The Times*. A day after the murder and many were already drafting up sensational headlines in their rush to get their own version of the story into print. Several would report incorrect or contradictory facts, but the overall fact remained the same: that of a horrific and barbaric murder in the small market town of Frome.

At this stage, the newspapers could only report versions of what those at Battle Farm had discovered and so far there was no indication as to the perpetrator. With the parents of the victim having been at the market all day, it was left to neighbours to provide statements to the investigating constables, and quotes to the reporters, but it soon became clear that no one in the vicinity had witnessed anything suspicious.

So the day ended, as it had begun, with the knowledge that a horrendous crime had been committed but no clue as to who had carried it out. It was hoped that when the inquest was held the following day and the post-mortem performed, answers would be forthcoming and an indication of the murderer's identity revealed. Until then, however, it was a waiting game.

3

The Inquest

The inquest into the murder of Sarah Watts opened on Friday 26 September 1851 at The George Inn, West Woodlands. This impressive seventeenth-century building was situated on the Frome to Maiden Bradley road, a little further along towards the village side from Weybridge Cottage and Battle Farm, but still in view of both. The George was also where the annual Court of Leet was held.

The use of such places as the George Inn for inquests was a common practice. Within many communities, especially rural ones like West Woodlands, inns or public houses were often the only readily available, large indoor spaces where such proceedings could take place. The establishments were also likely to have a sizeable table big enough to hold a body for viewing by the jury and for a post-mortem to be performed. The proceedings would normally be held upstairs or in a back room, sometimes with their own entrances so that the coroner and others in attendance did not need to pass through the public areas.

This arrangement was more than acceptable to the landlords of these places. They would earn extra money not only by hiring out the room but, dependent on the nature of the crime, would enjoy increased custom during breaks in the proceedings, with witnesses, jurors, reporters and magisterial professionals no doubt quenching their thirst, along with inquisitive locals trying to slake their curiosity. It can be assumed though, it was not always the most congenial surroundings, as the sounds of conviviality and the smell of alcohol and tobacco smoke would surely percolate through to where the inquest was taking place.

The George Inn also had a tragic history attached to it. Thirteen years earlier the landlord's wife had 'died of fright'. According to a newspaper report at the time:

> a quarrel took place between some persons at the George Inn, Frome Woodlands; and on the landlord interfering to restore order, his wife became so exceedingly frightened that she expired in a fit. The deceased has left five children, the youngest being only five weeks old. An inquest has since been held and a verdict returned, "Died from a shock given to the nervous system occasioned by fear".

West Woodlands and its neighbouring parish, East Woodlands, had a long history of lawlessness and disturbance and for centuries had attracted less salubrious inhabitants seeking refuge from the law within its densely forested interior. The woodlands belonged to the Longleat Estate and had done so since the mid-sixteenth century. Longleat House was the seat of the Thynne family – the head of which held the title of Lord Bath. The estate bordered the eastern side of the woodlands and many of the houses and farms within the twin hamlets had been purpose built for its workers and tenant farmers, during the eighteenth century. The owner of Longleat was also responsible for the erection of St Katherine's Church, in East Woodlands. It was built partly to benefit the god-fearing, law-abiding parishioners, who had previously to journey into the centre of Frome and St John the Baptist's Church to attend services, but also, like St Aldhelm previously, as an attempt to 'civilise' the less law-abiding folk of the region.

One notorious haunt for robbers and villains was an area called Dog Street that ran along the southern edge of East Woodlands, while certain remote backwaters elsewhere became known as workshops of the counterfeiter; either coining false money called Woodland Groats (one coin was equal to four pennies) or for paring, or clipping, genuine coinage of the realm. This illegal trade suffered a major blow towards the end of the seventeenth century when a detachment of soldiers, quartered at Frome, were ordered to enter the forest and attack the main counterfeiting gang. A major clash ensued, with the result that one 'coiner' was killed and the rest taken off for execution. Nevertheless, the practice carried on, albeit to a lesser degree, and in 1714, the year that St Katherine's was completed, Nicholas Andrews of Frome, along with two accomplices from Wiltshire, were hanged 'for counterfeiting Her Majesties Coyne.' Despite its disreputable history though, there were law-abiding communities in the woodlands and the murder on their doorstep of a 14-year-old girl was a huge shock. It was hoped that the inquest would now bring about a swift resolution to the crime.

Although similar to a criminal trial, inquests were held by a coroner, rather than a magistrate and in this case it was the coroner for East Somerset, Daniel Ashford, who oversaw proceedings. Ashford had travelled over from nearby Shepton Mallet, where the 42-year-old had a legal practice. He was relatively new to the coroner's role, having taken over the position from his father around twelve months earlier.

If the deceased's corpse was to be viewed by the jury, as in cases of murder, inquests were held as soon as possible after the crime had been committed, due mainly to the primitive techniques of storage and preservation of the time. The jury, who would view the body and deliberate on the circumstances of the death, consisted of twelve 'able and sufficient men', chosen from twenty-four who had received a warrant to attend. Unlike a criminal trial, however, the jurors had the right to ask questions.

The inquest opened and once the cheerless duty of viewing Sarah's body had been carried out, the initial witness was called. This was the father of the deceased. When John Watts took the stand it was possible his daughter's body was still in the room. He was sworn in and began his testimony:

> I live in the parish of Frome. On Wednesday morning last, a little after 9 o'clock, I left to go to Frome; my wife went with me; I left my daughter at home in charge of the house. I returned home about 4 o'clock the same afternoon. I went into the kitchen, and pulled off my gaiters, and I called Sarah; I observed some blood before me on the ground in the kitchen. My little dog ran into the milk-house, and was lapping. I went in to see what he had got, and I saw the deceased lying on the floor, her clothes turned right up over her head. I uncovered her face, and found that she was dead, and ran out of doors and met my wife coming in, and said to my wife, "the poor maid is dead." This was about ten minutes after I returned, and I told my wife the child was dead (meaning the deceased). I went to the turnpike gate to call the gatekeeper's wife, Mrs Court, to come down, for the little maid was dead. The child was 15 years old [sic]. I left no money in the house. I missed a coat and waistcoat from the house, and some cheese, about one pound and a half. I missed the cheese from the pantry inside the milk-house, and the coat, waistcoat, and shawl from a chest in my bedroom; the chest was not locked. There was an old silk figured handkerchief on the table in the kitchen, the same now produced by James Hoddinott; it has two initials in it (E.T.) in the corner. I cannot say whether the door of the house was open or shut when I first entered. I was so frightened. There is only that door to the house, and the party going in must have gone in at that door (the front door). In the coat stolen there was a blue cotton light spotted handkerchief, and a pair of man's size gloves.

John Watts stood down, emotionally shattered at recounting the tragic events of two days before. His place on the witness stand was taken by a youth, Alfred Allard, who lived on a neighbouring farm, and on the day of the murder had been working nearby.

He was probably the last person to see Sarah alive – apart from the murderer.

> *I am almost 13. I live near here. I knew Sarah Watts. On Wednesday last, I was going up with my master's dinner; this was nearly one o'clock. As I passed John Watts' farm, I saw the deceased going from the pig-sty to the muckton; she was about 50 yards from where I was standing. I saw no one near the house.*

Alfred then took his place alongside John Watts, as Francis Giles, the surgeon who examined Sarah on the evening she was murdered, replaced him.

> *I was sent for on Wednesday afternoon, about half-past six, to examine the body of the deceased. I arrived at the house at half-past seven. The body was laid out on the bed upstairs. I saw several bruises on different parts of the body; the principal one was on the right side of the temple, about the size of a half-crown; the bone felt as if it was depressed. On the right side of the face generally were more livid marks than the left; there was a streak of blood extending from the left corner of the mouth to about two inches in length; there were three horizontal scratches on the left side of the neck; there were three bruises on each elbow, just at the point; there was a slight bruise on the back part of the right arm below the elbow; there was a bruise on the outer side of the right knee, and another on the point of the left knee, near the cap. I saw nath [semen] on the private parts, to convince me that felony had been committed; she had not arrived at puberty; this felony had been committed before the circulation had ceased. The deceased must have been dead for some time before I saw her.*

The coroner then asked Giles if he could state the cause of death. The surgeon replied he was unable, at that time, to give a precise cause, as he could not be certain whether it arose from the blows to the head or through strangulation. From the external appearance of the body he suspected the latter, but would not be able to say for sure until he carried out a post-mortem. The inquest was then adjourned until the following Tuesday, to enable him to carry one out.

Although this seemed straightforward, a lesson had been begrudgingly learnt from the year before. During the inquest of Thomas George, who was murdered in Nunney by having his throat cut, the coroner, Daniel Ashford, had hesitated in authorising a post-mortem. This was due to the expense and his uncertainty of being able to reclaim the money back from the local magistrates. By the time a proper examination had finally been carried out by the local medical officer, with help from Francis Giles, valuable evidence had been 'lost' and so when a suspect stood trial, there had not been enough evidence to convict him and he was released. This time the coroner was not taking any chances, especially as the murder had already become so publicly known and a large reward offered – as soon as news of the outrageous crime had reached the seat of government, a £50 reward had been offered for information leading to the culprit being brought to justice. There was also a free pardon, if the informant turned out to be an accomplice to the actual perpetrator.

Now that the initial inquest was out of the way, newspapers carrying the story of the rape and murder soon hit regional and national streets, with sensational headlines and, at times, less than accurate reporting or telling of the truth.

The *Bath and Cheltenham Gazette* described it as 'one of the most atrocious murders that ever disgraced the annals of crime', while *The Times* said:

> *MURDER AT FROME – A shocking murder, accompanied with circumstances of most brutal atrocity, was committed on Thursday at West Woodlands, Frome, on a young girl only 15 years of age. The name of the victim is Sarah Watts, and at the time of the murder there was no one in the house but herself, she having been left in charge of it by her parents. From the appearances presented by the body there can be little doubt that the murderer first committed a capital felony upon her and subsequently destroyed life by striking her with a stick or some heavy blunt instrument. He likewise stole from the premises before he quitted a black cloth coast with metal buttons, a black cloth waistcoat, a shawl, and other articles. No one else has yet been obtained to his retreat, although suspicion attaches to a man who was seen about the place in the course of the day. A reward of 50 pounds has been offered by the authorities for the discovery of the murderer. Active exertions are also being made by the police, and it is hoped that he will not long escape justice.*

As other reports came thick and fast, several of these inaccurate details in *The Times* report would be repeated, along with fresh ones. These included the murder having taken place on the Thursday instead of the Wednesday, while the victim's age would be stated as anything between 13 and 16 years old, rather than her actual

14 years of age. These inaccuracies were mainly due to reporters who attended the inquest using shorthand to record the details and they were not always completely accurate when transcribing it later – especially if there was a deadline looming. At the same time, journalistic licence came into play, through dramatising certain events for their own purpose – that of making it as sensational as possible to sell newspapers. One example was the report of John Watt's inquest testimony, when he claimed to be 'frightened' on entering the farmhouse. Of course, when he came home he had no idea that Sarah was dead, let alone that someone had murdered her and might still be lurking about. He also would seemingly have not got his daughter's age wrong (as reported in several newspapers). One aspect the papers did get right, was when they wrote that 'Active exertions are also being made by the police'.

Since the constables had begun their investigation in earnest, several men from the local area had been hauled up before Frome magistrates the previous day on suspicion of the murder, although so far all had been released without charge. With the eyes of the nation now upon them though, the local magistrates, like the coroner, did not want to take any chances and so a request for assistance was telegraphed to the Home Office. They, in turn, contacted the detective branch of the Metropolitan Police Force, based at Great Scotland Yard. Their response was to send one of their top men, one who had been recently immortalised in an article, albeit under an alias, by none other than Charles Dickens. The magistrates of Frome could now perhaps sleep a little easier knowing that official help was on its way in the shape of Detective Sergeant Henry Smith.

4

Sergeant Henry Smith

The Detective Force organised since the establishment of the existing Police, is so well chosen and trained, proceeds so systematically and quietly, does its business in such a workmanlike manner, and is always so calmly and steadily engaged in the service of the public, that the public really do not know enough of it, to know a tithe of its usefulness.

So wrote Charles Dickens, in 1850, under the title 'The Detective Police', which perhaps, for the first time, brought this fledgling force into public consciousness and ignited a fascination for this particular type of law enforcer that has yet to be diminished.

The Detective Force had existed for eight years before Dickens's article, having come into being as a new department in the capital's Metropolitan Police force in June 1842. Within two months of its inception, it had become fully operational, consisting initially of two inspectors and six sergeants who were tasked with the job of 'infiltrating and detecting crime'. Their headquarters at Great Scotland Yard meant they effectively became part of 'A' Division, which covered the Whitehall district, but what made them different to their uniformed colleagues was the fact they could operate across divisional boundaries and in plain clothes.

Members of the detective branch had been recruited internally from the ranks of the Metropolitan Police, with each officer having shown many of the necessary traits required for their latest role, including: cunning, guile, and a good memory. The fact that they operated in ordinary attire and, if so disposed, it was said, engaged in all manner of trickery to bag their quarry, caused great concern initially. As their successes began to show their usefulness, and writers – like Dickens and others – sensationalised and dramatised their work both in fact and fiction, their presence became more acceptable to the public, and their professional status became elevated with an aura of mystery and glamour created around it.

One of the original members of this select group was Jonathan 'Jack' Whicher, who was fast on his way to earning his reputation as 'prince of detectives', but would eventually see his career sullied (although later vindicated) by his involvement in the infamous

'Road Hill Murder' case of 1860. This would take place nine years after the murder of Sarah Watts. The detective tasked with travelling to help in this current case, however, was one of Whicher's closest colleagues: Sergeant Henry Smith.

Smith and Whicher had joined the Metropolitan Police in the same year, 1837, and were assigned to 'E' division, responsible for policing the Holborn district. Whicher came from Camberwell, three miles south of London and had been a labourer before donning his constable's uniform, while Smith hailed from West Thurrock, Essex, and was a butcher by trade. Their 'beat' included the notorious area of St Giles, an eight-acre labyrinthine slum. But whereas his colleague's first reported arrest wasn't until December 1840, Smith began to make a name for himself immediately. The year after he joined, he was involved in investigating a case of counterfeit currency. Having brought a youth, accused of possessing fake money, to the police station, Smith attempted to retrieve a coin he believed to be hidden in the young man's mouth. When his charge refused to oblige, Smith landed an uppercut and after a brief struggle, retrieved the shilling.

Three years later though, while Smith was involved in a theft case, Whicher was seconded away to work in plain clothes as an 'active officer' – a type of proto-detective but one that had to be kept secret from the public for the time being. The next year, 1842, several of these 'active officers', including Whicher, came out of the shadows to become fully-fledged detectives. And it would not be long before Smith joined his old colleague as one.

Henry Smith's first case for the detective branch was while still a uniformed constable in 'E' division and took place a few months after the department had become operational. There had been 'extensive robberies of fabrics & silks', with much of the haul ending up at the Admiral Carter pub in Bartholomew Close. With this hostelry so near to Smithfield Market it was, unsurprisingly, frequented by butchers and so Smith, with his trade experience brought to good use, was chosen to infiltrate the thieves' den. Donning his old butcher's clothing again, he went undercover at the Admiral Carter, securing lodgings in one of the rooms there.

At first his 'Northamptonshire Yokel in the big city' act was treated with suspicion, but it was not long into his ten-week stay before he was accepted and so was able to observe the comings and goings of the patrons, as well as the landlord, James Deadman, who detectives believed was handling the stolen goods. Finally, Smith felt he had gathered enough evidence and gave the signal to his contacts in the detective branch. So effective was his 'yokel-butcher boy' act, that when the place was raided and he was arrested with the guilty parties – for appearance sake – the landlord insisted Smith was 'innocent' of any wrongdoing.

Later, after being 'released', Smith bumped into a man named Rawlings, who he knew to be one of the thieves involved but had not been at the pub. Invited to stay with Rawlings while he lay low, Smith instead went to his hideaway the next day with a colleague and arrested the man. Rawlings's surprise at this turn of events was complete, as was the surprise of the others standing trial, when Constable Smith of Holborn Division stepped into the witness box, having changed out of his yokel outfit into his high-buttoned police uniform. Groans of horror and dismay emanated from the accused in the dock, when they realised how they had been duped. Even worse was in store, as five out of seven were convicted and several were transported.

As for the 'smooth-faced' Smith (as Dickens would later refer to him) his ability to go uncover must have impressed the members of the detective branch he had been temporarily seconded to – which included his former divisional colleague Jack Whicher – because when a vacancy came up in the force not long afterwards he was asked to join permanently.

By the autumn of 1843 the former constable, now turned detective, Smith had renewed his partnership with Whicher. Together they set about tackling crimes with almost instantaneous results. In September they arrested a Henry Morley for the theft of more than 22yds of woollen cloth, and the following month they were in court giving evidence against Charles Johnson and Elizabeth Crowley, involved in the theft of goods from an Isaac Willis.

It was not all plain sailing, however. In 1845, Smith, along with Whicher, were reprimanded by their department head for 'not showing enough respect to superior, uniformed officers.' Despite this, the two of them and their fellow detectives were establishing a reputation for themselves. In 1846, the branch 'did itself proud' during the hunt for the killer of police constable Clark, while the following year, Detective Sergeant Thornton chased an Irish bank robber across the Atlantic (and arrested him on the other side).

Their most famous case came in 1849 and because of it, a series of articles which would establish their name and reputation. All eight members of the detective branch, including Smith and Whicher, were involved in what became known as the 'Bermondsey Horror'. It concerned the murder of Patrick O'Connor by husband and wife, Frederick and Marie Manning. O'Connor was a moneylender, among other things, and one who had become wealthy through charging exorbitant interest rates. He was also Marie's lover, but she had decided to kill him for his money and other valuables. Enlisting her husband, she invited the unsuspecting O'Connor to dine, but while eating, he was murdered and his body buried under the kitchen floor. After great detective work, Marie Manning was arrested in Edinburgh and her husband, Frederick, in Jersey. The capture made possible 'thanks to the energy and activity of our detective force in the first instance' said the *Morning Chronicle*.

The Mannings were tried, found guilty, and sentenced to hang. It was the first time a husband and wife had been executed together in England for nearly 150 years. Not surprisingly, the event attracted a huge crowd and among those watching was Charles Dickens. He had not only become fascinated with the case, as had most of the country, but also with the detectives behind the incarcerations. So fascinated, in fact, he decided to write about them.

Household Words was the magazine started by Charles Dickens the year after the Manning executions. It was published weekly and edited by Dickens himself – who also contributed articles. In the first edition it carried a statement which proclaimed:

> *We seek to bring to innumerable homes, from the stirring world around us, the knowledge of many social wonders, good and evil, that are not calculated to render any of us less ardently perse- vering in ourselves, less faithful in the progress of mankind, less thankful for the privilege of living in this summer-dawn of time.*

It took its name from a line in Shakespeare's *Henry V* – 'Familiar in his mouth as household words.'

The first article on the detectives appeared in July 1850 and was entitled: 'The Modern Science of Thief-Taking'. This was written by Dickens's assistant, William H. Wills. Around this time, Dickens invited the entire detective branch to the journal's office in Wellington Street. Six of them came: one inspector and five ser- geants, including Henry Smith, whom Dickens described as 'a smooth-faced man with a fresh bright complexion, and a strange air of simplicity'. The detectives sat in a semi-circle, as they lit cigars and drank brandy (but not too much) and shot the breeze, regaling Dickens with enthralling tales of their exploits. Smith, or Mith, as he would subsequently be called in the articles (Dickens slightly changed all the detectives' names) told the 'Butcher's Tale' centred on the Admiral Carter.

Smith returned to Dickens's office on another occasion, only this time with just one other sergeant, Stephen Thornton, and one of his bosses, Inspector Field. It was this latter detective, whom Dickens would immortalise in the character of Inspector Bucket in the novel *Bleak House*. It was also Field who gave permission for Smith to head to Frome, to investigate the murder of Sarah Watts.

Detective Sergeant Henry Smith arrived at Paddington Station on the afternoon of Sunday 28 September 1851, where he caught the train to Chippenham. Once there, he switched trains and began the next leg of his journey. As the train made its way through the various stations – Melksham, Trowbridge, Westbury – Smith could only observe as the urban landscape in which he had been used to solving crimes was replaced by a rural one, with its fields and farmhouses scattered throughout the vast tracts of land.

The train carrying Sergeant Smith pulled into Frome station late on the Sunday evening. The station had been built by one of Brunel's assistants, J.R. Hannaford and had only recently opened, the line from Westbury having been completed the year before. As Smith walked out into the autumn evening, he must have wondered what awaited him. He was used to theft and murder in the capital, with its slums and rookeries, but this was the rape and murder of a 14-year-old girl in a pastoral setting and in broad daylight, and emotions were bound to be running high. He would need all his faculties in full working order.

5

The Investigation

Detective Sergeant Henry Smith, sent down from the Metropolitan Detective Branch in London, began his investigation on Monday 29 September 1851, the morning after arriving in Frome. The first thing he did was make his way out to Battle Farm – along with the constable assigned to him during his visit, Edward Newport – and the scene of the crime. From the outset he knew it was going to be an uphill struggle to find the perpetrator, as no one witnessed the murder. Nevertheless, Detective Sergeant Smith got to work. Like the rest of his colleagues back in London, he had only three tools at his disposal: 'the gift of observation, knowledge of human nature and the ability to put together isolated facts'.

Using the first of these, he went into dairy room, where Sarah had been found murdered six days before, and began to look closely at the scene. On the side of the door leading to the kitchen from the dairy, he saw the distinct marks that Constable James Hoddinott had observed a few days before. Smith, though, concluded that the marks were those of four fingers and a thumb having been pressed against the wall (although sadly for Smith this was half a century before Scotland Yard possessed a fingerprint bureau to help solve crime). He compared his own hand against the prints and believed they had been made by a left hand.

Sergeant Smith then noticed another mark on the wall, which he deemed might have been made by the point of a shoe. He asked for the shoes the victim had been wearing at the time she was murdered and found an exact match; the mark was the same shape as the shoe. Looking more closely at the footwear, he noticed there was plaster between the sole and upper leather.

As he stood by the whey tub, placed on a stool, the murder sequence began to emerge in his mind. The distance between the tub and the wall was close enough to allow Sarah's feet to reach it and scuff her shoes against it, if her head was being immersed into the tub. Spilt whey on the floor, near the tub, indicated to the detective that the poor victim's head had been pushed into the tub at some point, while the presence of plaster on the shoe indicated a struggle had taken place as she kicked out her legs trying to get herself free.

Sergeant Smith now requested the wooden tub containing the whey be emptied. In the cheese making process, cow's milk is separated into solid (curd) and liquid (whey) by adding to it rennet – the natural enzymes found in a calf's stomach. The latter is then discarded, although as a valuable by-product was usually fed to pigs. After the tub was drained, Smith found signs of blood inside, confirming his hypothesis that Sarah's head had, at one time or another, been forced into the tub.

After his thorough investigation of the farmhouse and murder scene he began his questioning, starting with Sarah's parents. Although he had only been in Frome for less than twenty-four hours, a lot of 'local information' had reached his ears concerning the case. One of these pieces of information was that the Watts had kept a large amount of money in the house – one figure even putting it as high as £250. Although Smith dismissed such a large amount as being unlikely, the murder had occurred leading up to Michaelmas, 29 September – that very day, in fact – and so the possibility of there being some money in the house was a fair assumption. This was one of the quarter days when rent became due and tenant farmers, like John Watts, might have a large amount at hand, ready to pay the landlord. Watts, however, denied having any money in the house. Although his wife had inherited £50 a couple of years previously, it had been used to rent the farm and establish the herd, he told Smith.

After finishing with the Watts, Sergeant Smith toured the surrounding area to talk with several of their neighbours. Several men allegedly seen in the vicinity on Wednesday 24 September had already been in front of Frome magistrates but released without charge. Using the second tool available to him, the knowledge of human nature, Smith needed to account for this as he gathered testimonies. As well as potentially vindictive identification – if someone wanted to get rid of a person they disliked – there was also the aspect of greed; this potential complication having come about through an official government reward of £50 which had been offered for any information leading to the successful capture of the murderer (not long after, this would be increased by Lord Bath, of nearby Longleat, who doubled it. His wife, Lady Bath, also visited the Watts to offer her condolences).

As Sergeant Smith continued his investigation, widening his circle of enquiry to the outskirts and centre of Frome itself, the names of three men began to be mentioned on a regular basis, as being either near the farmhouse on that specific day, or elsewhere in Frome but under suspicious circumstances. The sightings in isolation might not be enough, but when put together – using the third tool available to Smith – with other information, the case seemed to have taken a turn for the positive.

It had also emerged that two witnesses claimed to have seen three men opposite The Woolpack Inn, which was situated on the route John and Leah Watts would have taken into Frome market. The men would, therefore, have known the couple were both away from the farm for the best part of the day. Later that morning, at around midday, it was also said, the trio were overheard arranging to meet in an hour, before heading off in separate directions. A couple of hours after that, around 2 o'clock, it was alleged that they were seen not far from, and moving in the direction of, the Watts' farm. One of the three was apparently in front, encouraging the other two on, although another witness, a little later, saw two of them without this third man.

Sarah Watts had been seen by Alfred Allard around 1 o'clock, still alive, and her parents had returned home around four. This gave a window of three hours for the murder to have occurred (although probably less as the body was already cold when discovered). Later sightings put the three men from the Woolpack in different clothing and passing something between them, while another witness claimed to have seen them in the town centre where he overheard a conversation which had included the phrase 'a watch but no tin' – which was local slang taken to mean that a watch had been found, but there had been no money (i.e. tin). The implication of this conversation was huge, as a couple of days after the murder the Watts had discovered a watch was also missing, presumably stolen. Watches, along with cheese, was one of the preferred item most often taken in robberies, as the former were usually valuable (while the latter could be easily stored).

The most damning piece of 'evidence' against the three was that several people had come forward to say one of them owned a handkerchief like the silk one found on the kitchen table by Constable Hoddinott – but by now handed to Sergeant Smith – on the day of the murder.

Despite all this potentially good news, when the second day of the inquest was held on Tuesday 30 September 1851, the day after Smith began his investigation, no one had yet been arrested for the crime. It took place at a public house in Keyford, along the road from Constable Grist's grocery shop, where John Watts had reported the murder. The Unicorn Inn was one of the town's principal inns and the building dated back to the eighteenth century. Like the George, where the first day of the inquest had taken place the Friday before, it had experienced its own share of tragedy and despair throughout its history. In 1801, the then landlord,

James Gully, went bankrupt and suffered the indignity of having all his belongings – including his marital bed – auctioned on the premises, while his successor shared in the same financial embarrassment a decade later. In 1818, Isaac Gregory, one of the town's constables at the time, reported that he was:

> *sent for to the Unicorn to stop fighting* [where he] *saw a man by the name of Pinchin in the kitchen stript to his shirt with his fists clenched challenging the company to fight. I ordered him to put his clothes on and behave peaceable, he refused and menaced me with his fists for a considerable time so that I was obliged to get assistance to take him to the guardhouse – on the road he made a desperate attack on my person – he kicked me in the leg and made a wound and aimed several blows at me.*

After another bankruptcy in 1832, the Knight family took over the lease and a succession of family members became landlord, including the latest incumbent, William, who at the time of the inquest was just 20 years old.

There was only one witness called on the inquest's second day and this was the surgeon Francis Giles, who was asked to report the findings of his post-mortem.

> *I made a post mortem examination of the body of the deceased on Friday afternoon last. I examined the head and on removing the scalp I found a large quantity of blood between the scalp and the brain on the forepart of the head towards the right side. On opening the skull I found that the bone was not fractured; the brain was very much congested but in other respects healthy. I examined the neck, and found two bruises beneath the skin, one in the middle line just over the windpipe, the other two or three inches distant at the left side. There were no other bruises in the neck. I examined the chest and found the heart and lungs very much congested but in other respects healthy. All the other viscera were healthy, the hymen was ruptured.*

Giles then detailed the remaining results of his investigation and reinforced his opinion that a capital felony had been committed shortly before death. She had been raped. At the same time, he believed the cause of death to have been pressure on her windpipe: she had been strangled.

The foreman of the jury then asked Giles if he was quite certain death had been produced by strangulation, to which the witness replied that he had no doubts about it. This was followed by a seemingly unusual question from the coroner Daniel Ashford: 'Is it possible that the girl could have strangled herself?' he asked. Giles was adamant in his reply:

> *It is quite impossible. I would add that the bruises on the neck were about the size of the point of the fingers of a man's hand, and fully bear out the supposition that death was caused by strangulation. The scratches on the neck might have been produced by a man's nails.*

Thomas Ivey, Chief Constable of Frome, then stepped forward to report that the clothes stolen from Battle Farm on the day of the murder, had been recovered that very morning and John Watts could be re-called to identify them if required. As the jury did not see how this would help in their enquiry to establish cause of death, the bereaved father was left to carry on his grieving in peace.

Coroner Ashford then said the law on the subject was clear. It was evident that the poor girl had been violated and murdered, but the evidence adduced did not fix the crime on any individual. The only course for the jury therefore was to return an open verdict: that the deceased was wilfully murdered by some person or persons unknown. The jury expressed their compliance in this course of action and the proceedings before the coroner were closed.

Whatever progress Sergeant Smith felt had been made so far on this barbaric crime in Frome, the official view, at least for the present time, was that they were still no nearer to finding the guilty party than they were the previous Wednesday, now almost a whole week ago. But for Smith, things were about to take a turn for the better.

6

The Arrests

Wednesday 1 October 1851 marked the first week anniversary of Sarah Watts's murder and despite the inquest's open verdict the previous day, and the fact she had been killed by 'person or persons unknown', Sergeant Smith had gained a large amount of information in the few days he had been in Frome.

As in many murder cases, various names of suspects had been brought to the detective's attention by local people, but he had to use all his experience to sift through this information to work out which of it could be relied upon and which was motivated by other means: malice, revenge, greed. As the new month began, he had whittled this intelligence down to just three suspects; a trio whose names and numerous sightings, in potentially suspicious circumstances, tended to suggest they should, at the very least, be located as soon as possible and questioned about their movements exactly a week before.

The names of the three suspects were William Maggs, William Sparrow and Robert Hurd. They were all notorious criminals known in the area, each having their own impressive criminal record and all having served time in prison for a variety of misdemeanours. Together, however, they were known as the Maggs-Sparrow gang which, according to at least one newspaper report, had 'infested Frome for a number of years'. The theft of milk, cheese, and bread, along with the odd instance of watches and other items was one thing – and all those hallmarks were there at Battle Farm – but would any of them be so depraved as to commit the rape and murder of a young girl? This was the question Sergeant Smith had to answer for himself as he began his more focused line of enquiry.

Sergeant Smith made his way down to Constable Newport's ironmongers shop in the Market Place, in Frome centre. Newport was the constable assigned to help Smith in his investigation. The constable had been told the names of the men suspected and so had summoned, through a third party, one of them to come to his shop. Smith had not been there long when Robert Hurd arrived. Although coming of his own accord, he was not happy. Sergeant Smith, as he was in plain clothes, introduced himself and told him the reason for his being there.

Robert Hurd was 37 years old, 5ft 11ins, with hazel eyes and dark brown hair. He had a scar on his upper lip and another on his chin. On the census ten years before he had given his occupation as 'labourer', but since then he had also earned money through prize fighting, going by the moniker of 'Frome Bob'. He had a ferocious reputation around the area and was known to punch people at the slightest provocation. On entering Newport's shop he had immediately announced to the constable that he would have knocked down the overseer, Lawes – the third party who informed him to go to Newport's place – but knew if that had happened, he (Hurd) would have been locked up for it.

Sergeant Smith, with notebook ready, asked Hurd about his whereabouts on the day of the murder.

> *I live at Little Keyford, near the Mount,* Hurd replied. *I left home at nine, by myself; came down to the Lamb and had one pint of beer – this was about half past nine; then went to the Unicorn and had rum and cider there; then to Singer's at the Crown; had rum and cider there; about 10 or 11 was down in town, and was about the town all day.*

Smith read his notes back to Hurd, to check he had got all the correct details and the latter nodded his agreement.

Hurd, as Smith would later recount, 'did not appear at all put out by my questions; his answers were short, but his manner was not confused.' Hurd also remarked that he wished the guilty party caught. As it would subsequently transpire, Hurd had also been the man outside the Crown Inn, who had met John Watts on his way out of Constable Grist's shop – after reporting his daughter's murder – and had bought the bereaved father a drink at the Woolpack Inn. For now, however, Smith was satisfied enough with Hurd's answers to let him go on his way.

The next person on Smith's list was one of the men who gave their name to the gang which had 'infested' the town for several years: that of William Maggs. He was a notorious burglar and thief and lived at a house in Feltham Lane, a little way out of Frome, in the direction of West Woodlands. He was 44 years old, stood 5ft 3ins tall and had grey eyes and brown hair. A scar adorned his forehead. He was married and had a family consisting of twelve children; ranging from the eldest of 25 years old, to the youngest being just 1 year of age. At the last census he had listed his occupation as a 'clog and patten maker' (a patten was a form of overshoe to protect normal footwear from becoming dirty outdoors).

When Sergeant Smith arrived at Maggs's house, the suspect was initially not so ready to answer the detective's questions as Hurd had been, as he and his wife, Maria, were not sure who this stranger in ordinary clothing at their door was. 'I wouldn't answer him – who is he?' Mrs Maggs told her husband. After being told exactly who this 'stranger' was, although still hesitating for a little time after, Maggs finally said, 'Well I'll tell you'. Smith asked his questions, as he had done with Hurd, and like the previous suspect, the detective observed 'no confusion in answering the questions [I] put to him'. Also like Hurd before him, Maggs denied any involvement in the murder and hoped the guilty party would be found. Although a burglar and thief, this did not mean he was a murderer. Smith, again with notebook in hand, wrote down his whereabouts on that specific day.

> I and Sparrow came into Frome about half past nine. We had gone up to the Mount at Keyford and from there to Frome. No other person was with us. We went down into the Market Place and waited for some time. I then saw William Payne. From there I then went by myself to the Angel public house at twelve o'clock. At half past I left there and went out into the market, waited half an hour, then to the Victoria Inn. There I saw Hurd, Wimpey [sic] and Sargeant. At four o'clock I went home and asked the little maid [meaning his daughter] if her mother was at home? She said 'No'. My way home was down by Bellows Hole across the fields into Feltham Lane. I did not go indoors. Then I went back to Frome by the lane to the Mount where I met Sparrow, no one else. Then to The Crown public house Keyford. Hurd, Sparrow and Sargeant were there. I waited till eight then left, came down the road to the Mount, down Feltham Lane and home.

Sergeant Smith read his notes back and Maggs agreed they were correct. Smith thanked him and, as with Hurd, the potential suspect was allowed to remain at liberty for the present time. Before Smith returned to the town though, he asked Maggs about the third person on his list, William 'Bill' Sparrow, who he was told currently resided at Maggs's house. Maggs confirmed this, but said Sparrow was not there now and he did not know where he was. As it transpired, Sparrow was in North Bradley, across the county border in Wiltshire, were he would soon find himself behind bars. He was arrested there on suspicion of possessing a stolen watch – potentially the one from Battle Farm was, of course, Smith's immediate thought on learning the news – and incarcerated at Westbury police station. As soon as the detective heard about the arrest, he arranged to go there.

On entering William Sparrow's cell on Friday 3 October, the prisoner mistook Smith for the prosecutor and, unaware of the wider implications, straight away launched into a defence statement: 'All I know is I bought it off Bob Hurd,' he pleaded. 'Will Maggs was with me and can prove it; I gave 27/– for it.'

Smith quickly enlightened Sparrow as to his real reason for being there and it was not long before he had another set of notes in his book:

> *I live at 19 Trooper St. Frome and lately at Feltham with William Maggs. I was at Feltham with Maggs at his home about 9 o'clock on the morning of the 24th, me and Maggs left home together along Woodlands Rd over to the bottom of the Mount, I saw William Sargeant and Hurd. Hurd then left and went into Frome and Sargeant went up the road towards the Mount. Me and Maggs went into Frome and there we met Hurd. We then went into Gales public house in the Coal-ash. About twelve o'clock Maggs and me left Frome. We went down Coal-ash away to Bellows Hole across the fields and came in the main road by Feltham Bridge up the road towards Woodlands way home. About 2.00 o'clock me and Maggs left home up Woodlands Rd to Lower Keyford. I went up to William Sargeant in the Square. Me and Sargeant went across the little lane to the Crown public house (Singer's) and there we met Hurd & Maggs. We left there about 7 o'clock; we all three went on the road to the Mount. We parted there and me and Maggs went home.*

Smith realised there were a few discrepancies between Sparrow and Maggs's accounts and indeed with that of Hurd's as well, but from the description the Watts had given of their missing watch, the one allegedly stolen by Sparrow, however obtained, was definitely not the same as that taken from Battle Farm.

On Smith's return to Frome, having left Sparrow in the police cell in Westbury, the detective sat down at his temporary lodgings in the town and began to look over his notes and weigh up the evidence that might connect Hurd, Maggs, and Sparrow to the crime. He took into account their reputations as criminals, but knew this didn't mean they were guilty of being rapists and murderers. One thing he needed to do, which he made a note of, was to talk to the other men – Payne, Whimpey, Sargeant – mentioned by one or more of the suspects. Although not able to locate any of them over the weekend, by Sunday evening Smith was certain in his own mind of the potential guilt of his suspects and so prepared to make his move the following day.

On Monday 6 October 1851, exactly a week since Sergeant Smith had begun his investigation, he drew the net in on those he believed to be responsible. His first port of call was The Lamb, up towards Keyford and not far from The Unicorn, where the second day of the inquest had taken place. Coincidentally these were both hostelries Hurd claimed to have visited on the morning of the murder. Here Smith asked Robert Hurd, alias 'Frome Bob', to accompany him to the magistrates' court, located back in town. Believing he was going to give a statement which would help establish Sparrow's innocence over the alleged stolen watch, for which he was still being held in Westbury police station over, the sometime prize fighter was obviously shocked and surprised – if not a little angry – when he himself was arrested and taken into custody for being party to the murder of Sarah Watts. From the moment this happened, Hurd protested his innocence: 'You don't mean that, be candid with me and tell me if you have no other charge than that.' Smith insisted, however, and then he and Constable Newport escorted their prisoner the short distance from the court to the main guardhouse, located next to the Blue Boar, in the Market Place. Here, prisoners would be held until they appeared once again before the magistrates or else were taken away to gaol. Hurd, ensconced inside the small rectangular building, was left alone to ponder the turn of events, which now saw him incarcerated and accused of being involved in the murder that had been the talk of the town for almost the past fortnight. He would not be in there alone for long.

The Blue Boar had a reputation of being one of the most infamous public houses in the town. It was situated at the north end of the Market Place and had been built towards the end of the seventeenth century. Ever since then it had attracted trouble like moths to a flame. When local shopkeeper Isaac Gregory had been Chief Constable of the town several decades earlier, he had frequented the pub almost as often as the locals. But whereas they were engaging in anti-social activities, heavy drinking and nefarious vices – it was notorious for the passing of counterfeit currency – he was there arresting them for it. It was to here that Smith and Newport now came for William Maggs. He offered no resistance to his arrest and soon found himself in the guardhouse, along with Hurd. Smith then returned to Westbury and took custody of Sparrow, bringing him back to Frome under the same charge as his two associates.

The news of the arrests spread like wildfire around Frome and the surrounding areas. Whether innocent or guilty of this particular crime, the local population could at least rest easier in their beds knowing three of the town's most prolific criminals were now behind bars and so would not be able to partake of their nocturnal and anti-social activities for at least the foreseeable future.

Criminal reputations apart, Sergeant Smith now had to compile his case to put before the magistrates and so needed to find out as much as he could about the men's movements on the day of the murder and since, and, as far as possible, find out what they had been up to in their lives until this point. He would have a lot to digest.

7

William Maggs

It could be argued that William 'Will' Maggs's life of crime was pre-determined from the moment he was born in 1806, in the small Wiltshire village of Horningsham. His parents were Joel, a lathe worker and Ann Maggs, formerly Trollop. He was part of a large family in the area and newspaper reports show his father and one of his brothers, George, spent time in prison. Another brother, Paul Lewey Maggs, was deported to Australia in 1820, when William was 14. In time, however, he would surpass them all by becoming head of one of Frome's most notorious crime gangs since the Howarth family had inflicted their reign of terror on the town in the early part of the nineteenth century.

When exactly William began his forays into the criminal world is not known, but if a newspaper account of a theft from 1819, concerning a William Maggs, *is* him, his debut appearance in court was around the age of 13; the year before his brother was deported.

The first event known to be *the* William Maggs took place at the Holy Trinity Church in Frome on 16 November 1824. This date saw the marriage of 19-year-old Maggs to 16-year-old Maria Gratewood. They began married life in the bride's home town of Warminster and not long after, started the family that would, by the time of his arrest in October 1851 for the Watts murder, encompass twelve children.

In 1827, a William Maggs was committed to Fisherton gaol for assaulting and ill-treating his child at Warminster, although the only evidence for this is a small mention in a local paper, so again it is not possible to be sure it is the right one. If it is the same William Maggs though, then the 'ill-treated child' would have been either Emily or Sarah, the two daughters Maria had given birth to by this time.

In all probability, William Maggs's life of crime was constant from his very early years, punctuated only by periods of time in various gaols. One such occurrence took place towards the end of 1833, when a William Maggs of Horningsham was sentenced to two months in the House of Correction at Devizes. His crime was breaching the game laws, presumably poaching. By the mid-1830s, however, the Maggs family – by now comprising five daughters and a son – had moved to Frome, and William was working, at least part of his time, as a 'hackle stock setter', a person who set and maintained the pins in the heckle – a toothed implement – which combed or 'carded' coarse flax for the woollen industry. This seemed to be a step up from his previous occupation of agricultural labourer.

An incident occurred in November 1836, however, that saw Maggs receiving a taste of his own medicine, so to speak. Making his way home from a local pub one night, he was robbed. The four muggers who accosted him stole a watch, pocketknife and twenty-four shillings. Whether this was simply a street robbery, or possibly a falling out between thieves, has been lost with the passage of time.

By the time of the 1841 census, William and Maria Maggs, along with a son and six daughters, were recorded as living at The Marsh on the outskirts of Frome. A seventh daughter – 15-year-old Sarah – was away at the time, in Shrewton, having secured employment there as a domestic servant. To what degree the rest of the Maggs family had engaged in similar nefarious activities to William up to this point is debatable, but certainly the rest of that decade would be marked by habitual thefts and robberies, offset by court appearances, custodial sentences and, at times, brutal punishments involving almost the whole brood.

In 1842, two of the eight children, Sarah and Mark, appeared at the Somerset County Sessions, held in Taunton, for theft. Sarah was given two months for having stolen 'three pounds in weight' of cheese from a John Miller, while her younger brother received three months 'hard labour' for stealing 'four pounds in weight' of cheese from a James Watson. He was also sentenced to be whipped, even though he was just 11 years old at the time.

The following year, their mother, Maria, who was by now 35 years of age and had given birth to nine children, was convicted of stealing 'six pounds in weight' of pork. Described as 'a labourer of imperfect education', she was given four months 'hard labour' at Shepton Mallet gaol. Charged with her was a 15-year-old accomplice, John Burton, who was sentenced to seven years transportation and was described, despite his young age, as an 'old offender'.

A few months after his mother's release, Mark Maggs, now 13, was charged with stealing potatoes. As this was his second offence he had given a false name – George Mood – when apprehended, but once his actual identity was discovered, he was, like Burton, sentenced to be transported for seven years. He was sent initially to Millbank prison, where he remained for a couple of years, but finally arrived in Australia in May 1847. In this same year, two of his younger sisters, Rosetta and Mary, each received four-month sentences – including a week in solitary confinement – for stealing several boas, and other property, from the furriers where they worked.

The year before all this, 1846, their father, William, found himself incarcerated as well. In a case of 'like father, like son' he had been caught stealing potatoes, this time from a nearby farm in West Woodlands. The offence had taken place in May and two months later he found himself in court at Wells in front of a Justice of the Peace called William Knatchbull.

One of the witnesses for the prosecution was the farm owner, John Shore, who swore upon his oath that:

> I was awoke about two o'clock by a noise which I heard in my barn close to my barton and on looking out of my window I saw the barn's door open. I called George Barnes my servant and we went together to the barn – the door was nearly closed but I saw the light of a candle in the barn. He remained on the outside while I went into the barn where I saw two men going from a heap of potatoes which I had left in the barn, the two were got up and running away. I caught hold of one of them whom I knew to be William Maggs living about two miles from me, he was just coming out of the barn from the potatoes. The other man escaped. I had left an empty basket in the barn last night and on going into the barn I found the basket partly filled with potatoes taken from the heap in the barn. I also found two empty sacks and a stick which were not my property. I secured William Maggs who kept calling loudly for "George" and on searching him found a screwdriver. I also found in his pocket four potatoes of the same quality as those I had left in the barn.

George Barnes, a servant to John Shore added:

> I locked up my master's barn with a padlock at about half past nine last night and went to bed at about half past ten, my master called me up at about two o'clock in the morning and on going to the barn the back door was open but almost closed. I stayed outside when a man came out and ran away from me...the potatoes were grown by my master and those in the basket were of the same sort as the heap in the barn called "The Champion".

Thomas Blackmore, a Frome constable at the time, then testified:

*I was called for about five o'clock this morning when I took
William Maggs in charge and took from his pocket four potatoes. I have compared the potatoes with those in the heap and
produce some from each sort – they both appear to agree. I also
took from him two pocket knives.*

The amount Maggs was attempting to carry off was judged to
be 'two pecks' and valued at two shillings. His calling out for
'George' might have been a simple ruse to throw investigators off
the scent of the real co-conspirator. If so, it worked, as no one else
was charged with the crime. The accused gave no defence and
was given six months 'hard labour', a common punishment at the
time and described as 'the exercise of irksome brute force, rather
than the application of self gratifying skill'. Hard labour could
include any number of activities, one of them being the smashing
of big stones into small ones with a sledgehammer. This seemingly pointless activity was in fact of great benefit to the community, as stone was needed in ever increasing quantities to build
and repair roads.

It is during this stretch inside that the first description of William
Maggs was recorded. In the prison register he was described
as 39-years-old, with grey eyes and brown hair. His school was
described as 'none', and his ability to read and write as 'imperfect'.
His height was recorded as 5ft 3ins and his complexion as being
sallow. A slight scar was observed on his forehead. His occupation as a 'Patten Maker' is interesting though, as on the census
return five years before, he was recorded as being an 'agricultural
labourer'; then, as now, one of the lowest paid occupations in the
country. Presumably the former job of 'hackle stock setter', mentioned even earlier, in 1835, had ended and he had returned to
labouring, or maybe one of his many arrests had cost him his job.
Whatever the reason, he seemed perhaps to be making more effort
to improve his situation as his family increased; although obviously
still also supplementing his family's needs by disreputable means.
If so, this latest arrest was a major setback.

Magg's new home, at least for the next six months, during the
summer and autumn of 1846, was Wilton gaol, which was situated
not far outside Somerset's administrative town of Taunton and had
not long taken over from Ilchester as the county's main prison. It
covered four acres of land and contained cells for 275 prisoners.
There were exercise yards, a hospital, chapel, workshops, store-
rooms and ... the treadmill.

Treadmills, or tread wheels, had been installed in many prisons since the 1820s by Stothert & Pitt of Bath, including the one

at Wilton. The prisoners had to tread the wheel like a hamster within a cage and it took practice for the novice not to get injured. Prisoners usually did ten minutes on and five minutes off, for up to ten hours at a time and were medically examined before being put to the wheel.

Male prisoners, like William Maggs, condemned to hard labour had to spend at least three months of their sentence on this wheel. Some of the wheels were even divided into compartments to stop prisoners communicating with each other, as a code of silence was enforced in several prisons. At Wilton, a system of gears powered a gristmill to grind corn, which was then sold to pay for the prisoners' keep and the prison's expenses.

Another activity that would no doubt have occupied some of Maggs's time there was known as 'oakum picking'. This was a great favourite in the workhouse as well, and involved the unpicking and untwisting of pieces of tarred rope from old ships, brought up from the dockyards. Once this had been done, the bits were sold back to the dockyards and used for caulking the planks of the ships; the tarry fibres being hammered into the gaps in between the boards to make the ships watertight. The wisdom of giving prisoners, such as Maggs, access to rope, can be called into question as will be seen later.

These activities were the main ingredients of Maggs's six-month 'hard labour' sentence. Not only was the work profitable for the prison, it had the supposed effect of tiring the inmates out to such a degree that they were less likely to cause trouble in prison and even perhaps deter them from returning to their old ways on their release. There were always exceptions, of course, and Maggs, when he finally returned to his family, turned out to be one of those.

Meanwhile, the eldest of William Maggs's children, Emily, had either decided to remain honest, or else was more adept at her nefarious activities than either her siblings or parents, as her name never appeared in any newspaper reports regarding court hearings. Her choice of husband, on the other hand, was not so deft. In October 1847, she married Isaac Ferris, a labourer living in Brandy Lane, Frome, at the same church in which her parents had married twenty-three years earlier. Two years later, and before they had started their own family, Isaac was in prison. In December 1849, Isaac and several other men had broken into Frome Vicarage and made off with a huge inventory of items, including 12lbs of tea, three sides of bacon, two hams, a turkey, and a leg of mutton. When the local newspapers reported the burglary, they commented that:

Every investigation was made to no purpose until Monday morning when in consequence of a quantity of fowls having been stolen from a stable in Frome a search warrant was obtained by Thomas Ivey, constable, to examine the house of Isaac Ferris, a labourer living in the parish.

This was a month after the robbery and there was not a chicken in sight, but the constables did find most of the goods from the vicarage which was identified by the Reverend William Bainbridge Calvert as his property. On 30 March 1850, Ferris and five others were sentenced at Taunton Assizes to be transported for ten years. Exactly a year later, and now without a husband, Emily appeared on the Frome census as head of the household.

By the time of the 1851 census, Emily's parents – William and Maria – and nine of her siblings, had moved to the house in Feltham Lane, so remaining in Frome and near the Woodlands area. Two of the eldest girls, Sarah, 24, and Mary, 20, were working as domestic servants, while the remaining seven, ranging in age from 15 down to 1-year-old, were recorded without a stated occupation. Maria's occupation is likewise left blank – although with so many children to look after this is perhaps hardly surprising.

William Maggs's occupation on the 1851 census was given as being that of a 'clog and patten maker'. To what degree he practiced this trade of patten making, with or without its addition of 'clog', is not known, but as it had been before he was sent to Wilton gaol five years earlier, he was no doubt up to his usual (nocturnal) activities to supplement the money needed to support his large family. Once more, however, this all came to a crashing halt six months later in October 1851, when he was arrested in the Blue Boar by Sergeant Smith for being party to the murder of Sarah Watts; a crime literally committed just down the road from his house.

8

William Sparrow

Of the three accused of the Watts murder in 1851, William 'Bill' Sparrow had the most evidence against him. He was also the one who had spent the most time in prison up until that point. He had been christened at the Holy Trinity Church in Frome, on 13 June 1819, making him, in October 1851, 32 years of age. His mother, named Elizabeth, was known as Betsey. His father, Thomas, was a journeyman dyer. The term 'journeyman' has nothing to do with travel, as might be supposed, but refers to a person who has passed their apprenticeship in a trade and is worthy of employment as a craftsman, but has not yet become a 'master' of his trade, nor able to employ others.

There is nothing in the official record about William Sparrow until the mid-1840s, but it can be assumed he began his life of crime, like Maggs, at a relatively young age. The census of 1841 records his parents as living in the Woodlands area of Frome and on that night, William's younger brother, Thomas, aged 18, is also with them. The 22-year-old William was not there at the time; possibly already staying with Maggs, but not officially recorded.

Predictably, perhaps, when Sparrow does appear in an historical record, it is as the result of the commissioning of a crime. This was in 1844, at the age of 23. On 9 October of that year, he and a co-defendant, John Payne, were up before Frome magistrates for the breaking into a house belonging to Edward Hoddinott. In court, Sparrow gave his version of the events that had occurred on the day before the burglary:

> On the Saturday evening I came out of the Unicorn Inn, Henry Wells came up close behind me and began with me about the house, he said he knowed there was the Missionary Box and a lot of money in it, I said I should see him in the morning, he said if he did not do that he must do something else to get some money for the races – he said he had got but half a crown for Anne and him to go to the races. He came down on the Sunday morning, I was down in the garden – he said that he had got tools down in the brickyard that he cut clay with and that would break open the door – he said I could go to the meeting and he would go and do it. I persuaded him not to do it. I never seed him again till the races at two o'clock.

The 'victim', Edward Hoddinott, then gave his version (Sparrow's co-defendant, John Payne, had elected to say nothing):

> *On Sunday the 8th of September I left my house at Blatchbridge at about six o'clock for the purpose of attending the Methodist Chapel at Blatchbridge ... in my bedroom upstairs I had two five pound notes of the Warminster Bank, one sovereign in gold and from three to four pounds of silver, five shillings worth of half pence tied up in paper, and three of four shillings in half pence in a bag, all locked up in a box in a bedroom ... I had also a small box belonging to the Methodist Missionary Society.*

Hoddinott then stated he had returned home a little before 8 o'clock that evening to find his doors had been forced and the money and the missionary collection box had gone. He continued:

> *Henry Wells worked at a brick farm below my house and passes by it every day on his way to work. William Sparrow lives about a hundred yards from my house and has some times worked for me. On the morning of the seventh of October I delivered William Sparrow in charge for being concerned in robbing my house. He told me he had received one five pound note and about a pound's worth of silver which Wells had given him on the race ground and he said if I would forgive him he would work it out.*

Stephen Wood Clarke, a cabinet maker in Beckington, and the brother-in-law of Edward Cooper, who kept the Woolpack in the same village, then deposed he had seen Sparrow with the others at the public house on 29 September 1844, where they were drinking gin and peppermint, and eating biscuits which they paid for with a £5 note. They then went by carriage to Frome. Some days later Sparrow and his friends were seen in the King's Head, in Frome, where Sparrow paid his bill from a purse containing at least half a dozen sovereigns.

Henry Wells was then called and told his version of events, which perhaps not surprisingly was slightly different to that of Sparrow's:

> *I saw William Sparrow the night before* [the burglary], *he said to me, I know of a job if you will go and do it tomorrow night. I asked him where, and he said "Go to Farmer Hoddinott's at Blatchbridge break into his house and take the money".*

According to Henry Wells, Sparrow had then gone on to explain that he would be at chapel with Hoddinott so that he could be seen not to be involved, as they were all wary of him since the break in at

James Garrett's house. He knew also that if he did not go to chapel, Hoddinott's servants would be left at the farm to guard the place; such was his (Sparrow's) reputation.

It seemed from the rest of the evidence that Wells and John Payne went to see Sparrow about the job at 11 o'clock on Sunday morning, along with the tools needed for the burglary. Sparrow went to chapel and the two others broke in and made off with the money which they hid in a field until race day, when they met up with Sparrow and gave him some coins. The £5 notes were hidden at the brickyard until Sparrow asked for them; he sold one to a man at the Ship Inn, in Frome, for £3 and shared out the remainder with Wells and Payne.

Unsurprisingly they were caught and Constable Thomas Grey gave evidence to state he had arrested Sparrow at Hoddinott's house, where Sparrow was asking Hoddinott to forgive him and promising to 'work out what money he owed'. Sparrow finally confessed and told the whole story. He was remanded to Wilton gaol where, two years later, Maggs would undertake his six-month 'hard labour' sentence. Sparrow was charged with receiving stolen goods and the amount of money involved was a very large sum for those days.

The Frome magistrates decided the case should go to trial. Sparrow denied his involvement when tried at the County Sessions in Wells a couple of weeks later, but by then it seemed Henry Wells had turned Queen's Evidence (as he was not charged). Payne was acquitted, but Sparrow received fourteen years.

On entering the gaol following his conviction, Sparrow's details were entered into the prison 'description' book. He was recorded as being 5ft 5ins in height, of fair complexion with hazel eyes, brown hair, unmarried, and with a slight scar on his forehead. His occupation was that of labourer. In the quarterly returns the prison surgeon says that he was healthy and his behaviour had been 'Good'. In January 1845 he was transferred to Millbank Prison, on the banks of the Thames, in London, where the 14-year-old Mark Maggs was incarcerated, waiting for his transportation sentence to be carried out.

Sparrow was still at Millbank when William Maggs served his own sentence, in 1846, back at Wilton, but a couple of years later, he was transferred again; this time it was on board a prison hulk, *Justitia*, anchored at Woolwich. This was an old East Indiaman type ship and one of the first to be converted for convict use. Once there, Sparrow petitioned for release. This was the second time he had done so; his first application, in May 1846, had been refused, as was this one. Why he thought he should be let out after such a short way into his sentence is unknown, although possibly it was connected to Payne having been acquitted at the trial and him feeling he had been unfairly treated. Whatever the reason, he applied for a third time the following year, although once more without success.

Sparrow spent the rest of the decade moving from prison to prison, remaining healthy and apparently still being well behaved. In the summer of 1849, he was 'removed' from the *Justitia* and transferred to another rotting hulk, the *Warrior*, moored just off Woolwich dockyard. This seventy-four gun ship was more than sixty years old and in such bad shape its ribs hardly held together – a few years later it would be described in a government report as 'rotten and unsound from stem to stern [and] beyond any repair.' It could hold 450 men, had a convict-staffed cobblers and tailors, and held education classes (although its seems Sparrow did not take advantage during his six months there!) as well as boasting that it was lighted by gas, owing to its proximity to the shore.

On 22 January 1850, now back on terra firma, William Sparrow was transferred to Shorncliffe Barracks Convict Station, near Cheriton in Kent. This was an army barracks, used partly as a prison and as a halfway house for those awaiting imminent depor-tation or pending release. It proved to be the latter for Sparrow, as on 2 May 1850 he received a pardon, having served a little less than half a dozen years of his fourteen year sentence.

There are no further details around his release, although possi-bly he had a case from the very beginning and someone in author-ity finally considered it. Alternatively, his premature release might have been a by-product of the new thinking that concerned the way in which punishments were carried out. Over the next couple of years, physical transportation was used much less often and it was judged that a sentence of seven years abroad was equivalent to four years penal servitude at home. At the same time, periods of fourteen years or less nearly always saw the prisoner remaining on home soil.

Once at liberty, William Sparrow made his way back to Frome and teamed up with William Maggs again, to create the infamous self-titled crime gang. When questioned at the time of his arrest, in October 1851, Sparrow gave his address as 19 Trooper Street, Frome. This was the home of his younger brother Thomas, his wife Mary Ann and their 1-year-old daughter Emma. The young fam-ily seemed respectable and hard working and indications are that Sparrow used this as his 'official' address, but in reality was perma-nently with the Maggs family. Wherever he was staying in March 1851, he made sure he was not there come census night; as his name is not recorded at either address.

Although there is nothing in the official record for Sparrow (or Maggs) for the seventeen-month period between his release in May 1850 and arrest the following October, the fact that the gang he co-headed became notorious enough for the newspapers to say it had 'infested' the town must mean he was up to no good for most, if not all, of that time. It was no wonder the people of Frome breathed a sigh of relief at the news of his latest arrest.

9

Robert Hurd

Out of the trio of prisoners on remand for the murder of Sarah Watts, or even the whole criminal fraternity of Frome and surrounding areas, Robert Hurd, alias 'Frome Bob', was one of the most colourful characters ever to walk its streets and frequent its public houses. That is not to condone his life of crime, but he seems to have been so much more than a mere petty felon like his co-accused, Maggs and Sparrow, and even had he not become involved in the Watts murder case, his name would demand mention in books on Frome and far beyond.

Robert Hurd was baptised on 19 February 1814, at St John's Church in Frome. His parents were Job and Catherine (Kitty) Hurd and his father, at that time, was described as a soldier in the 2nd Somerset Militia. Although there are few facts around his formative years, he nevertheless grew up a strong healthy boy with a thirst of adventure and by the time he was 15 years old he was working as a labourer. It seems that this was not enough money or excitement for him though, and so he began a life of notoriety and crime.

Hurd was first arrested in June 1829, and remanded in Shepton Mallet gaol, for the alleged burglary of a house during which a watch and several other items were taken. After a couple of months in gaol awaiting trial, he was acquitted in August and discharged. This brush with the law did not deter him; in fact, his acquittal might have given him confidence in his own ability to evade justice. One year later, in April 1830, he was charged with stealing nine umbrellas but was again acquitted after a short spell on remand in Wilton gaol – an even luckier escape, perhaps, as his co-defendant was gaoled for seven months

At the age of 22, possibly inspired, or encouraged, by his father and the tales of army life, the lure of adventure took him all the way to Spain and a part in a little known aspect of European history. In summer 1835, Lieutenant Colonel Sir George De Lacy Evans, MP for Westminster, began to organise a British Volunteer Corps to help the liberal cause of Queen Isabella the Second against the claim of Don Carlos to the throne of Spain. Known as the First Carlist War, things were not going well for the Queen's side and she appealed for help from her allies; the French sent their Foreign Legion. Britain declined to intervene officially but felt it should do something practical to defend its interests there and so in June of 1835, it was decided to form a military volunteer corps; in other words, a band of mercenaries. One contemporary source recorded:

> *The force was very emphatically a mercenary force, not in the mere sense of one serving for pay but also of one serving for pay only. All the nobler feelings of patriotism, of anxiety for the approbation of his countryman which enable the British soldier to face danger and to endure hardship were wanting to the legionary. His government had distinctly refused a contingent of regular forces and his engagement was a mere commercial transaction the noblest feature in which was the characteristic love of adventure.*

By the end of summer 1836, a force of 9,000 men, under the command of De Lacy Evans, arrived in San Sebastian; the majority being volunteers from British line regiments organised into English, Scottish and Irish brigades. Despite many having served in the regular army, they were untrained to work as a unit under these circumstances and had no time or space in which to complete any proper training. Insubordination and discontent became rife, with the continuing lack of pay a constant grievance.

Their presence was also not well received by opposing Carlists, as one former soldier observed:

> *To our foes, we of the British Legion were the most odious of all; strangers, mercenaries, heretics, scoffers, polluters of their sacred soil; so they did term us. For us there was no quarter; in the heat of battle, or by cold judicial form, it was all the same: to fall into their hands was certainly a tortured death.*

If Robert Hurd was in Spain from the start of the campaign, and there is no reason to believe he was not, he would have fought in several battles around the Basque regions of the country. In 1837, however, they suffered a serious defeat at Oriamendi, with so many casualties that the unit had to be dissolved. Things were little better for those who returned to England. At the end of this year, the *London Dispatch* reported that:

> *The Spanish Legion can scarcely be said to exist at present. Those who still remain in Spain have the name of receiving pay, nothing more. As to the wretched men now shocking the eye of humanity in London, they have no chance whatever of being paid.*

Court reports also tell of starving ex-volunteers in ragged uniforms begging in the streets as the promised pay had not materialised.

Robert Hurd's involvement in the First Carlist War is only known through later descriptions of him as a 'Spanish pensioner', and an assertion, made at one of his arrests, that he lived on a pension of 9d per day from that campaign. Records of it do not seem to have survived, either from misfortune or design, so there is no knowing how long he was out there or what part he played, but the third clause in the final terms of service allowed for state pensions to be given to wounded soldiers, so it seems he stuck it out long enough to receive injuries that ensured a reasonable pension and for the final terms of service to be agreed that granted it.

He was certainly back in England at the end of 1838, as he married Charlotte Hayward, the daughter of a blacksmith, on 24 December, in her parents' village of Shaston St James in Dorset. He gave his occupation as a 'licenced hawker'. By the time of the 1841 census, however, he and Charlotte had moved to his family home, in Little Keyford, Frome. In it, Robert is recorded once more as a labourer, while Charlotte assisted her father-in-law as a weaver. Also recorded that night were, supposedly, four siblings: two sisters and two brothers, although there is the possibility that at least two of these might have been Robert and Charlotte's own children, though there is no official documentation to support this.

The cliché of 'going out a boy and coming back a man' was likely to be true in Robert Hurd's case and whilst away he would have met adventurers like himself out in Spain. He would have fought beside them, seen them cut down in front of him and listened enthralled to the stories of their pre-legion experiences, mainly from London, and others from the regular army just like he had heard from his father. A quiet, married life in the small town of Frome with his parents, wife, and possible young family, was not what Robert Hurd had in mind for the future. And he was soon to change all that.

How long Robert Hurd stayed in Frome after that census night in 1841 is not known – he may even have only been visiting briefly – but the spirit of adventure and travel had taken hold and he was soon on the move again. In February 1845 he was in Oxford; it is here that he received what is thought to be his first press report since his return from abroad:

> Robert Hurd who had been in the service of the Queen of Spain was brought up with being disorderly and fighting in the street the preceding night. On promising to leave the town he was

discharged; the mayor cautioned him against being seen in the bad company he had kept.

After this he began to make a name for himself; the newspapers were always keen to print stories about him and those reports that do survive are obviously the ones known about through official channels.

In October 1845, the same year as his Oxford court appearance, his nickname 'Frome Bob' appeared in print for the first time and had a crime attributed to it. The now somewhat transient 'Frome Bob', described in the local newspaper as 'a travelling vagabond [going] from fair to fair', reportedly attacked a gentleman named Munday, who was steward to Lord Bolton. The incident took place at the Globe Inn in Andover, Hampshire. Hurd knocked Munday down and attempted to steal his pocket book. Bystanders came to the steward's aid, although Hurd managed to escape – through the help of several accomplices – with some loose silver. These accomplices were described as being 'two other men, a woman and a cart drawn by three large dogs'.

By the time of his next press report, in August 1846, Hurd or rather 'Frome Bob' was now an established prize fighter. The newspaper reported that he had been, along with a young woman, Caroline March (possibly the 'woman' from the previous report), arrested for being drunk and disorderly. This again took place in Hampshire. The arresting constable claimed that when Hurd was being searched, he swallowed a coin that had previously been in his pocket (and was claimed to be counterfeit). Hurd ridiculed this idea and claimed that it was a Spanish coin that he accidentally swallowed during the tussle that occurred at the time of his arrest (although he also later claimed that he had not swallowed it at all). He then turned on his accusers and asked them why he, an ex-soldier, who received 9d per day as a pension (the equivalent to around £20 in today's money), would do such a thing? It seemed to work, as this time the authorities were lenient and the pair were discharged with just a caution, and this vocal, swaggering attitude Hurd showed throughout the rest of his life had now begun.

This court appearance does throw up a couple of interesting aspects though, regarding his life at this time. Firstly, when 'enlightened' during the proceedings, by the magistrate, as to the consequences of his immoral conduct becoming known to the authorities in London, Hurd seemed nonchalant about this possibility and replied that they would not concern themselves with his conduct. This suggests he had some kind of reputation in London which needed to be protected – possibly connected to his prize fighting. Secondly, it revealed him still in receipt of a pension from the Spanish escapade, a decade after the event, which would imply he had conducted himself honourably whilst abroad and so was not dismissed, deserted or behaved too badly. This is further reinforced by the fact that the pension continued for the rest of his life.

If he had been a model soldier in Spain, he soon changed his ways on his return to England. There is an air of mystery and glamour around his life from this point on and one example appeared in October 1846, in the personal column of *Bell's Life in London*, a sporting newspaper published every Sunday. A brief message read: 'Frome Bob had better write to his friend Ashborne of Wimborne'. Was this a coded message about a piece of skulduggery, an 'in joke', or something more sinister, perhaps even a death threat? After this passage of time, it is most unlikely that we will ever know. Trouble was never far from his door though and the report of a trial at the Old Bailey of that year described how Hurd met two old acquaintances at a pub in Westminster, during which time, in a befuddled state, he exposed two watches and a quantity of gold and silver. An argument developed between Hurd and the pair of acquaintances that resulted in a fight during which he was badly beaten and his valuables taken. At the trial though, his evidence seemed confused and uncertain – so much so his 'attackers' were acquitted. This does not seem to be the 'Frome Bob' of the court appearance a few months earlier, so was there more to this case than meets the eye? Perhaps it was even connected in some way to the cryptic message which had appeared not long before in the personal column of *Bells' Life*.

In September 1848, at Wimborne Fair, Dorset,

> *An unusually numerous muster of light fingered gentry was about, and met the watchful attention of the police. Robert Hurd of some notoriety as a prize fighter under the name of Frome Bob and another fellow, calling himself Francis Harvey, were committed to three months hard labour for the stale trick of thimble rigging, by which they succeeded in obtaining from one simpleton £2/10/-. When before the magistrates, Hurd urged that the latter deserved to share the punishment for being duped.*

This is Hurd's first recorded prison sentence, and it seemed that the Old Bailey experience was now forgotten, as we once more hear the fearless bravado that was to mark his career – whether in the ring, public house, or courtroom. He was sent to Dorchester Prison and was described, while there, as a married man from Taunton working as a 'seller of fish', aged 34, and of 'imperfect education'. His behaviour during his time inside was recorded as 'orderly'. Giving his hometown as Taunton was a puzzle and something that he would repeat later in his life; possibly he was distancing himself from something in which his alter ego 'Frome Bob' might have been involved.

A couple of years later, back in Frome, his crimes had escalated and so had the punishment. At the spring Quarter Sessions in Wells, on 29 March 1850, not long before Sparrow would be prematurely released, Hurd was charged with theft. He was alleged to have taken a purse containing five half crowns from a man named John Moon, who was drinking in the Unicorn Inn, in Keyford. Hurd came in and asked the man about a watch he had heard he had for sale. In the court appearance, Moon continued the account:

> *I put my hand to my pocket and found my watch was gone. Hurd said "You damned old fool you got your watch in your pocket." He then put his fingers into my watch pocket and pulled my purse out. I saw the purse in his hand … there were five half crowns in my purse and I am not certain whether there was a sixpence or a shilling in the purse besides. Then I said, "Now my purse and watch are all gone!" I was sober at the time. I went within an hour after this happened to find a constable."*

If an accurate account of what had happened, this shameless example of daylight robbery earned Hurd a sentence of six months 'hard labour' in Wilton gaol, where both Maggs and Sparrow had already served time.

These later press reports of Robert Hurd's 'career' do not give a home address for him, but since the last census, in 1841, when he was recorded as being in Frome, he had spent time and been arrested in: Oxford, Andover, Southampton, London, and Wimborne. Whether he was still based in Frome and travelled out to these various fairs and crime scenes, perhaps staying at local inns, is not known, but what is officially recorded is that on the night of the 1851 census, 30 March, he was in London, staying with a John Canning, an old acquaintance and fellow ex-soldier and pensioner from Spain. This was a lodging house located at 30 Old Pye Street, which at the time of the census had eighteen lodgers and was situated in an area known as the 'Devil's Acre'. Historians and social commentators have struggled to find hyperbole strong enough to describe this part of London and its inhabitants. Occupied by prostitutes, beggars, thieves, conmen, charlatans, and any combination of these, Charles Dickens, in the first edition of his periodical *Household Words* – which would later feature the articles on Sergeant Smith and his colleagues of the detective force – commented:

> There is no part of the metropolis which presents a more chequered aspect, both physical and moral, than Westminster. The most lordly streets are frequently but a mask for the squalid districts which lie behind them, whilst spots consecrated to the most hallowed of purposes are begirt by scenes of indescribable infamy and pollution; the blackest tide of moral turpitude that flows in the capital rolls its filthy wavelets up to the very walls of Westminster Abbey.

This gravitation towards the more 'squalid' areas of a town or city 'begirt by scenes of indescribable infamy and pollution' is another aspect which seemed to repeat itself throughout Hurd's life.

Perhaps coming up for (fresh) air, six months later, in early September 1851, Hurd was again in Southampton when he became embroiled in another bizarre case. It involved a James Collins, who was allegedly duped out of a huge amount of money by the landlord of the Barleycorn beer shop. The details are convoluted and included an intended trip to London to see the Great Exhibition, but what is of interest is that at the trial, one of the customers in the Barleycorn was asked if he had seen 'Frome Bob' on the premises. The witness replied he was a stranger at the pub and so therefore did not know him. It was then suggested that the case be adjourned in the hope 'Frome Bob' would be apprehended; although exactly what part he was supposed to have played was never explained.

Possibly Hurd was involved in some way though, and felt the net closing in on him in Southampton, because by mid-September he was back in Frome and staying at his parents' address at 3 Mount Lane, in Little Keyford. By now, his parents were elderly and in the census earlier that year were recorded as 'paupers'. He could only have been in Frome for a short time before the dreadful events unfolded on Wednesday 24 September and then, less than two weeks later, was arrested for his supposed part in them.

PART TWO

(7 October 1851 – 4 April 1852)

10

The Magistrates' Court

Whether someone was usually arrested in Frome, they would either be locked up in the blind house, a small guard-room sans windows – hence the name – located in a corner of St John's churchyard, at the bottom of Church Lane, or else they would be taken to the town's main guardhouse, next to the Blue Boar, until their appearance before the local magistrates. The seriousness of this crime, however, meant that William Maggs, William Sparrow and Robert Hurd, alias 'Frome Bob', were to be remanded a dozen miles away, to await their day in court.

The town of Shepton Mallet lay twelve miles to the west of Frome and its house of correction was one of three in Somerset, the others being in Taunton and Ilchester; the latter was also home to the county gaol. Houses of Correction, such as Shepton Mallet, usually held persons awaiting trial (or the magistrates' court, as in the case of the trio from Frome) prisoners who had been committed indefinitely through lack of sureties, or else those sentenced to lesser spells of imprisonment – usually with the inclusion of hard labour – for minor offences.

Shepton Mallet's House of Correction had opened near the beginning of the seventeenth century and initially men, women, and children were put in together. By the end of the eighteenth century, when the prison was expanded, separate areas were introduced. By 1851 it had the capacity to hold nearly 300 prisoners and although reformers had pressurised the authorities into improving conditions, they were still far from ideal. A government report in 1770 resulted in a scathing attack on the prison system nationwide:

Many who went in healthy are in a few months changed to emaciated, dejected objects. Some are seen pining under diseases, expiring on the floors in loathsome cells of pestilential fevers and the confluent smallpox. The cause of this distress is that many prisons are scantily supplied, and some almost totally unprovided [sic] with the necessaries of life.

As for Shepton Mallet itself, it was described as a 'shocking place', built on a marsh with primitive sanitation and cells like pigsties.

Eighty-two years later, in 1842, another report, instigated by Queen Victoria, was still critical of Shepton gaol:

Scanty accommodation for prisoners [with only] *32 single cells, 12 larger cells, and 12 day cells, for male prisoners … a large majority of the prisoners sleeping in what may be called dormitories, where several pass the night in company together, and into which the turnkeys* [gaolers] *are almost fearful of venturing at night; nor can this prison be placed in a good state of discipline until this evil is remedied. It is bad enough when three prisoners sleep in the same cell, but still worse when seven or eight are thus place together. And the evil is not confined to the insecurity, the wilful contamination and the amusement, but the health also is liable to suffer from the impurity of the atmosphere thus created.*

Luckily for Maggs, Sparrow, and Hurd, they were only to spend a week there, at least initially, as the date for the hearing had been set for Monday 13 October 1851. Their appearance in court would be in Frome, as it was the normal procedure to hold it within the locale where the crime had been committed. There was also a requirement that a minimum of two magistrates be available before the case could be heard.

Magistrates were appointed by the Crown for each county and were, for the most part, gentlemen who owned or occupied land to the value of at least £100 a year. As the position was unpaid, it meant magistrates were largely from the middle class and above, often local employers or professionals. They were normally unqualified layman, but supposedly well educated enough to listen to cases and dispense justice impartially. A magistrate was entitled to sit in any part of the county but, in practice, tended to remain local.

Frome had a number of magistrates it could call on for this particular case and these included: Dr Thomas Sunderland Harrison, a surgeon from Lancashire, but who now lived at Innox Hill House; William Hulbert Sheppard, a factory owner who resided at Keyford House and member of the influential local textile family; Reverend G. Rous, vicar at nearby Laverton Church and a prominent member of the Poor Law Commission; local businessman and non-conformist John Sinkins, whose abode was at Wallbridge House, located on the town's outskirts; and Lord Dungarvan, otherwise known as Richard Boyle, 9th Earl of Cork, who owned a substantial amount of property in Frome and whose home was nearby Marston House. In addition, there were several former military gentlemen, such as Major William Trevillian, Colonel William Boyle (younger brother of Richard), and Colonel Arthur C. Phipps (the latter now a solicitor based in Wells).

If the case was of a lesser degree the magistrates could try it themselves. If the charge was more serious, known as 'indictable', they conducted a preliminary investigation to establish it was a reasonable one. This included hearing evidence from police and several principal witnesses. As this crime was murder, the latter therefore applied. Once brought before the court, Maggs, Sparrow, and Hurd, would have the charges read out to them and then be asked for their plea – 'guilty' or 'not guilty'. If they answered with the latter, the magistrates would invite the prosecution to call evidence from witnesses, including the arresting officer, in support of its case.

As the magistrates were mostly laymen, they were assisted in matters of law by an appointed clerk. In Frome, this was from the firm of solicitors Wickham & Cruttwell. Their offices were in Bath Street, the large thoroughfare cut in 1810 to the south of the town centre, but they also occupied a building at the end of Edgell's Lane, these days called Justice Lane and where the market car park now stands, which was used as the magistrate's court. It was centrally located and literally a minute's walk from the main guardhouse. It was not uncommon in many parts of the county, at least until the introduction of a specific Act in 1849, for cases to be heard in the private house of one of the bench, a hired room or even in a public house like the inquests – but Frome was fortunate in having its own court a long time before that.

While the three prisoners languished in the prison at Shepton Mallet, Detective Sergeant Smith had travelled once more across the county border; this time to investigate potential 'evidence' against Sparrow that had recently come to light. The ancient Wiltshire parish of North Bradley lay between Trowbridge and Westbury, although its far parochial reaches extended west to the Somerset boundary. Each year the village held a fair in May and September. The latter had originally been held on the Monday after Holyrood Day, which traditionally fell on 14 September, but by the mid-nineteenth century the date had been moved to end of the month. It was still predominately for the sale of cattle and cheese, but there were many organised activities, including horse racing and bowling. The first day of the fair, Monday 29 September, had coincided with the one on which Sergeant Smith had begun his investigation, back in Frome.

Sparrow had made his way over and secured a room at the New Ring of Bells public house. He was still staying there when arrested three days later and taken to Westbury Police Station on the suspicion of possessing the stolen watch.

While in North Bradley, Sergeant Smith discovered two important pieces of 'evidence' against Sparrow. The first were conversations Sparrow had engaged in with several of the locals, during the
fair, and the other concerned a fight in which he claimed to have
been involved.

On the second evening of the fair, after people had found out
that he lived in Frome, Sparrow had been asked about the murder. He claimed to have seen Sarah's corpse the day after, having
been out to the Watts' farmhouse. He described her injuries and
the whereabouts of her body – it was downstairs in the dairy room
he said – as well as certain other details. As Smith was only too
aware, the body had been taken upstairs on the actual day of the
murder, where it had remained until the inquest two days later. At
the same time, several details Sparrow had mentioned, Smith had
only recently found out for himself. Either the suspect was making
it all up, exaggerating details he heard around the town and from
the newspapers, filling in the rest from his own imagination, or
else he knew all of this because he had been directly involved in
the robbery, rape, and murder – either as the main perpetrator or
a willing participant.

The other potentially incriminating 'evidence', the fight, was
where Sparrow claimed he acquired a wound to his left thumb. He
had been questioned about the injury on his arrest and an examination by a police surgeon had taken place the following day. His
version was that it had been inflicted during a fight at the fair on
the Monday evening. In his defence, there had been a brawl at the
pub where he was staying and it was a common practice during
that time to crush an opponent's thumb between the teeth, which
would cause extreme pain and often turn septic, even to the point
of requiring amputation. Sergeant Smith talked to several people
who had been present when the altercation had occurred, but discovered they were prepared to swear under oath that Sparrow was
not involved. His version of events had already been called into
question when his thumb had been examined by George Shorland,
the police surgeon. In the doctor's opinion, the injury to the thumb
was much older than the four days claimed by Sparrow, possibly
around as many as ten days. If this was the case, it would mean
Sparrow had acquired the wound on or around 24 September –
the day of the murder.

By the time Sergeant Smith returned to Frome, several
witnesses from North Bradley had agreed to testify before the
magistrates' court and the detective's investigation seemed to be
reaching its culmination. It was all starting to add up to Sparrow
being the main culprit and the other two, Maggs and Hurd, guilty

by association. Incarcerated in Shepton Mallet gaol, there was little the three of them could do but wait until their court appearance the following week.

On Monday 13 October 1851, Maggs, Sparrow and Hurd, were escorted back to Frome for their appearance at the magistrates' court. On their arrival in the town, the trio were marched through the centre to the main guardhouse. Hundreds of people lined the route, straining to catch a glimpse of the men accused of the hideous crime that had dominated conversations for the past three weeks.

The prisoners were secured in the guardhouse, with separate cells and silence imposed, to await their brief journey across the road to the magistrates' court. If a prima facia (literally 'at first sight') case could be established, the trio would be returned to Shepton gaol, where they would stay on remand to await the sitting of the next assize court. While there, access to legal representation would be at the discretion of the prison authorities, who often insisted that a prison officer or constable be present. As for time to prepare their case, this would be a matter of pot luck for both defence and prosecution, as the next assizes could sometimes be a mere few days away and appeals for more time were not usually treated sympathetically. In this case though, and if sent to trial, the next assizes would be held the following April; plenty of time for the two teams of solicitors to prepare their cases. On the downside, of course, this meant Maggs, Sparrow and Hurd would have to spend the next five months in prison.

When everything was ready at the court, the prisoners were brought out of the guardhouse, marched across the bridge in the direction of North Parade and then directed into Bridge Street for a few yards, before turning left into Edgell's Lane. Their destination was the last building on the right, at the end of the small lane: the magistrates' court. Once more, crowds lined either side of the route, while others stood in the doorways and craned their necks out of windows of the private dwellings that made up the rest of the lane's buildings. The small party reached the court and went inside: the crowd outside could now only imagine the proceedings taking place within.

11

Day One

On Monday 13 October 1851, William 'Will' Maggs, William 'Bill' Sparrow, and Robert 'Frome Bob' Hurd, were brought into the magistrates' courtroom in Frome and escorted to the dock, where they stood to await the proceedings. The bench consisted of five local magistrates: Dr Harrison, Mr John Sinkins, Colonel Boyle, Mr W.H. Sheppard and Major William Trevillian.

A local solicitor, Thomas Hawkes, whose offices were in nearby North Parade, applied for permission to be present on behalf of the prisoners. The magistrates, however, decided against the request on the grounds that it was only a preliminary inquiry to decide on the presented evidence, and therefore he would not be needed; although they allowed him to remain in court. The public was excluded from the proceedings on the magistrates' orders though, and the witnesses were also excluded at the request of the prisoners – the most vocal among them being Hurd; they would be recalled one by one to give their testimony.

As on the first day of the inquest, held two days after the murder, the initial witness was the victim's father, John Watts. He repeated the testimony he had given before the coroner – recalling the sequence of events on his return to the farm about 4 o'clock and finding his dead daughter. He added though, that having been into town to find the doctor, he had called at Constable Grist's house in Keyford, to give him the details of the murder. As he was leaving, at about 6 o'clock, he met the man whom he now knew to be one of the prisoners – Robert Hurd – outside The Crown, which was next door to the constable's house. Watts then explained that Hurd had asked him to have a glass of beer with him and that they had gone to the Woolpack Inn on Culver Hill. He then stated that he had not known Hurd at the time and did not think he had seen him before.

The next witness, also as at the inquest, was 13-year-old Alfred Allard. He was in the employ of a carpenter named John Chedzey on the day of the murder and, through his testimony, was likely to have been the last person to see Sarah alive, other than the murderer or murderers. Like John Watts before him, he repeated the evidence he had given earlier, although he added that he was about two 'lug' (approximately 30ft) from the victim when he saw her and she was not wearing a bonnet. He also said he had not seen anyone else near the house.

The first 'new' witness was Mary Wheeler, who lived at Tytherington but was visiting a nearby farm when the Watts returned home. She was one of the first to comfort Leah Watts, after the discovery of the body.

> *On Wednesday 24th I was at farmer Pickford's and was outside the front door when ... I heard Mrs. Watts say, "She has been dead these hours"*

Mary Wheeler ran over to the farm and once inside,

> *saw Mrs Watts upstairs, crying and she said her child was dead. She came downstairs and we went into the dairy, and I saw the child lying down. She had two bad blows on her temple and a cut or scratch on her cheek; it looked as though she had had a blow to the side of her left ear; the skin was broken, there was no blood. I considered that she had been put into the whey or that whey had been thrown over her; there was a bad mark on her knee and another on her elbow as if it had been done with a stick; there was a small dark place on her bosom; I observed blood on her person and one spot upon her petticoat and another on the outside of her frock; when I found her she was lying on her back and her clothes all up over her head. There was blood under her upon the floor; the body was quite cold all over and quite stiff; there was a spot of blood in the kitchen. When we were upstairs the mother discovered that several things were missing and that her house had been robbed; after we had washed her and laid her out on her back, blood & corruption ran out of her mouth.*

Sarah Battle, a neighbour whose family owned Battle Farm but rented it to the Watts, then corroborated Mary Wheeler's testimony, while Francis Giles, who had examined Sarah the first evening and performed the post-mortem, repeated the evidence he had given on both days of the inquest. He finished his testimony, as before, with his belief that the victim had been violated before death.

The next few witnesses were all concerned with various sightings of the three prisoners on the day of the murder. If Alfred Allard's declaration was true, and there was no reason to doubt it, Sarah had been killed between 1 o'clock when he saw her, and 4 o'clock, when her parents returned home. The fact that the body was already stiff – according to Mary Wheeler and others

– indicated that death had probably been before 3 o'clock or even earlier. This gave around a two-hour window for the crime to have been perpetrated and so the whereabouts of any of the prisoners at any given time on that day – but especially during and immediately either side of this specific period – was of great significance.

One of the many sightings of the prisoners that emerged, placed them at the Marston Gate turnpike, between 1.00–1.30 pm, which was within that 'crucial' time period and around a twenty minute medium-paced walk from Battle Farm. The toll gate was situated on the Frome road, coming in from the direction of Nunney. The first of the witnesses who saw them there was Joseph Watts, a horse doctor.

> *I live in Tytherington Lane and have known all three prisoners more than ten years. I recollect seeing them on Wednesday the 24th of September as I was coming down the lane from my house to Marston turnpike gate about half past one o'clock in the afternoon. I saw four men in the lane but I don't know who the fourth man was. They were sitting under a bush close by the toll bar. Hurd got up and beckoned the others on and they all went on together to a heap of stones between the gate and Sandy Hill. When I came up to them William Maggs spoke to me and shook hands with me, William Sparrow also spoke to me and Hurd, who was standing at a gate a little beyond, beckoned the others on as if he was the leader of them. They then turned down Sandy Hill Lane and looked over the two gates on each side of the way. Afterwards they went on till I lost sight of them. They went in a direction towards farmer Wellet's house.*

A plan of the neighbourhood was then produced in court for the magistrates to study and to understand the geography of the area, in relation to the murder scene and the sighting of the prisoners.

Robert Hurd then addressed the witness (Joseph Watts) and said: 'I guessed the time by hearing the Rectory bell. It rang at 1 o'clock and it was about half an hour afterwards that I saw you.' He then asked several more questions, one of which Watts answered: 'I know Farmer Brine of Gare Hill; I did not go there to see anyone else; William Brine is no relation of mine; I did not say on my former examination that I went to see my relations.' Joseph Watts then requested the depositions should be produced and examined, which they were, but no such statement was found. 'From the time I first saw them,' Watts continued, 'to when I saw them go down the lane was about a quarter of an hour.'

Richard Babey, the toll collector at the Marston Gate turnpike was called next. The 64-year-old corroborated the previous witnesses' testimony, in that he had also seen four men near the gate about the time stated by Watts. He said he could not identify any of the prisoners, although one was taller than the rest and this man had beckoned the others on – it was noted that Hurd was much taller than Maggs and Sparrow. Two of them went on through the gate, Babey recalled, and shortly afterwards he saw Joseph Watts go on towards Frome and overtake the quartet near the heap of stones. The men went on together. The toll collector recollected that Reverend Boyle's carriage had passed the gate in the direction of Marston around the same time, but whether it was before, or after, he witnessed the interaction, he could not say.

Despite Hurd admitting he had seen Watts after the rectory bell had rung, the three prisoners solemnly declared they were not the men seen by the witnesses. Sarah Cox, the kitchen maid at the Marston Rectory House, residence of the Reverend Boyle, was then called to state that the ringing of the dinner bell was at 12.30 pm (and not 1 o'clock as Hurd had claimed) and at two minutes before 2 o'clock on 24 September. The second ring, she added, was for the family luncheon.

Another sighting of Maggs, Sparrow, and Hurd, along with a fourth man, had occurred earlier in the day, during the morning, and opposite the Woolpack in Culver Hill. Although well outside the probable timeframe of the murder, this was significant, as the beer house was on the route that John and Leah Watts had taken into the market and, according to one of the witnesses, had been observed by the prisoners. This witness was Sophia Cornish, landlady of the Woolpack. Her husband, Benjamin Cornish, was also a witness to the sighting. When called to the stand, the latter stated he had seen the three prisoners and another man – this fourth man Cornish named as William Sargeant – standing opposite his shop (beer house) window. The four stood together in conversation for about twenty minutes, before separating:

> I cannot say which way the others went but I afterwards met Hurd near the Unicorn as I was going to Frome. He passed me and I met him again coming out of the churchyard from Gentle Street. I saw no more of any of them until nearly ten o'clock at night when I saw Hurd in my house. He appeared to be sober and spoke to me of the murder saying he hoped it would be found out. While the four men were standing together in the forenoon near my house, Mr Watts the father of the deceased, passed by towards the market.

The timings given by the two witnesses collectively placed the men outside the Woolpack sometime between 10 and 11 o'clock, the period in which the Watts had passed by on their way to Frome town centre.

Several more afternoon sightings were then described by witnesses in relatively quick succession. Benjamin Mines, a farm labourer said:

> *I know the three prisoners and recollect seeing them with a man named Whimpey* [sic] *on the day of the murder at the door of Mr Gale's public house.* [This public house was the Victoria Inn, located in Christchurch Street East] *Hurd and Maggs were holding a conversation during which they proposed and promised to meet each other in an hour. I saw Hurd take out his double case watch and look at it. Hurd had a dead goose hanging by his side. At the time I saw them it was nearly two o'clock. I could not hear where they appointed to meet.*

Joseph Noble, a thatcher then stated:

> *I have got some potatoes in a field just by the road near the Mount. Sparrow and Maggs came up to me together on the day of the murder … They were coming from the direction of Feltham and proceeding towards the footway that leads across the field to Quaking Bridge. Maggs had on dark clothes and Sparrow was dressed near in the same way as he is now.*

Another witness to their journey back into Frome, presumably from Maggs's house in Feltham, was Harriet Morgan:

> *I live at the Mount; I went out to serve the pigs and saw Sparrow and Maggs walking up under the hedge in the Blatchbridge road, near the Mount on this side of Moss's cottages coming from Blatchbridge; this was between two and three o'clock – it might have been after three.*

A third witness to this journey was called. Thomas Harding recounted that:

> *On the day of the murder I was going to Woodlands. I went along till I came to Bellows Gate when I crossed the fields. When I reached the Asylum it was about three o'clock. Three men came towards it across the road from Woodlands.*

The only problem with this witness, in terms of the prosecution's case, was when asked to look around the room to see if he could identify the three men, he could not – even when his attention was directed towards the prisoners.

The prosecution's focus then switched to Sparrow's arrest, his wounded thumb, and his attendance at the North Bradley Fair. William Staples, an inspector with the Wiltshire County Constabulary and the officer who had arrested Sparrow, was called to give his deposition:

> On the 2nd of October I apprehended the prisoner Sparrow at Westbury on a charge of stealing a watch at Frome; He stated that he had bought the watch last Wednesday at the Victoria public house; he said he agreed on the price, but not having the money with him, William Maggs and he went home to his lodgings and got it. They afterwards met Robert Hurd and paid him for the watch, 37/- he said first and afterwards he said 27/-; he said William Maggs owed him for ten days work and that was the money with which he purchased it, but that not being enough money he pawned a waistcoat and coat at Frome. When I took him [in] I observed that his thumb was in a very bad state; I asked him how he got it and he said in reply, "I hardly know but I think some of the Southwick chaps bit it at the fair. His thumb was examined by a surgeon on the third of October ... it was in a bad state - like a boil and breaking.

As for to Sparrow's attendance at the fair, a local gardener, John Jackson, said:

> I was at Bradley Fair on Wednesday the 1st October. I saw Sparrow on 29th and 30th September and on the 1st October, at the fair; I went to a public house and saw Sparrow there. Knowing him to be a native of Frome I asked him if he had heard anything about the murder? He said "Yes he had." There had been two or three taken up on suspicion but they couldn't make anything out of them; I asked him if he thought it would ever be thought out, he said no, for it was only one man that did it; I asked him if he knew how the murder was done; he answered yes, she was at first struck on the head with a stick and then put into the whey lead, she was dead, taken out and left on the floor; during the time he was talking, the knot of his handkerchief worked around by his ear, and he said, "Do you think I am going to be hung?" He also said he knew the people that lived in the house where the murder was committed well but I did not hear him describe it ... I did not see that his hand was tied up on Monday, I saw that his hand was

bad on Tuesday and he said he got it done on Monday but no one believed it because it was evidently an old sore that had been done for some time. On Tuesday morning I observed his thumb myself and it appeared to be an old bruise. I call it a bruise when anything has been squat or pinched very badly. It appeared as if it had white matter under it from which I thought it had been done some days. I believe there was some row in the house called the Ring of Bells where Sparrow was on the Monday night. On the Monday evening, Sparrow said during the talk I had with him, that he had been at Westbury races the week before.

Sergeant Smith then announced that he did not wish to offer further evidence at that time and so wished for a remand. The room was cleared and after a consultation of about twenty minutes the prisoners were recalled and remanded until 20 October, the following Monday. They were then taken out of the court and returned to Shepton gaol for a further week's incarceration.

12

Day Two

O
n the morning of Monday 20 October 1851, the three
men suspected of killing Sarah Watts, Maggs, Sparrow
and Hurd, were again returned to Frome from Shepton
Mallet and brought up in front of the local magistrates. This time
the bench consisted of six magistrates, two of them being new to
the case: Colonel Phipps and Mr L. Ludlow. The remaining ones
were Mr W.H. Sheppard, Dr Harrison, Major Trevillian and Mr
John Sinkins. Once more a large crowd had gathered to catch sight
of the prisoners.

Prior to the commencement of the proceedings, Robert Hurd
requested, as he also had on the first day, that all witnesses be sent
out of court. This was done. The first witness to be called to testify this time was an agricultural labourer by the name of Robert
Hilliar. Not only did he share a first name with Hurd, but also an
address; he lived next door to the prisoner's parents.

> *I live in* [No 2] *Mount Lane near Mr Sheppard's* [the magis-
> trate presiding] *house in the parish of Frome,* Hilliar began.
> *I was working for Mr. Doswell on Thursday last week* [this was,
> in fact, the Thursday before, on 2 October] *at the Woodlands,
> cracking stones. I was coming up Blatchbridge between six and
> seven o'clock in the evening from my work; when I was coming
> up the hill I sat down to rest a bit; I saw William Maggs come
> out of Burchill Lane; he went on up the hill towards Frome
> and then he made a cross turn and went up the lane; I knew
> that Maggs* [and] *Hurd and others were blamed for the murder
> then; I went on as quick as I could into the lane that leads to
> my house and just to the side of a stave gate, I went into a field;
> I went into that gate and close up after the lane, and when I
> was going up after that hedge, I heard another man coming
> down; it appeared so by his steps, and he met Maggs opposite to
> another little lane that leads to Blatchbridge Lane; I was under
> the hedge when they were talking; I saw Maggs; the other man
> was taller than Maggs; Maggs asked this man if he had heard
> anything fresh to day. The man that I did not know told Maggs
> that he had heard that Bill Sparrow had told the London officer*
> [Detective Sergeant Smith] *who had done the murder; that*

the London officer had been to Sparrow and said, "Ah my good fellow, I am glad thee hasn't done the murder, thee wot have a free pardon and £50;" Maggs said he will neither have a free pardon nor the £50, for it was Bill Sparrow who killed the girl, and that he would not have killed her, only she knew him.

Hilliar then explained why he had not come forward with this information beforehand.

I was afraid that I should be murdered or I should have told this before. On Saturday night last, since I gave this information, I went down to Cornish's [The Woolpack Inn] with my wife and daughter to have a pint of beer; a man who is first cousin to the prisoner Sparrow, was there, he sat opposite me, he said to me, "When theest go in and say anything about my cousin I'll hit your neck out of crook". I have four miles to go before daylight to my work and return again that night and I was afraid to tell this before. I live next door to the prisoner Hurd; I have known Maggs for the last two years.

Maggs addressed Hilliar, regarding them having known each other for two years, and said:

'I have known you for 20 years; we worked together at Nunney'.
'I never spoke to you before', Hilliar replied.
'How long have you been working this four miles from your house?' Sparrow interjected.
'Two weeks and four days'. Hilliar answered.

The first constable at the crime scene, James Hoddinott, was then called and the focus of the prosecution changed to the handkerchief which had been found at the crime scene.

I am a constable of Frome. I went to Watts's house at half past six on the night of the murder. I went into the kitchen. I saw a small spot of blood about two or three inches broad on the floor near the fireplace. I asked the woman if anything was found in the house and she said: "Yes, a handkerchief was left on the table," it is now in my possession; it is marked 'E. T.' in the corner, the same I now produce. There were no stains about it; but when he first had it there was a little wet on it as if it had been put into a person's mouth.

The prosecution wished to show the handkerchief belonged to Sparrow and to draw attention to his wounded thumb, so several witnesses were called to give evidence in these two areas. The first one was Elizabeth Elliot.

*I am the wife of William Elliot [and] I live at Burr's Lane
Farm; my husband keeps the Burrs Lane Bar turnpike in the
Woodlands. I know William Sparrow, he called at my house on
the 14th September a few minutes after 3 o'clock; to light his
pipe his nose was bleeding when he came in; he took out a red
sort of handkerchief with white edges; to stop it, it looked very
dirty; in the corner of the handkerchief there was a slit and a
little further down another; the handkerchief produced is like
one he had; the slits are similar; it was very much such a handkerchief; I noticed the threads in it. I would rather say it is the
handkerchief than is not. My impression is that it is the same.*

In response to the testimony of the witness, Sparrow shouted from
the dock: 'I have not had a silk handkerchief for the last seven
years'.

Caroline Bryant was then called:

*I was at North Bradley Fair about a fortnight or a week ago
with my husband. I saw Sparrow there. About 4 o'clock. In the
evening he came down and laid down under my stall and I saw
some blood on his finger. I asked him what was the matter with
his thumb? He said it was only a scratch.*

The injured thumb became the sole focus of attention now and
another witness relevant to this was called. Martha Watson was the
daughter to the landlord of the New Ring of Bells where Sparrow
stayed while attending the fair.

*My father keeps a public house at North Bradley. I assist
him in his business. I recollect the last Bradley Fair. I saw the
prisoner Sparrow at our house on Monday and Tuesday. On
Tuesday 30th of September I saw he had a bad thumb, he was
showing it in the taproom. On Wednesday morning he showed
it to me, as he was going by he held it up to me; he said it was
bit in a fight at the fair. It was in a very bad state there was
matter on the thumb nail.*

She then recalled Sparrow's knowledge of the murder, through his
telling of having seen the body:

*On Wednesday October 1st we were at breakfast. My father
asked if it was true a girl had been murdered at Frome, he said
it was quite true, he had seen the girl himself. I said "Do you
mean to say you have seen the girl yourself since she has been
murdered?" He said he had on Thursday morning and that*

there were ten constables there when he saw her. Father asked him if they had any suspicion of any one and he said he did not know and that there had been four persons taken up and set at liberty again, among them the girl's uncle. He said "I do not think the girl's uncle murdered the girl more than you did," meaning me and father. He said she had a blow on the head with a stick, as he thought, and she was put in the whey tub after that. I asked him which it was that caused her death, whether the blow to the head or being put into the whey, he said he didn't know, that the whey was quite stained with blood that came from her head; he added he did not think the murderer would ever be found out as he thought there was only one concerned in it; adding that when she was found she was lying in the back kitchen with her clothes over her head.

Through these testimonies the prosecution was obviously trying to show that Sparrow knew all this information because he had been involved in the murder, and it was not a work of his imagination. There was, of course, another option – that of him actually being at Battle Farm on the Thursday morning, the day *after* the murder. But the fact he claimed to have seen the body while it was still downstairs seemed to rule this out. Several witnesses also testified to say they had not seen him at the farm on that day. One of these witnesses, who took the stand, was Sarah's mother, Leah Watts:

I was at home on Thursday morning, the day after my child was murdered; the prisoner Sparrow to the best of my knowledge did not come to the house on that day. I left about four o'clock in the afternoon. My husband was at home when I left. In the evening of the murder, after the child was taken upstairs I missed my husband's coat, waistcoat and a shawl. I had the shawl safe in a chest on Monday. I believe I saw his watch on that day. I did not miss the watch until the following Saturday.

The emphasis then shifted back to Sparrow's injured thumb and when exactly the wound had been inflicted. George Shorland, surgeon of Westbury, then gave his testimony:

On Friday Oct 3rd I was called in by a police constable to see the clothes and person of William Sparrow. I did so at the offices of the magistrates' clerks in Westbury. I did not discover any traces of blood on his dress, but I perceived patches of stains and matter on his shirt; he accounted for them by stating he had a bad hand, and that they were occasioned by keeping his hands in his trouser pockets; there were similar stains in his pocket which corresponded with those on his shirt. I examined his left hand and found two contused wounds on his first and second knuckle of his thumb and on the second knuckle of his forefinger, there was also a contused wound on the extremity of his thumb; he said he got his injuries at the fair. The matter was fully developed and covered with a scabby eructation. I am of the opinion that the wounds must have been caused at a period anterior to that stated by the prisoner. Judging by the position of the marks I should think 8 or 10 days prior. I consider they must be occasioned by the hand being in contact with some hard substance, a bite would no doubt produce similar injuries, especially the wound at the end of the thumb which was more lacerated. If it had been done on the Monday matter would certainly not have appeared under the nail by Wednesday morning.

Before these facts could sink in, however, Hurd announced to those assembled in court, in what had become his regular courtroom flamboyance, he wished to make another statement:

I made out my statement a fortnight ago tomorrow, he exclaimed. *Mr Sheppard cautioned me at the time, that if I said anything now, it might be an injury to me. I made out my statement correct, from ten in the morning until dark. I should wish for Mr Smith, the detective to take my statement and to go every place I said I was at. Of course if any one denies it that person will be chief witness against me. Gentlemen, when our time is come to call forward our witnesses we shall not be able to have them; I should wish to subpoena them for me to have justice. I want no man or woman to swear anything but what is right for me. The Sergeant of Marines could clear me in a minute.* (This was a recruiting sergeant who Maggs and Hurd claimed to have met in the Victoria Inn).

After this brief outburst by Hurd, Sergeant Smith came towards the magistrates and requested the prisoners be further remanded. After a short consultation, the magistrates agreed to adjourn until the following Monday.

The case had by now generated much excitement – as one newspaper would later report – that when Sergeant Smith went through the Market Place with the trio of prisoners, somewhere between 1,200 and 1,300 people lined the route. With the main evidence against Sparrow mounting, the net seemed to be closing in on all three accused.

13

Day Three

The morning of Monday 27 October 1851 dawned and for a third time, the trio accused of the Sarah Watts murder were brought to Frome from the place which had been their residence for the past three weeks: Shepton Mallet gaol. There was surely some hope on the part of the prisoners, at least, that this would be their final appearance before the magistrates and they would be set free. Things, however, did not go as they had hoped.

On their arrival at the magistrates' court, they found that they were joined in the dock by a fourth suspect – William Sargeant. He had been the fourth man outside the Woolpack Inn, on the morning of the murder, and had also been seen with his now fellow prisoners several more times during that day. Sargeant was a 46-year-old edge tool maker, at least this was the occupation recorded on the 1851 census. He had in fact only recently been released from Shepton Mallet gaol, having served eighteen months for assaulting constables while they were attempting to arrest Robert Hurd at the Unicorn pub over the 'Moon theft' case.

The reason for Sargeant's arrest and appearance was the bundle of clothes that had been stolen from the Watts' farm the day Sarah had been killed. They had been found on the day of the second inquest, Tuesday 30 September, hidden in a field near to where Sargeant lived, at Butts Square. Although only circumstantial evidence, Sergeant Smith had nevertheless found two witnesses who would support the prosecution's argument that it had been Sargeant – a well-known associate of the other three – who had stuffed the bundle under a hedge in the field. With these witnesses in place Smith felt free to arrest the suspect on the morning of the third court appearance; and like Maggs before him, Sargeant had been picked up while inside the Blue Boar; conveniently allowing himself to be apprehended about a stone's throw from the magistrates' court.

Sitting on the bench this time were eight magistrates; five of whom had sat on the case previously, along with three others who could perhaps bring a fresh eye to the proceedings. The new members were Lord Dungarvan, Reverend Rous, and Mr W.F. Knatchbull. If the case was unfamiliar to the last magistrate – although he would surely have read the newspaper reports or been briefed by his fellow magistrates – one of the prisoners was only too familiar. Magistrate Knatchbull had met William Maggs before, in Wells in 1846, when he had given him six months hard labour for stealing potatoes. The remaining quintet of magistrates consisted of Dr Harrison, Mr Ludlow, Mr Sinkins, Major Trevillian, and Mr Sheppard.

The first witness called that morning was Sophia Cornish. She was, of course, married to Benjamin Cornish, landlord of the Woolpack Inn on Culver Hill. Her husband had given his testimony the week before and recalled having seen all four men in the dock outside his beer house when the Watts had passed by. Now it was her turn. The prosecution's supposition, in calling these two witnesses, was that the four prisoners knew John and Leah Watts would be away from their farm for the whole day and so saw an opportunity to burgle their home. Mrs Cornish took the stand and straight away backed up her husband's statement:

> I remember the morning of 24th September, I saw all four of the prisoners together between 10 and 11 o'clock in the morning, opposite our shop window; I know the whole of the prisoners. Whilst they were standing together I saw Mr Watts pass.

Sophia Cornish then gave details of two more sightings later that day. The first concerned Sparrow, who she saw around 4 o'clock in the afternoon,

> coming down the Mount towards the Asylum; there was a short man with him; Sparrow had, in the morning a very nice green Jim Crow on; when I saw Sparrow again he had a black hat. The other sighting was of Hurd the same evening… He came in with Mr Watts the father of the girl murdered; he asked for some beer and I bought him some; he said that the murder was a horrid deed and he hoped the rascals will be hung and quartered; he said the girl was found dead on her father's going home, and that the murder was done when the parents were at the market; I did not hear any conversation between Watts and Hurd; Watts did not speak whilst he was in the house; Hurd stayed there whilst Watts sat there.

At this point, acting as his own counsel, Robert Hurd theatrically leapt up and addressed the witness in somewhat of an aggressive tone:

> 'Do you remember looking up and saying it was a bad job?'
> 'I might have said so,' replied Sophia Cornish.
> 'Did you say so or did you not?'
> 'I think I did.'

The prosecution now switched their focus briefly onto William Sargeant, for the next witness, although she also gave evidence about another sighting of Sparrow. Ann Hiscox lived at Butts Square and was a neighbour of Sargeant:

I remember the 24th of September; Sparrow asked me whether Sargeant lived this way; after 2 o'clock. I was standing at the bottom of the square; I showed him the house and he went up to it and went in, and staid there a few minutes and then came out with Sargeant and he went up the Frome Road; I know that on the day there was a murder committed; I have had some conversation with him respecting the murder; I told him about Sparrow asking for his house; he said that Sparrow asked him to go down to the Crown and he refused but did go with him and stayed about an hour and then came home after; I did not see that they had anything when they left the house; Sargeant said it was a rascally shame to serve the poor child so.

A sighting of the other two prisoners – Maggs and Hurd – was the focus of witness Henry Keene:

I live at the Butts and work for Mr Case. I remember the 24th of September at about 3:30. I saw Maggs and Hurd together; they were going up a lane towards the Asylum from Little Keyford. They came down from the direction of the beer house. I was about 20 lengths from them. I saw Maggs give Hurd something; he took it out of his pocket; couldn't see what it was; they kept moving on slow.

If they were heading away from the Woolpack at 3.30 pm, then they did not get very far, as according the next witness, Joseph Singer, they had come back past the beer house and were drinking in another pub, nearer the town centre, by the time the hour was out:

I keep the Crown Inn at Keyford. I remember the 24th September, I saw all four prisoners at our house about 3:55 o'clock. I saw them come in; they stayed there together; I think they left separately; they all went at 7 o'clock or within a few minutes after; I can't say in what direction they came.

It was now Sparrow's turn to question a witness:

'*Did you see anything about my hand on the Sunday after the murder?*' he asked, menacingly.
'*I didn't notice it,*' the landlord replied.

This was 28 September, and the night before the fair at North Bradley that Sparrow attended.

For now, the focus of the next witness was on Sparrow's alleged ownership of a handkerchief found at the Watts farmhouse, rather than any possible 'confession' at the fair:

> [My name is Mary Francis and] *I am the wife of Henry Francis who keeps the Horse and Groom at the Woodlands. I remember the 24th of September; I heard of the murder. I saw Sparrow at my house* [this was presumably an earlier date]*; He came in the afternoon and stayed there two or three hours before he went away. He had an old dirty silk handkerchief. On the 20th he was again drinking at my house, I saw the same handkerchief on his knee and on his hand. I was close to him; it was ragged at the corner; he left it on the settle whilst he went out. I examined it and I observed some slits in it. I noticed it more when it was spread out on his knee; I saw him at the house again on Sunday* [the same evening that he had also visited The Crown Inn at Keyford]. *I believe I should know the handkerchief,* [at this point the handkerchief found at the farm was shown to Mrs Francis. There was no hesitation on her part]; *this is the same handkerchief I saw in Sparrow's hand on the 13th and 20th; we were sitting talking together and I assume it is the same. I heard a great deal of talking about a handkerchief and this is the reason that I came forward today. I have not seen the prisoner since.*

Sparrow once again addressed a witness, only this time he was more animated:

> 'You never saw me with that handkerchief, I never had it.'

The exhibit shown to Mary Francis had been produced by James Hoddinot, the constable who had attended the crime scene on the first evening, and who now himself took the stand:

> *I found* [the handkerchief] *on the table at the house where Sarah Watts was murdered. I first went into the house about half past six on the 24th of September; after I entered the house the first thing I saw was a spot of blood below the fireplace, on the floor, then I looked on the table and found the handkerchief I now produce; I examined it and then put it into my pocket. I then saw two or three spots of blood on the wall; then went into the milk house and saw the floor all bloody, a large pool of blood all over the ground just under a trendle which was half full of*

whey and it appeared to be bloody as if some had been tipped out with something covered with blood.

Several more witnesses were called to prove the finding of the handkerchief in the house. These included the victim's father, John Watts, who was later reported by one newspaper as looking like a very old man and appearing deeply affected while he gave his evidence, especially when describing his arrival back at the farm.

My daughter was murdered on the 24th of September, [I] *returned home on that day about 4 o'clock* [and] *observed the whey in the milk house before I went out and I also saw it when I came back; then tipped the tub up containing it, and I saw that the water was bloody as if something covered with blood had been dipped in it.*

A relative, Hannah Watts, who lived in Button Street, Frome, then debunked any possibility that Sparrow had been at the farm on the Thursday.

I remember the 24th of September [and] *the morning after the murder,* she said. *I was at the house at a quarter before six and staid there all the day. I was in the house all day up to seven o'clock* [in the evening]. *I never saw Sparrow before, and I am quite sure he did not come to Mr Watts's house the whole of that day; if he had I must have seen him.*

The attention of the court was now brought back to the bundle of stolen clothes and the possibility Sargeant had been involved in hiding them in the field near his house.

On Tuesday, after the murder [this was 30 September – the day of the second inquest] *I found the bundle now produced, about ten minutes to six in the evening in a field on the Butts Hill,*

stated John Butcher, a saddler who lived Behind Town, in Frome.

It was a misty morning with a little rain. I should think it must have been about an hour before as this was raining very fast about 5 o'clock the same morning. I should have seen it if it had been there then; it would have been wetter. The clothes could not have been thrown where they were from the road but some one must have got over the hedge and placed them there. A person might go from Butts Square to where the clothes were found in a few minutes.

The clothes were produced and identified by John Watts as his property. He confirmed that they had been stolen on the day his daughter was murdered. John Butcher's place was then taken on the stand by Thomas Vesey, a labourer, whose own testimony seemed even more damning for Sargeant:

> *I live in the Butts Square Frome. I know all four of the prisoners. Sargeant lives near me about four or five doors away. On the morning of the 30th of September I heard someone go down the square about 2:30 in the morning and return about half an hour later. Sargeant lives at the top of the square. There is no thoroughfare through the square. Sargeant lives at the top about three doors along; anybody going up to where Sargeant lives must pass my house.*

There were to be no more witnesses called that day and all four prisoners were remanded to await their next appearance. This, however, was set to be on the following day and would see their fate decided.

14

Day Four

Tuesday 28 October 1851 became day four of the magistrates' examination of the Sarah Watts murder case and on this day they were due to decide whether the suspects, Robert Hurd, alias 'Frome Bob', William 'Bill' Sparrow and William 'Will' Maggs, along with a fourth man arrested the day before, William Sargeant, should be sent for trial.

As on the previous day's session, the bench consisted of eight magistrates, who were Colonel Phipps, Mr Sinkins, Reverend Rous, Mr Knatchbull, Dr Harrison, Mr Sheppard, and Mr Ludlow. The eighth and final magistrate was Colonel William Boyle, whose attendance in this case was his first.

The excitement around town that had accompanied all the prisoners' previous appearances was now reaching fever pitch, as an outcome was expected that very day. Before that happened, however, there were more witnesses to testify, and first in the stand was Robert Singer:

> *I work for Joseph Singer at the Crown at Keyford, [and] on Sunday after the murder I was in the taproom of the Crown at Keyford; Sparrow came in the evening; I saw something bound around his finger or thumb it looked like a bit of rag; I am quite sure this was on the Sunday after the murder.*

If this was true, then Robert Singer had observed something his employer had not and would be proof once and for all that Sparrow had sustained his thumb injury *before* going to North Bradley. This seemed to be damning evidence.

The next witness, a labourer named William Butler, who lived near the murder scene in West Woodlands, merely confirmed that he had seen an earlier witness – Robert Hilliar – working on the Maiden Bradley road, breaking stones, on the second day of October at about 9 o'clock. This was the day that Hilliar had testified that, on his way home, after work, he heard Maggs and another man talking about Sparrow having been approached by Detective Sergeant Smith.

The story Hilliar told was that Sparrow had been offered, in a roundabout way, a reward and free pardon in exchange for naming the guilty party (which Maggs was alleged to have said was

Sparrow himself). It was now the turn of Detective Sergeant Henry
Smith to take the stand. The reason the four men were standing
in the dock was solely down to his presence within the town. He
now recounted in detail for the first time the full details of his
investigation:

*I came to Frome on the 28th of October. On the morning of the
29th, in company with Newport, constable of Frome, I went
to the house of John Watts at Woodlands where the murder has
been committed; I examined the house and saw two or three
spots of blood in the front kitchen, one on the door leading to
the milk house. On the wall near where the latch catches I
observed four finger marks and one apparently of the thumb,
with some blood just below the print; I have compared the mark
with my own hand and I'm confident it was the left hand of
some person being the shortest mark and the lowest; the person
must have been going in to make such a mark* [it was the
thumb on Sparrow's left hand that had been injured]. *I
went into the milk house* [and] *I observed a tub standing on a
stool containing milk; near that were marks on the wall six in
number; I compared the left shoe of the deceased with the dent
in the wall and I am of the opinion that it was caused by the
feet of the deceased, as the toe of the left shoe filled the hole in
the wall; there was mortar between the sole and the upper part
of the shoe. I did not examine the tub having seen nothing at
the time to cause me to do so. On the Thursday following the
tub had been emptied and appeared to be stained red; I then
commenced making enquiries in the neighbourhood and for the
purpose of tracing out the murder; I was led to suspect the three
prisoners – Hurd, Sparrow and Maggs.*

*On Wednesday noon, October 1st, I was in the Market Place,
Frome, in the company of Newport,* [when] *the prisoner Hurd
came in to Newport's shop; I told him I was an officer and
wanted to ask him some questions respecting the murder at West
Woodlands; I said, "You can do what you think proper about
answering them, but what you say I shall take in writing." I sat
down and he made the following statement:- "I live at Little
Keyford; I left my home about nine by myself and went down
to the Lamb public house in Frome and had one pint of beer it
was there at 9:30; afterwards I went to the Unicorn and then to
Singers at the Crown at Keyford, where I have some rum and
cider between 10 and 11 o'clock. I was down in town; about the
town all by myself all day". I told him I meant on the day when
the murder was committed. On Monday the 6th of October I*

apprehended Hurd in Frome; I told him that he was charged with Maggs and others with the murder; he said, "that's not the charge you apprehend me on; be candid and tell me;" I told him that it was. He replied "I know nothing about it."

Smith then gave details of his initial encounter with Maggs:

On the [Friday] *3rd of October, I went to Magg's house at Feltham; I told him who I was and that I wanted to ask him some questions as to where he was on the day that the murder was committed. Maggs said: "I and Sparrow went into Frome about 9:30, up to the Mount at Keyford and from thence into Frome; no other person was with us; we went down into the market place waited there some time and saw William Payne; from there went to the Angel public house at 12 o'clock; at half past left and went out into the Market, waited half an hour, then went into the Victoria Inn there I saw Robert Hurd, Whimpey, and a sergeant of Marines; at 4 o'clock I went home and asked the little girl* [one of Magg's daughters] *if her mother was at home and she said no; my way home was down Bellows Hole, cross the fields and up Feltham Lane; I did not go indoors but went back to Frome by the lane to the Mount where I met Sparrow and no one else; we then went to the Crown public house at Keyford; Hurd, Sparrow and Sargeant were there; we waited there till 8 then left and went down the road to the Mount and down Feltham Lane home.*

Like his meeting with Hurd, Smith did not take any further action against Maggs until the next Monday, when he arrested them both.

On Monday 6th I apprehended the prisoner Maggs in Frome. I told him that he was charged with Hurd and others on suspicion of committing the murder; he said he knew nothing about it; at the time I took the statement of Hurd and Maggs – I read it over to them, and they said it was right; Newport was present at the time.

Smith then described his arrest of the third suspect: William Sparrow, who was, of course, already behind bars, having been picked up in Westbury a few days earlier over the allegation of possessing a stolen watch.

On Monday 6th [this was actually Friday 3 October] *I went to Westbury* [where] *the prisoner Sparrow was detained there on suspicion of stealing a watch; I saw him in a cell at the lock up; when I first went to the cell he thought I was the owner of the watch, he said, "All I know of the watch is that I bought it off Bob Hurd I gave him 27 shillings for it; Will Maggs can prove that he was present when I paid the money." I then told him I wanted to ask him some questions respecting the murder; I told him who I was and gave him the same caution as I have given Hurd; he said, "I live at 19 Trooper Street Frome and lately with William Maggs; I was at Feltham with Maggs at his home about 9 o'clock in the morning on the 24th; I and Maggs left home together along the Woodlands Road; when at the bottom of the Mount I saw William Sargeant and Hurd: Hurd then left and went into Frome, Sargeant went up towards the Mount; and Maggs went in to Frome and then we met Hurd; we then went to Gale's public house* [the Victoria Inn] *at Coalash. About 12 o'clock Maggs and I left Frome, we went down Coalash Way across the fields and on to the main road just by Feltham Bridge* [and then] *up the road towards Woodlands Road which was on our way home. About 2 o'clock Maggs and I left home we went up the Woodlands Road to Lower Keyford; I went up to Sargeant's in the square; I and Sargeant went across to Singers* [The Crown Inn] *and there we met Hurd & Maggs; we left there about 7 o'clock; we all went on the road to the Mount and parted there and Maggs went home".*

On the 9th [This was the 6th, so possibly an error in the newspaper report when the reporter was transcribing his shorthand account] *I apprehended the prisoner Sparrow at Corsley; I told him he was charged on suspicion of being concerned with Hurd and Maggs in the murder; he said he knew nothing about it. At the time he was detained at Westbury. I examined his left hand and found he had a very bad thumb, as it was festered and there was matter; there were two small marks on the side of the thumb and two of the knuckles were sore; on the wrist was a dry scab with a little matter; I asked him how he got his hand hurt; he said he had been fighting at the Ring of Bells North Bradley on the fair night and that the Bradley man had bit him. I asked if he knew his name or where he lived. He couldn't tell me but said he should know him if he was to see him; I went to Bradley but could not find any person that he had been fighting with. I went to the house of Maggs on Saturday 18th to ask for Sparrow's things; Mrs. Maggs gave me a green Jim Crow and a silk pocket handkerchief; she and I put them together, and I said I would call again for them; on Saturday last I went again with Newport and Mrs Maggs gave him the Jim Crow. On Monday 27th when*

Sparrow was in the room he stated that he had not had a silk pocket handkerchief for seven years with the exception of the ones around his neck; the handkerchief found in Watt's house has been in my possession since [Constable] Hoddinott gave it to me and he marked it in my presence; the handkerchief produced before the magistrates on Monday last is the same.

Attention now focused onto the fourth and most recently arrested man: William Sargeant. Smith recounted the details of their interactions, up until the time that he had taken the suspect into custody:

On Thursday the 2nd of October I met William Sargeant near the railway station; I told him who I was, that I wanted to ask him some questions respecting the murder; I cautioned him as to his saying anything, he said, "I live at the Butts; I left home on 24th September in the morning about nine o'clock; and went to the Mount into the field to dig docks and returned home about ten o'clock; I remained at home until 1 o'clock; then I went to the Crown public house; I was there by myself; I left about 2 o'clock then went home; I never left my house after that time; Sparrow, Maggs and Hurd were at the public house when I left".

Smith finished his testimony by giving details of the previous day's arrest of Sargeant:

On the 27th of October I apprehended Sargeant at The Blue Boar, Frome, I told him he was charged with Hurd, Maggs and Sparrow with committing murder at Woodlands. He said he was innocent as a baby and knew nothing about it.

Taking on the role of defence counsel once more, Robert Hurd stood and began to ask Smith several questions, although many, as one newspaper would later report were 'quite immaterial'.

'When I came into Mr. Newport's shop on Wednesday did you observe anything as if I had been put out?'

Smith replied to Hurd he *'was not sufficiently acquainted with you at that time.'*

'Can you remember that I said that Mr Newport had sent for me by old Lawes the relieving officer?' Hurd now asked.
'Yes, you said he had collared you and you had a mind to knock him down.'
'Did you say, "Is your name Frome Bob?"'
'Yes,' replied Smith.

For whatever reason, Hurd now became annoyed and still address-ing Smith said: 'It is no use to ask you any questions,' and promptly sat down again. He would not remain seated or silent for long though. As the depositions of several of the previous witnesses began to be repeated, Hurd angrily stood up and addressed the court in general as the testimony of John Watts, the victim's father, was being read out.

'May God be my witness and prove my innocence,' exclaimed Hurd. 'I declare that Watts has perjured himself with his own words.' He then turned on John Watts, who sat nearby, although still seemingly addressing the magistrates.

'I wish to ask Mr Watts if, when the old man came out of Mr Grist's shop, he [Grist] wasn't talking about the murder?'

'I believe he was,' John Watts replied in a somewhat shaky voice.

Hurd was now joined by the other three prisoners in questioning witnesses, and through this, additions were then made to several of their statements. This included Richard Babey, toll collector at Marston Gate, whose statement had added to it the fact he had seen Joseph Watts, the other 'Marston Gate sighting' witness, a few days later and 'from what took place I made a memorandum, which I now produce'.

Various other depositions were read out again and confirmed before the session came to an end and the room cleared. The mag-istrates conferred and before long reached their decision: there was enough evidence for the case to go forward and therefore Maggs, Sparrow, and Hurd, would stand trial for the murder of Sarah Watts. However, the fourth man, Sargeant, was to be discharged.

The prisoners were brought back in and told of the magistrates' decision. Both Maggs and Sparrow remained silent, but Hurd was not so compliant. 'If Christ were to drop down in this court at this moment,' he said, 'I know there are parties here that would crucify him.'

Nevertheless, Hurd's protests made no difference as the mag-istrates' decision was final: Robert Hurd and his two associates, William 'Will' Maggs and William 'Bill' Sparrow, were to stand trial at the Lent assizes, to be held the following April; meaning that they would remain behind bars for at least the next five months. It would then be up to a jury of twelve men to decide whether they were guilty or not guilty of the murder of Sarah Watts.

PART THREE

(5 April 1852 – 7 April 1852)

15

The Assizes

At one time all manner of legal proceedings – civil and criminal – were heard by the Lord of the Manor in their own locality, but by the nineteenth century, various courts had been created to oversee an entire county. The main ones were the Quarter Sessions and the assize court. The former as its name would imply, being held four times a year: at Epiphany, Easter, Midsummer and Michaelmas. These would hear both civil and criminal cases, but would be concerned only with lesser offences. The more serious ones, such as murder, would be heard at what became known simply as the assizes.

The assize court in England and Wales was normally held twice a year, Lent and summer. These courts were under the control and organisation of the Clerks of the Assize. Judges would travel around several neighbouring counties, at the set times, to hear cases and administer justice. This gave rise to the 'circuits' and in England, by the mid-nineteenth century, there were a total of six of them: Home, Norfolk, Midland, Northern, Oxford and Western. Each circuit included anything between four and eight counties and when the assizes were in session, each would be visited in rotation, with a certain number of days allotted for it.

Frome, being in Somerset, came under the jurisdiction of the Western Circuit, which also contained Hampshire, Wiltshire, Dorset, Devon, and Cornwall. The next assize after Maggs, Sparrow and Hurd's appearance at the magistrates' court was the one at Lent – the spring of 1852 – when they would be tried for murder. It would be held in Taunton Castle in the county's administrative centre (the summer sessions being held at Wells or Bridgwater). The opening of a session was accompanied by a great amount of ceremony, with the under sheriff meeting the judges at the county boundary; after which they entered the town with an escort of javelin men and fanfares of trumpets.

Defendants at the assizes had the right to a copy of the witness statements against them (depositions) arising from the committal (magistrates) hearings, but no right to view any statements made post committal. This could, therefore, be used as an advantage by the prosecution, as they could keep witnesses back until the trial, limiting the time available for the defence to prepare its case in light of this 'new' evidence. In these cases, the magistrates were shown just enough to commit to the higher court but vital evidence could be held back for the 'killer' blow in front of the jury at the assize.

Trials at the assize courts would take place in the county in which the crime was committed, with a jury drawn from the same area. At the start of the trial the prisoner would first be 'arraigned' or have the charges read to him and then asked to plead either 'guilty' or 'not guilty' to the charge they faced. If they pleaded not guilty a jury would be chosen from the twenty-four men who had been summoned; these were men between 21 and 60 years old who had certain property qualifications and quite often they were shopkeepers or small landowners. The accused had the right to object to individual jurors, if they had good reason, but once everyone was satisfied, the jury was officially empanelled and the trial began with an opening speech by the prosecuting barrister.

The prisoner could not give evidence in defence; not because the system was bias against him or her, but because it was deemed unfair to them. Being legally 'untrained', or so it was assumed, meant if they were cross-examined, they might unintentionally incriminate themselves. They could however, issue a sworn statement of the facts as they saw them and call witnesses to support their case.

Similarly, it was quite common for the accused to be refused representation in the lower court (the magistrates) as this was thought of as obstructing justice and preventing the bench from doing its job of assessing the evidence by potential constant interruption from the defence lawyer. This is, of course, what had happened back in Frome the previous October, when Thomas Hawkes's request to represent the three prisoners was denied (although he had been allowed to stay to listen to the proceedings).

As is often mentioned, a prisoner was presumed innocent until the prosecution had proved its case. This normally included calling witnesses to strengthen the evidence presented by the prosecution, so as to persuade a jury of the accused's guilt. The judge was there to advise the jury on matters of law, while the jury itself was there to decide on the facts of the case. A criminal trial was not held to establish the *truth* of a matter, but rather to test the *evidence* presented in front of a jury by two opposing teams, each putting their own 'spin' on a set of events; playing down the facts which did not support their position and emphasising those which did. The judge acted as the 'referee' between the two, as well as advising all parties on the law, with the aim of ensuring that both sides abided by certain rules and the evidence was presented as fairly as possible before the jury. This was known as the adversarial system, in which there would be a 'winner' and a 'loser'.

Reports of the assizes would appear in local newspapers (and national ones if the case was deemed sensational enough) and they would often send their own reporters. These reporters would take a type of shorthand, as evidence was given or officials spoke. This gave rise to slightly differing reports and sometimes errors in names, places or times, but overall the essential details tallied. In fact, it is surprising how little contradiction occurred on reading through the various reports of this case. Any differences there were usually concerned unimportant omissions, due to shortage of space or small points thought not worthy of recording. The reporters would be squeezed into an undoubtedly packed courtroom and scribbled away as best they could. On occasion they would no doubt have misheard parts, or got details wrong (as had happened the previous autumn with several newspapers' initial reports of the murder case), not understood sections of the evidence, or had to nip out to answer nature's call and suchlike.

Evidence given before the magistrates could be expected to be much the same as that given later at the assizes, but normally there was enough of a difference for both transcripts to be of use to the historian. Not all witnesses gave evidence in both courts – the opposing teams selected those that they thought would be most effective. Some accounts were longer and more detailed in the higher court; with changes in emphasis or added detail, and some were dropped entirely.

The Somerset assizes at Taunton for Lent 1852 was set to begin the week of Monday 5 April. An unpleasant case of baby poisoning, alleged to have taken place in Bath the previous summer, was to be the first case heard, and this was to be followed by the Frome murder.

Since their incarceration in Shepton Mallet gaol, Maggs, Sparrow, and Hurd, had to simply wait out their time. Meanwhile, Detective Sergeant Henry Smith had returned to London with the gratitude of the Frome magistrates (and no doubt the law-abiding section of the population) still ringing in his ears and early in the New Year, he received an additional gesture of appreciation in the form of a handsome silver watch and gold guard with the following inscription engraved on the inner case: 'Presented to Sergeant Henry Smith, by the inhabitants of Frome, in testimony of his intelligence and activity in investigating the circumstance of a murder in their parish in Nov, 1851,' Whether the wrongly attributed month was merely within the newspaper report of the gift or had indeed been inscribed on the case, it is impossible to know. What is certain, however, is that along with the cost of the watch, the case, and its inscription, Smith's services while investigating the crime, had cost the authorities of Frome the grand total of £29.

With Smith having fulfilled his duty for the time being, it was left to the prosecution – and defence – barristers to build their respective cases for the jury to listen to and so decide the fate of the prisoners. To a great degree, the former had merely to repeat its case with committals from its numerous witnesses, many of whom had testified as to seeing the prisoners moving in the direction of, or near by, West Woodlands on the day of the murder.

The key witnesses, in terms of narrowing down the actual time of the murder, it seemed, were Alfred Allard and Robert Walter; the latter being a new witness found since the magisterial hearings. Allard had already given his testimony at the inquest and then again before the magistrates. He had seen Sarah alive at about 1 o'clock, which meant she had met her unnatural death sometime after then and 3 o'clock (as she was already stiff and cold when her parents returned at 4 o'clock). The other witness, Robert Walter, who had been found by the prosecution after the committal hearings, most likely had seen the murderer – a lone figure going away from the farm – although he could not identify the person as he only observed them from the back. He did establish a time though, and this was between 2.30 and 2.45 pm, which fitted in with the proposed time of the murder.

Knowing the case against them, the defence had to establish three things: the whereabouts of the prisoners at the crucial period – between 1 and 3 o'clock – the ownership of a handkerchief found at the farmhouse and the cause of the wound on Sparrow's thumb. If Robert Walter's account was correct, although the defence would not be aware of this witness at present, the evidence seemed to point to Sparrow as being the lone perpetrator (due to the wound on his thumb, his 'confession' at North Bradley fair and 'ownership' of the handkerchief) and the other two – Maggs and Hurd – being accomplices, although not having taken part in the actual murder.

The magistrates obviously thought there was enough evidence for all three to stand trial with a good chance of conviction and with it, no doubt, the death penalty; but it would now be up to the jury to decide whether the prisoners were to live or die.

16

5 April 1852

The assizes proper began on Monday 5 April 1852. If the occasion, with all its pomp and ceremony was not imposing enough, then the building in which the trials were to be held made it dramatically more so.

Taunton Castle had been built to defend the town it took its name from, and its history had been a long and bloody one. Its origins went back as far as Anglo Saxon times, but it was the Normans, in the twelfth century, who built the stone structured castle. A Great Hall was located on the first floor of the keep, over a stone vaulted undercroft. In 1216, Bishop Peter des Roches, a supporter of King John defended the castle during the first barons' revolt, while later that century, during a second revolt, it was used as a prison for the son of Simon de Montfort, the Barons' leader. Throughout the First English Civil War, Taunton, and its castle, remained in Parliamentary hands, although both were heavily besieged on several occasions by Royalists. After much loss of life on either side, the defenders were finally relieved by forces commanded by Thomas Fairfax, after his victory at the Battle of Naseby.

Probably the bloodiest and most infamous episode in the history of the castle followed the Monmouth Rebellion. After the Duke of Monmouth's attempt, in 1685, to depose his uncle, King James II, and seize the Crown finally failed at the Battle of Sedgemoor, the castle's Great Hall was the setting for what became known as the 'Bloody Assizes': the series of trials in which Monmouth's supporters had been tried for treason. More than 500 rebels were brought in front of the court over just two days – 18 and 19 September 1685 – and out of these, 144 were hanged, drawn, and quartered; their remains then displayed around the county so that people understood the fate of those who rebelled against the king (the majority of the other rebels were transported). If these particular assizes became notorious, then so did the judge who presided over them. Lord Chief Justice Jeffreys was the 40-year-old, Welsh-born judge who, through his merciless and harsh sentencing, became known to history as 'The Hanging Judge'. After the Glorious Revolution three years later, he was incarcerated himself, in the Tower of London, and remained there until he died the following year, in 1689.

After this, the Somerset assizes, or at least the ones held at Lent, remained at Taunton Castle. The judge who would oversee the week's cases was a little less iniquitous than his pitiless predecessor. Sir William Erle QC had become a judge in 1845, after being the (Whig) MP for Oxford. He held the position for one term only, between 1837 and 1841, as he chose not to stand for re-election. As a judge he had acquired a reputation for thoroughness, rather than brilliance, and was regarded as fair and impartial (unlike a certain judge before him) with a rapid grasp of the facts of a case. His speech was deliberate, even monotonous, with a faint regional accent. The defendants that week, which included Maggs, Sparrow, and Hurd, could have done a lot worse.

The crowds gathered early on the first morning and there was a palpable buzz of excitement at the thought of the proceedings to follow. But it was not for the Sarah Watts murder case. The initial hearing of the assizes that week was of an alleged poisoning in Bath; the victim being a 4-month-old baby. The child had been born the previous year, on Tuesday 10 June 1851. The heavily pregnant mother had come to the city the Saturday before and secured a room above a chemist, run by a Mr and Mrs Searle. Two days later, her 'husband' had arrived and the morning after, Mrs Slater, as she called herself, gave birth to a baby girl they named Elizabeth. Shortly afterwards, the couple left for London and an agreement was made with the Searles to look after the baby.

Mrs Slater came frequently to visit her baby, but every time she left, Elizabeth would suffer from terrible vomiting and diarrhoea. This became such a regular occurrence that the Searles became suspicious and contacted the police. After a covert surveillance operation, during Mrs Slater's next visit, she was arrested and taken to Bath police station. Back at the Searles, baby Elizabeth once more became violently ill, only this time her condition deteriorated to such a point that she died. She was 4 months and 1 day old.

During the police investigation into what had now become a murder case, it transpired that 'Mrs Slater' was really Elizabeth Catherine Lewis, a member of a respectable Bristol family who had obviously come to Bath to give birth away from prying eyes. The father of the baby and 'husband' to Mrs Slater was, in fact, Thomas Crosby, a well-to-do solicitor, also from Bristol.

The prosecution's case was that the mother had conspired to poison the child with arsenic when she visited her, as this substance had been found in the baby's internal organs and on her teats.

The defence argued that the baby had also become ill when removed to the country for a short while – and had not been visited by her mother – and as the Searles were chemists, there was the possibility that some of the arsenic sold in the shop could some-how have contaminated the teats, rather than being administered by the mother. This latter fact seemingly reinforced by the fact that no arsenic had been found on the mother upon her arrest, nor was there any residue on her fingers or gloves when examined. The inspector carrying out the covert operation had not witnessed the accused administer any poison. Also, it was claimed, the baby seemed to have been a naturally sickly child from birth, having refused all types of food before the first visit by the mother.

After the two sides – prosecution and defence – had stated their cases, Judge Erle summed up for the jury's benefit. He told them that although each of the prisoners was charged with the intentional murder of their daughter, Thomas Crosby was only an accessory before the fact. They, the jurors, therefore had to think carefully about all the evidence that had been presented and unless they could be certain, and without any reasonable doubt, that the defendants were responsible for the death of their child, they should not deliver a guilty verdict. In this, then, they should ask themselves the following questions: were they satisfied that the baby's death had been caused by arsenic poisoning? If the answer was no, then 'not guilty' would be the only possible verdict, but if they were satisfied that arsenic had been involved, had Elizabeth Lewis given it to the child? If she had, then the third and final ques-tion to be answered was had Thomas Crosby been an accessory to this fact?

It did not take the jury long to consider all the evidence pre-sented before them and return the verdict of 'not guilty' for both defendants. At this, Elizabeth Lewis slumped forward in a dead faint and had to be carried from the dock, followed by a tearful Thomas Crosby. This first trial, or session, did not finish until late into the evening and the judge adjourned the session for that day. Was this verdict an indication that Maggs, Sparrow, and Hurd, were in front of a fair jury and one not over impressed by the value of circumstantial evidence?

The following morning it was the turn of Hurd and his two confederates to attend court, although there was not

> quite so great a concourse of persons anxious to obtain admit-tance to the Hall on Tuesday, when this trial came on, as on the previous day. Nevertheless, the atrocity of the crime, and the horrible circumstances of brutal barbarity which preceded the act of murder, drew great numbers to the Castle yard at an early hour, and whenever either of the doors of the Hall was opened, a tremendous rush was made to obtain places within.

At nine the place was crowded; and at that hour the learned Judge (Erle) took his seat on the bench.
Somerset County Gazette, 10 April 1852

The prisoners were brought in and placed at the bar. The winter months in Shepton gaol had seemingly done little to change Hurd's style, according to one newspaper, as his nonchalant and insolent manner had remained intact.

They are persons of somewhat forbidding aspect, especially Hurd, whose conduct in the dock was much calculated to prejudice the Jury against him. He is evidently a daring, unscrupulous fellow, capable of resorting to violent means to accomplish an object where other measures might prove abortive. As soon as the jury was sworn, the report continued, *Hurd took from his pocket, with an air of confidence and an assumption of pomposity, some writing-paper and a pencil,*

William 'Bill' Sparrow 30, William 'Will' Maggs, 44, and Robert Hurd, alias 'Frome Bob', 37, were then charged with the murder of Sarah Watts and when called to say how they pleaded, they all answered in a firm, resolute tone: 'Not guilty.'

Mr Moody and Mr Everett appeared for the prosecution while Mr Edwards and Mr Cole represented Maggs and Sparrow. To begin with, there was slight confusion over Hurd's counsel, and he addressed Judge Erle: 'My Lord,' said Hurd, 'I humbly hope you will allow some learned gentleman to watch this case on my behalf. I have petitioned Sir George Grey.'

The judge replied that 'his thoughts were then upon the subject on which the prisoner had spoken.' Judge Erle asked one of the defence counsel, Mr Edwards, if it would interfere with the course he intended to adopt with respect to the other prisoners if he undertook the defence of all three, and, being answered in the negative he informed Hurd that 'Mr Edwards would defend him'.

The prosecution, in the form of Mr Moody, expressed his satisfaction that the prisoners would all have the benefit of Mr Edwards's assistance.

A model of Battle Farm and a plan of the surrounding countryside were then brought into the court, both having been created by Frome surveyor William Mansford, who swore to their accuracy. Mr Moody then rose to address the jury and state the case for the prosecution.

17

Prosecution: Preliminary Address

Gentleman, I have the honour to appear before you, the jury, to lay before you today the grounds on which you will be asked to say whether the prisoners are guilty of the crime of wilful murder. It would be superfluous of me to address observations to you with a view to bespeak your attention to the momentous importance of the case, for it is impossible that you could be without a deep sense of the great responsibility under which you will have to act.

But I must forewarn you that the closest application of your understandings and faculties will be required in this case, on account of the nature of the evidence on which I seek to establish the charge against the prisoners; this evidence being purely circumstantial. You, the members of the jury, will have to look at a vast variety of minute circumstances. You will though, have to first listen to a preliminary address which I will make and in which I shall endeavour to give you such a notion of the whole case as should enable you to examine and investigate every detail of evidence as it is presented before you.

When you have heard me, you will have the labour of hearing every part of the rather large amount of evidence that will be produced, and then to inform your minds as to the conclusion to which you should come and say whether, from the facts adduced you, indeed the conclusion is that the prisoners are guilty of the crime imputed to them. In this, as in every other case, the first question will be whether or not the crime was committed by anyone. I will, therefore, shortly state the circumstances surrounding it, so as to put this question out of the reach of all difficulty.

Sarah Watts, the poor girl who was murdered, was a child of about 14 years of age. She was the daughter of John and Leah Watts, who occupy a dairy farm at a place called Woodlands, about 2 miles from Frome, in this county. The house is situated about 100 yards from a road which passes in front of it. Mr Watts and his wife left their house on the morning of the 24th of September last to go to the Frome market. They left their child at home, and only that child.

They were in the market up to time enough to return home at four o'clock in the afternoon. When they reached their house the father called to his daughter, but she did not answer. The first thing which attracted the father's attention was some blood on the floor of the kitchen and hearing a dog, which belonged to them, lapping up something in the dairy, he went there, and saw that the animal was lapping some whey that had been spilt upon the floor. He then saw his daughter laying on the floor, with her clothes much torn, her body bruised and bloody and her person exposed and quite dead.

Soon afterwards she was taken upstairs, and the evidence of the surgeon, who saw her at about seven o'clock that same evening, would be conclusive as to her having met her death by violent means. There were marks of such violence upon her person as she could not possibly have inflicted upon herself, and the natural conclusion was that it was inflicted by other hands. Therefore, you, the jury, will have no difficulty as to the first proposition, that the child had been murdered. Further than this, I am now able to state that murder was not the only crime committed upon her. The surgeon will state that in his opinion the child had also been ravished. Nor were these two the only crimes perpetrated, for the house was also robbed.

The parents were of course greatly alarmed, and their attention was soon attracted to the fact that some bread and butter had been taken, and the cheese cut in such a way that they were sure the child could not have done it. On going upstairs they then found the house had been ransacked, and several articles carried away – among them a watch, which will prove an important fact in going through the evidence.

I will now draw attention, in detail, to circumstances which will be material in bringing home the crime to the prisoners; and here it will not be improper of me to make some remark upon the peculiar nature of the evidence which will be offered. This robbery, which was probably the original object of the persons who committed the murder, was so skilfully contrived and executed that, though effected in broad daylight, within a hundred yards of a highway, and close to some other dwelling-houses, I am not in a position to produce either an eye-witness or ear-witness of the transaction itself. No one saw the deed committed; no one heard the child cry; no one saw the guilty parties enter the house or go from it.

I have therefore to rely upon what is called circumstantial evidence – a description of evidence which, as you, the jury, have probably been present during many of the trials at these assizes, must have seen, and which was relied upon in a great measure in most cases, and in some entirely so. The value of circumstantial evidence is not to be found in any single fact, but in the combination of many facts. When different facts – be they trivial or important - in connection with a certain crime are found to agree in throwing the guilt upon a party – though neither can perfectly fix it – evidence of that kind is considered as conclusive and satisfactory as the positive testimony of an eye or ear witness.

I shall now describe the house in which the murder was committed, and shall illustrate my remarks by using the model of it, lying on this table. In the corner of the dairy was a tub of whey, which stood upon a trundle. When the father entered the dairy he saw blood upon the floor, just under the child's head, and at a subsequent time he observed that the whey was discoloured, as though with blood – from which it has been inferred by some that the child, having been beaten about the head, had been thrown into the tub, and afterwards withdrawn from it, for her clothes were wet with whey.

Nothing was said as to this inference, however, for some time; and I draw attention to this fact because it will be found important in connection with a statement made by one of the prisoners. As might be well supposed, a matter of this frightful atrocity attracted the immediate attention of the magistracy in the locality; and the first thing they did was to apply to the Home Office for one of the metropolitan police to be sent down to investigate the affair.

A person named Smith, of what is called the Detective Force, arrived therefore on the Sunday at Frome, but he did not enter up on his enquiry until the following day, the 29th, and his exertions forwarded the discovery of the perpetrators of the deed in a very considerable degree.

In pursuing his inquiries he found, at the left-hand side of the door leading from the kitchen into the dairy, a distinct mark of a hand – four fingers and thumb, the latter being bloody. This indicated that the struggle had taken place. Smith also observed there was a mark upon the wall, like that which would be produced by the point of a shoe; and on comparing the girl's boot with it he found the toe to correspond exactly. There was also mortar between the sole and the upper leather of the boot.

On the 1st of October the whey tub was emptied, and at the bottom of it was observed a large red spot, which the father thought was produced by blood, but of this there did not appear to be perfect certainty.

Having stated these facts I think it will be convenient to give a short history of the prisoners from the morning of the 24th of

September, as far as the materials I have in my possession, up to the time of their apprehension.

I have already stated a robbery was committed and I believe I can produce such evidence as will show that in this all the prisoners were perpetrators. The child was seen just outside the house at one o'clock; and it is evident the murder took place between that hour and four. The prisoners were seen in company with each other on the morning of the 24th, apparently intent upon some important transaction, and about two o'clock all three of them were seen going in the direction of Watts' house and within half a mile of it.

Mr Watts and his wife, having left their house at about nine o'clock on the day in question, pass on their way to Frome a beer-house kept by a person called Cornish. When they pass, the three prisoners are standing near the door of the beer house, in company with another man. They must have seen Mr Watts pass, and soon afterwards they go away in different directions. Two of them, Maggs and Sparrow, are soon afterwards seen at the Marston turnpike gate, whence they go in the direction of Watts' house; but are not seen closer to it than half a mile. At that time the murder could not yet have been committed. Sometime later, they are seen in the Victoria Inn, with another man named Sargeant; and there they make an appointment to meet again within an hour.

Soon after two o'clock they are seen to pass through Marston turnpike-gate and to stop at a short distance from it; Hurd goes in advance and then beckons to the others to follow. They proceed down a lane, and Hurd parts from them, and is not identified with them again until after the time at which the robbery must have been committed.

Maggs and Sparrow are next seen to go through a field to a place about half a mile distant from Mr Watts's house, this being about two o'clock. There is no trace of them any further at this time; but the next fact to be mentioned is that a man is observed leaving Mr Watts's house, running away in a shuffling manner, with something in one hand, and this man had on a smock frock. Now, it will be shown that on the morning of the 24th Maggs wore a smock frock, and Sparrow a Jim Crow hat. Whether the person running away was Maggs or no, no one can say; but it is an important fact, that soon afterwards he is again seen in Sparrow's company, with different clothes on. This is between three and four o'clock.

They are next found together in Frome market; all the prisoners and another man, and some of their conversation is overheard – something about a watch, the expression used by one of them being "a watch but no tin."

They are then traced to the Crown Inn, where they remain from about four o'clock till seven. When old Mr Watts discovers the robbery, he goes into Frome for a constable; and as he is in the house of the constable, Hurd, who appears to be watching from outside, fell in with him and, apparently sympathising with him, invites him to go into a beer-shop and have a pint of beer, which Mr Watts did. What motive actuated Hurd to do this, if he was in any way connected with the robbery, you, the jury must infer.

I will now refer to some facts individually applicable to the prisoners. With respect to Sparrow, he states that he knew the premises, although it does not appear that the child could have known him, as he has not been at the house for many years. When old Mr Watts entered his house he saw on the table in the kitchen a silk handkerchief, and it will be shown that this belongs to Sparrow – a fact which will be testified to by three witnesses. Sparrow has also volunteered to the constable a statement, to the effect that he has not had a silk handkerchief for the last seven years.

There is also another important fact for consideration: a person who had not been at the scene of the murder, when it was first discovered, could not possibly know all the details respecting it; but Sparrow, who it will be proved was not present at that time, nor during the next day, had at a public house in North Bradley, on September the 30th, stated the circumstances down to the smallest particulars.

In addition to this, Sparrow had a wound on his thumb when at Bradley. This will be proved to have been caused in the struggle with the poor girl, and to have made the mark on the side of the door, as already spoken of. When asked how he had got it, Sparrow answered he received it in a fight at Bradley fair, though from the state of the wound, it was evident he must have had the injury some days before. His statement is that he had got it bitten in a certain fight which took place in an inn there on the 29th; but it will be shown that it must have been caused four or five days previously; and, more than that, it appears that at the time of the fight in question he is quietly seated in another part of the house.

As to Maggs, a few days after the murder was discovered, an old man, who will be called before you, the jury, overheard a conversation which Maggs had with another person. Maggs said "Well, have they found out anything more?" The other answered, "No, but they say that Sparrow is going to peach; that the constable has been and told him that he shall not only have a pardon, but shall also have fifty pounds," on which Maggs said, "he can't get the pardon nor the fifty pounds, for he was the man that killed her; and he said he would not have done it but that she knew him."

Now, coupling these things with the fact that the two prisoners were traced almost to the house, and that Maggs had on a smock frock, which he afterwards changed, it will be for you to say whether conviction is not brought home to your minds as to their guilt.

With regard to Hurd, you will see that the evidence assumes a milder aspect and seems to show that he was an accomplice to the robbery, but not that he participated in the murder.

I will now call on the first witness of many that have been assembled for this case, in order to give weight to the evidence outlined in this preliminary address. And through their testimonies believe that you, as the members of this jury, will come to no other conclusion than to find all the prisoners guilty of the crimes they have been charged with.

I thank you.

18

Opening Witnesses

As had happened before, the first witness called by the prosecution was the father of the murder victim: John Watts. The 62-year-old, having suffered the initial ordeal of finding his dead daughter, followed by having to relive it all at the inquest and magistrates' hearings now had to go through it once more in front of a jury.

Robert Hurd had already inflicted somewhat of a verbal tongue-lashing at the magistrates' court, calling out that Watts had perjured himself, and now, in court, he transfixed his intense glare at the frail, almost broken, John Watts, as the old man made his way across the courtroom and into the witness stand.

My name is John Watts and I live at Battle farm in Frome; I am the father of the deceased. On the 24th of September I went to Frome market; I left my house a little after nine o'clock in the morning. My wife went also to market; she left a few minutes before me, but I overtook her. We passed the beer-house together. We left my daughter at home; we returned home a little before 4 o'clock. I did not see whether the door was open or shut. When I went in, I called my daughter to bring my boots, that I might put them on but she did not answer. As I was taking off my gaiters I saw spots of blood on the floor of the kitchen. I sat opposite the fireplace; she did not answer, and, hearing a lapping in the milk-house, I went in to the milk-house and there saw my daughter lying on the floor, with her clothes disarranged – at first I thought it was a bundle of clothes – with blood over her face. She was lying near the door, and behind it, or across it rather; with one knee up and the other straight down. One arm was across her breast and the other at her side – her clothes were very much torn, and her appearance indicated that she had struggled a good deal; the floor was wet; I just put back her clothes, and saw that she was a corpse and that her face was much bruised, I went out to let my wife know and met her at the Turnpike Gate.

I did not examine her further and I went out and called someone; from the time I went out to the time I went back no one had been in the house, because I did not go away from the door. My wife came in, and then I went to the turnpike house, and returned in five minutes with Mrs Court. Several persons were by then in my house.

I then went out to some beasts, and returned again very soon, in about half an hour. Some tea was made for my wife, and then we missed some bread and cheese and butter. I then went upstairs with my wife and we missed a coat, waistcoat, and shawl; I afterwards went to Frome, where I gave information; I returned about nine o'clock or past – it was dark then.

I saw Robert Hurd standing at the door of the constables' house, near the Crown Inn; I did not know Hurd, but he asked where I had been. He asked me if I was going to Woodlands and he said he was going to the Mount. He asked me to go with him to the beer-house and have a glass of beer; I went with him to Cornish's and had a pint of beer, and went home about nine. I had not drunk anything before for the day and very little of anything else; I had no conversation with Hurd. I did not know any of the prisoners. I have seen the clothes which were stolen; I saw them at the office of the magistrates; Hurd paid for the beer.

On the 25th of September I went away from home; I went to Warminster. I returned about one or two o'clock; I remained home the rest of the day. During that day I did not see Sparrow there; there were two or three constables there; on the 1st of October the whey was turned out of the tub, and I saw something like blood in it; this was a week after the murder.

John Watts was then cross-examined and asked several questions; the first one concerned the immediate surroundings of the farm and his neighbours.

There are several houses near mine but none within 200 yards. The Turnpike house is near; there are others around – three in all, separate from each other, and on the three sides of mine. A person named White lives in one of them, he is a labourer; in the other a farmer, named Pickford, lives – he has some grown up sons. These people, my neighbours, ordinarily dine about one o'clock and would generally be at home about that time.

I left my dog at home that day; it was accustomed to bark at strangers, but I have not known it to bark since; it was not at all injured, that I know of; my daughter had no acquaintance but children at school; she was very small for her age; at first we thought my poor daughter had died of fits; we had not at first any idea that she had been murdered; a suspicion was awakened by the discovery that articles had been stolen. Up to the time I went into the dairy nothing attracted my attention but the blood on the kitchen ground. I did not notice anything upon the table.

Near the door of the dairy was blood on the wall, and above, four marks of fingers; the blood was underneath the mark made by the thumb; it was a patch of blood, not a drop; the body was moved from the dairy, but I don't know by whom. I did not take notice who carried the body upstairs; several people were there; I can't say if there was much blood on the child; I didn't look much at her [and] there was very little blood in the milk house; it was only on one small place; they had no difficulty, that I saw, in carrying the body through the doorway.

A great many people were there, and many conjectures were made as to how the girl met her death; I don't remember hearing anyone say the whey was bloody, but I thought it had a bloody appearance; there were also a great many people there next day, and the house was nearly full sometimes; I could pay no attention to them; my grief was such I hardly knew who was there.

Mr Hoddinott was there several times and I remember his pointing my attention to the handkerchief. My wife said there was no handkerchief left, but I don't think she said anything about the handkerchief until after he had asked whether anything had been left in the house by that person supposed to have committed the murder. My wife found the handkerchief and she asked me if it was ours; she had asked me this before Mr Hoddinott put the question; I had no handkerchief at all like that; I therefore at once saw it had been left there by someone.

Mr Moody, the prosecutor, then went over certain parts of the testimony with the witness, to clarify several points for the jury; John Watts continued:

When I returned from the turnpike house, I was asked by my wife about the handkerchief; I don't know that I spoke of blood being in the whey when I observed it; the blood on the wall was close to the mark made by the thumb; There were four finger marks of blood on the wall and the mark of the thumb; the blood ran down the wall about half an inch below the thumb mark. Farmer Pickford lives about a stone's throw from mine.

It was again the turn of the defence to ask the witness questions. The first concerned Watts's encounter with Robert Hurd:

I had never spoken to Hurd before I saw him at the beer-house. I had been to the constable's before I saw him; it was well known that a murder had been committed; there was great excitement all about, in consequence of the murder. It was after I had been for a constable that I met him; I can't say whether he said anything to sympathise with me; he said something like this – he hoped the scoundrels would be found out and their necks wrung for it. He walked along quietly with me.

The next witness was then called.

My name is Leah Watts and I am the wife of the last witness. On the morning of my child's death, 24th September, I went to market, having left just before my husband; we left at a little past nine; I passed Cornish's beer house in going. On our return, my husband got home first, and I found him coming out of the house; I did not find any persons in the house then; I went in, and took off my shawl, laying it on the table; there was on it an old silk handkerchief.

I then went into the milk-room and found my child dead; she was removed upstairs about a quarter of an hour after; we found that bread and butter had been taken, and that induced us to make a search. The drawers and chests had been forced open and some clothes taken; my attention was not drawn to the watch before Saturday morning, when my husband having asked about it we found that it was gone. I think I had seen it on the Monday before the death of my child.

I was home all day Thursday, all the time my husband was away but don't remember seeing Sparrow there at any time that day; I never saw him before we were in the magistrates' court. The whey-tub was emptied the Wednesday after the murder; I had noticed something in the whey – a little colouring, like blood, but it disappeared soon after; when the tub was empty and I observed a little "pitching" at the bottom, not clots, something like blood; Mr Hoddinott spoke about these marks, but I don't know that anybody else did; there is a wooden latch on the wall near where the finger marks were.

She was then cross-examined and, like her husband, asked several questions.

The latch is a large wooden one; I don't remember whether I saw these marks before or after the body was removed; [Detective Sergeant] Smith drew attention to them, but I don't know if this was the first time I had seen them.

I never knew my daughter to have had fits before her death, but my general impression was that she had died naturally, until we missed bread and butter; it was then that, for the first time, I thought someone had broken in. None of the chests or drawers had been locked; the watch was kept in the chest, under the clothes; I have not heard any tidings of it since.

There were not many people in the house on the evening of the murder; those who were there suggested different modes as to how the girl was killed, but I was so much frightened I hardly knew what they said; I did not think anyone would murder my child in daylight till I found the house had been robbed. We found out that she must have been murdered, because her head was very much bruised, though no blood came from it.

I have been twice before the magistrate on this case, but did not mention about the handkerchief the first time; I did so the second time; Hoddinott took possession of it. None of the things taken away were under lock; we had nothing locked up; the boxes in the room were all open but we did not miss anything from them; we have never seen the watch which was missed. The boxes had nearly all been opened, there had been a complete search both in my room and in the one in which my child slept; there seemed to have been great hurry and the things were tossed about.

Leah Watts then stepped down and her place was taken by Mary Wheeler; she was the woman visiting a nearby farm when she heard Leah's cries and was the first across to the farmhouse to comfort the distraught mother.

On the 24th of September I was at Farmer Pickford's house, near John Watts's. In the afternoon I heard someone call out, "She's dead, she's dead – been dead this hour," it was Mrs Watts. At a little after four o'clock I went over, and saw Mrs Watts above stairs; I saw the body in the milk-house; laying by the whey treadle. It was lying more on the back than the side; the body was cold; I assisted in laying it out. Edwin Pickford assisted me and we carried the body upstairs and laid her out almost directly; no blood at all came from it as we removed it; I observed some in the whey treadle and observed marks of heavy blows about the child's temples head and face; on one side of the face, as though some flesh had been pinched out, there was a very severe one. She had one mark on her knees, and elbow, and another on her shoulder. I did not feel the marks on her; there was some blood about her, and some about the floor under her; three persons assisted in carrying her up, and I was one of them; we removed her as we found her, not having altered her clothes in any way; at first I thought she had died in a fit, but her mother said she never had had one; I had not then seen all the bruises about her body.

I was not there when Hoddinott came that I remember; there were many other persons there. The girl was quite dead and stiff before I saw her, and her lips as purple as a purple ribbon; there was some whey about the floor, as though it had been spilt over from the tub. There was a large piece of skin off her temple, and I said the blood must have come from that place. There were many people in the house when we carried her up. There was as much as a bucket full of whey on the floor and on her clothes. I mentioned to the people that the blood must have come out of her head.

Francis Giles, the surgeon who had attended to Sarah Watts that first evening and who had carried out the post-mortem, now took the stand.

My name is Francis Giles.

I am a surgeon, and was called on the 24th to see this child; I was there about half past seven in the evening; I found her upstairs, laid out; there were several persons below, and two or three above; I found on the body the principle bruise on the right side of the forehead; there was another also on the forehead; the face was swollen and livid; three scratches were on the left side of the neck; I saw Nath, on the private parts, to convince me a felony had been committed; she had not arrived at puberty; this felony was committed before the circulation had ceased; I made a post-mortem examination on the 26th; I found outside the skull, and beneath the scalp, some clotted blood corresponding to the bruise outside; inside the neck were two bruises, each about the size of the top of my finger.

I have no doubt whatsoever that she died of violence, committed by some other person; I ascribe the death to suffocation; the marks in the neck were such as would be made by the thumb and finger; on the windpipe this pressure would of itself be quite ample to produce death. Her brain was congested, but not sufficiently to have caused death; suffocation produces congestion of the brain; the marks on the head were not enough to have caused that congestion of the brain. At the inquest I attributed the death to pressure on the windpipe; I said nothing about the death having been caused by drowning, but I think someone else spoke about it. If she had been put in the whey pail, death would have been assisted.

The last person to see Sarah alive, apart from the perpetrators of the crime, was then called.

> *My name is Alfred Allard and am thirteen years old. I remember the 24th of September; was working for Mr Chedzey; was going down the road towards the Woodlands at about one o'clock for my master's dinner; I past Watts's house and saw Sarah Watts there; she was just outside, and had no bonnet on at the time; I came back that way, but did not see anyone.*
>
> *A great many people are always about the road leading to Woodlands but not the road near Watts house; I have not met a great many on that same road, but there are generally a good many on further; I don't remember that I met anyone I knew on that road; I only met a wagon by the gate, and farther up I met people; I had frequently seen the girl as I passed; I knew her, but did not speak to her; and I am quite certain that I saw her on this day. I was going along the road when I saw her; the road on which many people go is not near Watts' house.*

19

Henry Smith

The next witness to be called was the London detective, Sergeant Henry Smith. It was he who had carried out the investigation that had led to the arrests and the present hearing at the assize court.

On the final day of the lower court proceedings, back in the previous October, the magistrates had expressed to Smith their unanimous approval of the manner in which he had put the case together; which they said reflected much credit on him. Smith had returned to London to carry on his duties within the Detective Branch to which he belonged at the Metropolitan Police Headquarters: Great Scotland Yard.

Once the New Year dawned and Lent approached, his thoughts no doubt turned back towards the West Woodlands case and the three suspects that would stand trial, based on his investigation, for the murder of an innocent 14-year-old girl. Although he had outlined the details of that investigation for the magistrates' court, he would now do so again for the benefit of the jury:

My name is Henry Smith. I am a Sergeant in the Metropolitan Detective Police and was sent down to investigate the murder. I arrived on Sunday evening the 28th of September, and commenced my investigation on the following morning, when I went to the house and examined it. I saw some blood in the kitchen, a little from the fireplace, on the left-hand side, going into the kitchen from the milk house. There was blood on the door and on the wall; I examined this part carefully, and found a mark of a left hand; about three quarters of an inch below the thumb-mark was a spot of blood; it was evidently a left hand and fingers were close together; the hand appeared to have been a little cramped; it seemed as if someone had been pressing against the wall to get a purchase to open the door; the blood touched the end of the thumb-mark, and extended downwards.

In the dairy was the whey-tub, on a stool, and on the wall were six marks, as if someone had been pushing against it to get away; as if something was going down the wall, such a mark as a shoe would make. [Sarah's shoe was then produced in court]. *I found it corresponded with the mark in the wall;*

in the shoe was some mortar, between the upper leather and the sole; the whey-tub was near enough for the child's head to be put into it while her feet reached the wall; there was some water between the upper leather and the sole in the toe part. These marks were near enough to have been reached by the child supposing that she had been put into the tub with her face downwards and alive struggling.

There were some marks on the floor but I am not able to say if they were blood or not; the whey was in the tub at the time; there was no appearance of blood in the whey that I saw. I saw the tub emptied, and there were something like blood on the bottom; but I can't say what it really was. I saw the state of the rooms upstairs; they were in a very confused state.

In a day or two afterwards, my suspicions alighted on the prisoners at the bar and other persons some short time after, from what I had heard. Being in the shop of Newport, a constable, I saw Hurd first. Hurd came in there of his own accord; I told him my business, and said I wanted to know where he was on the 24th; I also said that I should take down in writing what he might state, and that he might make a statement or not, as he chose.

Smith then read out the statement Hurd had made regarding his movements that day. According to the prisoner, he had left his house in Mount Lane around nine in the morning, engaged in a mini-tour of three pubs – The Lamb, The Unicorn and The Crown – and then headed down into Frome centre sometime between 10 and 11 o'clock. Once there, he remained 'about the town' on his own, for the rest of the day. Whereas the first half of his statement was minutely detailed, times, places, even the drinks he purchased in each public house, the latter half was vague and would be contradicted not only by several witnesses but also his fellow prisoners.

It was now the turn of Maggs's and Sparrow's statements to be read by Smith and even between the two of them there were contradictions. They were both in agreement that they had left Maggs's house in Feltham Lane around 9 o'clock – the same time Hurd was leaving his in Mount Lane – and that their journey into the centre had been via the Mount. But whereas Maggs claimed there was 'no other person with us' (and Hurd had stated he had gone straight into town after visiting the last of the three pubs on his mini-tour) Sparrow contradicted both when he stated that 'off the bottom of the Mount I saw William Sargeant and Hurd'.

Although Sparrow did not state it explicitly, the Woolpack Inn was located at the bottom of the Mount and so it can be assumed he is confirming one of the important early sightings which took place that day. It was here, of course, the landlord and landlady of the pub had testified before the magistrates, they had seen all three prisoners – along with Sargeant – between 10 and 11 o'clock in the company of each other, opposite the Woolpack, for around twenty minutes. If this sighting was accurate and it seemed that Sparrow had now confirmed it, then it was also true that the quartet had seen the Watts pass by and would have known they would be at the market all day.

Sparrow had stated that: 'Hurd then left and went [to] Frome' which tied up with the latter's assertion that he had gone into town around that time on his own (and would also again confirm part of the testimonies of Benjamin and Sophia Cornish of the Woolpack). He (Sparrow) and Maggs then went into the centre together (thus corroborating this part of Maggs's statement).

The fourth person – William Sargeant – had, according to Sparrow and the relevant witnesses, headed off back up towards the Mount (before possibly turning right and heading back home to Butts Square). Once in the centre of Frome, Sparrow's statement seemed to be the most enlightening and accurate of the three – giving an insight into their movements during that part of the day. He stated he and Maggs met up with Hurd again – while Hurd, in his statement, merely said he was 'around the town'; although he did state it was 'on his own'. Maggs's statement of this time had been merely vague, as opposed to contradictory.

The fact all three men asserted they were in town – whether together or alone – between 11.00 and 11.30 in the morning, is confirmed by several of the Frome constables. At 11 o'clock Maggs and Sparrow were seen by Constable Newport, as well as Chief Constable Ivey, and half an hour later, at around 11.30, by Constable Hoddinott.

Hurd was also seen by Chief Constable Ivey, around 11.10, coming across the North Parade Bridge before he headed into the Blue Boar pub (where Maggs and later Sargeant would be arrested by Smith). The prosecution claimed that the prisoners, in order to set up alibis, had deliberately let themselves be seen. Whether this was the case or not, the sightings did happen, and so acted as a reference point to anchor their movements during the day.

While still in town, Maggs then stated that he saw William Payne, but Sparrow omitted this. Whether Payne saw them is not mentioned and possibly does not matter. Then, according to Maggs, either on his own or with Sparrow (although Sparrow does not mention this part), the Angel in the centre was visited. This was around midday. The visit lasted around half and hour and then Maggs stated that after leaving the public house he stayed in the market place for another half an hour – thus taking the time to about 1 o'clock. He then went up to the Victoria Inn, in Christchurch Street East, which was back up towards Keyford. Maggs's and Sparrow's statements now both contradicted that of Hurd (who supposedly was 'on his own' all day) as they stated that they met up with him again; with Maggs's statement specifically having named the Victoria Inn. With Hurd, according to Maggs, was a man called Charles Whimpey, along with a recruiting sergeant for the Marines.

Now their stories parted company, and interestingly this was into the crucial time period when Sarah Watts was murdered. Sparrow stated that he and Maggs left the Victoria Inn around twelve – an hour before Maggs said that they arrived! Maggs himself stated that he left on his own at 4 o'clock. Therefore, he is saying he was in the Victoria Inn the whole time that the farmhouse was robbed and Sarah attacked (and contradicts witnesses who testified to seeing him in Feltham Lane around 3 o'clock).

What seems likely from their combined statements is that Maggs and Sparrow did part company at some time during that period: Maggs returned to his house in Feltham Lane and Sparrow headed off to see Sargeant at his house in Butts Square, before the two of them came back into Keyford and met up again at The Crown. When Maggs reached home he reportedly asked one of his daughters if her mother was at home, but when told 'No', he came back up into Keyford via the Mount. He then went to The Crown, where he met up once more with Sparrow, Hurd and Sargeant. All four stayed here, according to Sparrow, Maggs, and the testimony of the landlord of the pub, for a length of time between 'four and seven or eight o'clock'.

The quartet then left sometime between 7 and 8 o'clock in the evening, and headed back up towards the Mount. Here they all parted company, Maggs and Sparrow going back down Feltham Lane and Maggs's house, Hurd to Mount Lane, and Sargeant no doubt back to his home in Butts Square.

If the three were concerned enough to set up alibis by 'being seen' on purpose, as the prosecution had suggested, this would imply that they were expecting to be questioned and if that was the case, then surely they would have got their stories word-perfect and in unison. The fact that they had not, perhaps went in their favour. But taken together though, there did seem to be some cohesion in their statements, although it would be up to other witnesses – both those called by the prosecution and defence – to corroborate or contradict the statements of the three prisoners.

Sergeant Smith now outlined the rest of his investigation, just as he had done in the magistrates' court, and explained how he had

come to arrest the prisoners. He was cross-examined by the defence
barrister and asked about his interactions with the prisoners.

> *My suspicions alighted on several* [other] *persons; I was busily
> occupied from the 28th of September to the 1st of October in
> making inquiries up to the time I took Hurd in charge; on the
> first Hurd came into Newport's shop of his own accord after
> me; he first spoke to Newport, who is a constable; he asked
> what Newport had sent for him for; he said also that the over-
> seer, Lawes, had collared him, and that he* [Hurd] *had a mind
> to knock him down; he also said that if he had collared Lawes,
> he should have been locked up for it; he did not appear at all
> put out by my questions; his answers were short, but his man-
> ner was not confused; at other times I heard him say he hoped
> the guilty party would be found out; Maggs did not answer so
> readily; his wife said to him, "I wouldn't answer him–who is
> he?" (That was, myself) and after hesitating for some time he
> said, "Well I'll tell you"; I did not observe that he was at all
> confused by the questions I put to him; he said he knew nothing
> about it and that he hoped the guilty person would be found
> out. I had him left at liberty from the 1st to the 6th.*
>
> *I left Hurd at large from the 1st to the 6th and Maggs from
> the 3rd to the 6th. Sparrow also gave me his answers in a plain
> straightforward manner, and did not seem confused; all three
> have always denied that they knew anything of the matter, and
> expressed a wish that the guilty party might be found out. I had
> in custody a person named Sargeant, who was detained about
> a fortnight. The depositions were read over to the witnesses in
> my hearing yesterday. We were before the magistrates six or
> seven times; I can't say who were present on each occasion; I
> had the handkerchief in my possession two or three days; I gave
> it to Mr Parrott, constable; this was, I think, before Mrs Elliott
> was examined; I did not give it to anyone else; a man named
> Hellier* [sic] *was examined before the magistrate on two occa-
> sions; on the second the deposition he made on the first was read
> to him; I have read it over to him since then, and have read to
> some other witnesses the depositions made by them respectively;
> I have heard them read by others; I was before the magistrates
> on the first occasion; he did not say he did not know Maggs or
> Hurd, nor did the magistrate point them out to him.*

Smith then stepped down from the witness box. It was now the
turn of those witnesses he had rounded up to give evidence as to
the movement of the three prisoners.

20

Sightings

Now that the prisoners' statements had been read out, and their movements during the day of the murder explained for the jury's benefit, the prosecution turned their attention to the witnesses who claimed to have seen them at various times during the day.

The crucial time, of course, was between 1 and 4 o'clock in the afternoon – when it seemed that Sarah Watts had met her death. Hurd claimed he was 'around town' all day – which implied he was also in town during that specific period; Maggs claimed to be in the Victoria Inn for the entire three hours, along with Hurd and Sparrow; and Sparrow – whose statement seemed the most open of them all – stated he was with Maggs, then Sargeant, and then all four of them (the fourth being Hurd) in the Crown during the period under scrutiny. It would now be up to the prosecution and their witnesses to disprove this and place either some or all of them near Battle Farm during that critical time.

The evidence of the first two witnesses concerned the morning sighting outside the Woolpack, which was also important to establish a key fact: the prisoners knew the Watts were at the market all day. These witnesses, of course, were Benjamin and Sophia Cornish, landlord and landlady of the Woolpack Inn, respectively. The former was first to the witness stand:

My name is Benjamin Cornish, and I am a beer-house-keeper of Culverhill, Frome: I keep a beer house on the Frome side of the Mount between Woodlands and Frome. I saw Sparrow, Hurd, Maggs & Sargeant standing in front of my house on the 24th; between ten and eleven o'clock in the morning; they remained together about 20 minutes; while they were there Watts passed by on his way to Frome. That is the way in which Mr. Watts goes to market. Hurd had on a coat similar to the one he now wears; Maggs's clothes I did not observe; Sparrow was dressed somewhat similarly to his present dress; they were together, and were going towards Frome. I did not see them separate. As I was going to market Hurd passed me on the Unicorn Hill in the direction for the market and three or four minutes after in the market; there are various roads from Maggs's house to

Frome, and I saw him on one of them; Hurd came to my house on the Thursday night [the day after the murder] *there was no one with him then; it was between nine and ten at night and had a smock frock on; he had some meat in a bundle.*

Cornish was then cross-examined and asked to give further details regarding the prisoners' attire on the morning of the murder: 'When the prisoners were opposite my house Hurd had on a 'wide awake' and a palacot, Maggs had a long coat and Sparrow a 'Jim Crow'.'

Benjamin Cornish then stood down and his place taken by Sophia:

I am [the] *wife of* [the] *last witness; on the 24th of September I saw the prisoners and another man called Sargeant opposite my house. I knew Hurd and Sparrow before this, and I had also seen Maggs, but did not know his name; Watts passed by as they were standing near our house. In the afternoon I again saw the prisoners with another man; this was between three and four; Sparrow was going from the Mount, by our house; he had on a black, common-shaped hat; it was not the same as he had in the morning – he then had on a green Jim Crow. I saw Hurd again on that day, they came to my own house for a pint of beer, this was after nine in the evening when Watts was with him; he said he was very sorry for the murder-they were d_ _ rascals who had done it, and he hoped those who were guilty of it would be hanged, drawn and quartered. Hurd paid for the beer. With the exception of Sparrow's hat I did not see any change in his dress; the murder was of course the subject of general talk.*

Throughout these testimonies, as well as the ones that followed, Robert Hurd...

was constantly employed ... in taking notes of the evidence and handing down remarks upon it to the learned counsel for the defence. His manner had some influence upon the others; and the whole three, though they paid great attention to the testimony delivered by the various witnesses, seemed disposed to make a show of bravado and of confidence that the crime with which they were charged could not be brought home to them.

At the same time, Hurd's confrontational attitude towards the witnesses continued, but this eventually became too much for the judge and he was 'ordered to turn around and face the bar'.

William Bailey was then called. He had been a witness to a couple of later sightings:

My name is William Bailey and on the 24th of September I was working for Stephen Wheeler, who lives near the Asylum at Keyford; he saw the prisoner Sparrow going towards the Woodlands about 12 o'clock and I saw the other two prisoners with Sargeant and Sparrow, standing near Cornish's beer house [before] they separated; Hurd went towards Frome, Sargeant towards Tytherington and the other two going towards Woodlands about 12 o'clock. A few minutes after I went to Mr. Cornish's for a pint of beer and afterwards saw them standing at the bottom of the hill this was about ten minutes after; they were talking to one another; I saw them separate. I [also] saw Sparrow and Maggs coming direct from Woodlands about quarter to four o'clock, and going towards Frome.

Bailey had not given evidence at the magistrates' court, a point the defence counsel, Mr Edwards, decided to pursue in the following conversation:

"So, may I ascertain where you currently live and if you have delivered this testimony at any time beforehand."

"I have lived in Frome since this murder, but have never been before the magistrates."

"Mr Bailey, can you elaborate for this court the circumstances why this is the case?"

"I heard people talk about it, but I did not go to give my evidence ... I have remembered ever since I saw them about 12 o'clock, but I never went to the magistrates because I did not know I was to do so; I spoke about the matter to Mr Cruttwell [the Frome based solicitor and clerk to the magistrates there] *and probably that is the reason I am here; I was working near the asylum at this time; I looked at the clock when they passed; I did so because I had a right to; I went to look what time it was, and they passed; I was working upon my own account at the time."*

Mr Moody, the prosecutor, then asked the witness to clarify the point. 'I was at Bruton in a public house talking about this matter [after which] Mr Dyne sent for me and took down my statement in writing. The next day Mr Cruttwell sent for me.'

Another 'new' witness was Martha Stephens, who lived at Marston Gate, near Frome:

I am the wife of George Stephens, and live near Frome; on the 24th of September, I saw two of the prisoners; I had known them before; Sparrow ... ever since he was born; I also knew

Maggs; I saw them cross the road and get over Marston gate; this was about a quarter before twelve o'clock; they crossed the road, and went into the ground opposite my house; it is farmer Hoddinott's ground; one had a coat on, and the other a sleeve waistcoat; did not observe the hats they had on; they were going towards Woodlands.

Again, Edwards rose and questioned the witness about any previous testimony she had given:

"I never was before the magistrates to give evidence," she said. *"I was called on about six weeks ago about these facts."*

"And what about the day in question, can you tell this court anymore about it?"

"I saw many people that day, but I didn't notice them; I am quite sure, however, it was the prisoners I had seen; I had seen them before; they lived at short distances from me."

"And please remind me at what time did you say it was when you believe the prisoners crossed the road?"

"I looked at the clock just when I saw them, and it was about a quarter to 12; I don't know if our clock was quite right, but I believe it was."

"And were they in possession of anything that you noticed?"

"The prisoners were not carrying anything."

"Thank you, Mrs Stephens. No more questions, m'lord."

Benjamin Mines now took the stand. He had given evidence at the magistrates' court on the first day of the proceedings.

I have known the prisoners seven years, and saw them near the Victoria Inn, Frome on the 24th of September; they were together; it was about half past one; I heard them agree to meet each other again in an hour that afternoon; Hurd took out his watch; after this they parted company.

The witness was then cross-examined.

"And this was at one-thirty you saw them?"

"It was at a quarter or half past one."

"And where exactly was this?"

"They were in the market when I saw them."

"And how far is this from Marston?"

"It is about a mile and a quarter from the Marston turnpike gate."

"You say you had known the prisoners for a number of years; can you describe what clothing they were wearing on that day?"

*"Yes, I had known the prisoners before; Maggs had on
a short cloth jacket, a dark one; it had some stripes in it;
Sparrow had a dark coat, which, so far as I know, was the
one he now has."*

"Thank you, I have no more questions."

Ann Hiscox then took the stand. Like the previous witness, she had
also given evidence at the magistrates' court the October before,
and her sightings came within the crucial time period. Her testimony concerned Sparrow's movements:

*I live at Butt's Square, in Frome; on the 24th of September
Sparrow came there, between five and ten minutes before two;
he enquired for [William] Sargent and went to Sargent's house
and remained there a quarter of an hour; and then went out in
the direction of Frome; I saw them go away together, and I did
not see them afterwards; Sparrow had a blue coat and yellow
buttons.*

On being cross-examined, she added that Sparrow 'seemed to be
much as usual, I should think; he asked his questions in an ordinary way, and did not appear to be in any hurry; Butt's Square is
something less than a mile from Marston Gate.'

The Marston references in terms of distances between it and
the locations of the sightings, during the defence's cross-examination of the previous two witnesses, were important as the testimonies of the next two placed all the prisoners there at the start of the
crucial period.

The first witness resided on the same long stretch of road as
Battle Farm. He had also given his testimony at the magistrates'
court:

*My name is Joseph Watts, I live at Tytherington Lane, and
know all the prisoners; on the 24th of September I saw them in
the lane, with another man I did not know; they were under a
bush; the lane leads near to Marston Gate; they were together;
I saw Hurd go through the gate and beckon to the others, who
then immediately went after him, and they all went to a heap
of stones in the road leading to Frome; I spoke to Maggs and
Sparrow but no one else, and shook hands with Maggs. I saw
Robert Hurd hold up his hand a second time; I went on with
them to the corner of Sandy Hill Lane; I saw Robert Hurd
beckon with his hand a third time they went down the lane,
and I left them; I heard the Rectory bell about half an hour
before I first saw them.*

Bulls Bridge, where Robert Walter saw the murderer 'shuffling' away. (*Authors' collection*)

Frome police station, where Joseph Seer confessed to the killing. (*Frome Museum*)

A typical court in session: the trial of the suspects charged with the killing of Sarah Watts took place at Taunton in April 1852.

Sarah Watts was found murdered in the dairy room of Battle Farm.

Keyford, which was part of the route John and Leah Watts took on their way to market. (*Frome Museum*)

Shepton Mallet Gaol: All suspects charged with the killing would spend time here, awaiting appearances in court. (*Authors' collection*)

The murder makes national news: *The London Daily News* 29 September 1851.

A smock coat similar to the one worn by the man seen running away from Battle Farm by Robert Walter.

St.John's Church (*c*1860s), in front of which the Watts sold their cheese on market day.

Pub. by S. Cugner, Froome

The West front of the Old Church of S. John Baptist. Froome-Selwood.

Frome market – early twentieth century, but still very much as it would have been fifty years earlier.

Illustrated Police News graphic, from a review of the case in 1889.

Frome Market Place from the direction of the Blue Boar and main guardhouse. (*Frome Museum*)

Frome Market Place 1860s. (*Frome Museum*)

CROWN INN

Pub. by Langford & Butler

Kershaw & Son, London, No.885.

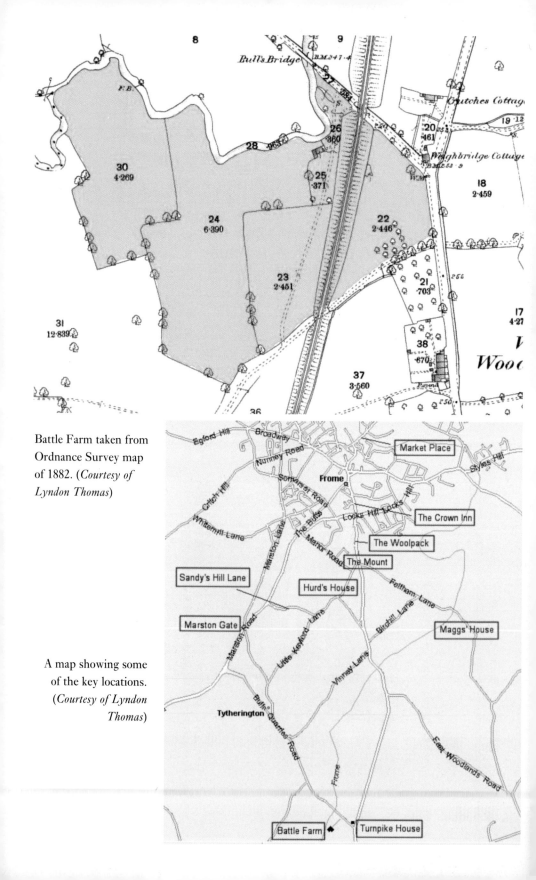

Battle Farm taken from Ordnance Survey map of 1882. (*Courtesy of Lyndon Thomas*)

A map showing some of the key locations. (*Courtesy of Lyndon Thomas*)

The Toll House near Battle Farm, present day. (*Authors' collection*)

The present-day entrance to the remains of Battle Farm. (*Authors' collection*)

The Market Place Guardhouse not long before it was demolished in 1965. (*Frome Museum*)

Trudoxhill Congregational Chapel. (*Authors' collection*)

The Woolpack
photographed in the
1950s. (*Frome Museum*)

The George,
West Woodlands,
scene of the inquest.
(*Authors' collection*)

Sir William Erle, assize trial judge in 1852.

Frome Magistrates' Court, plot 1687 from a map of 1838. (*Frome Society for Local Study*)

Aerial view of Dartmoor prison, where Sparrow spent ten years before his release in 1862. (*Authors' collection*)

Frome Post Office in Vicarage Street, scene of the 1855 robbery by Sarah Watts's namesake. Now a car park. (*Frome Museum*)

CONVICTS FORMING A MORTAR BATTERY IN THE WOOLWICH MARSHES.

Convicts at work at Woolwich, where Maggs was held for a time. (*Meyhew & Binney*)

Taunton Castle, scene of the 1852 Assizes. (*From an old postcard*)

The Unicorn Inn, Keyford in around 1914. (*From an old postcard*)

Richard Grist's grocery shop and The Crown public house to its left. (*Authors' collection*)

The Blue Boar in the present day minus the guardhouse, to its left, which was demolished in the 1960s. (*Frome Museum*)

Frome Bob's letter to court, 16 September 1861. (*Authors' collection*)

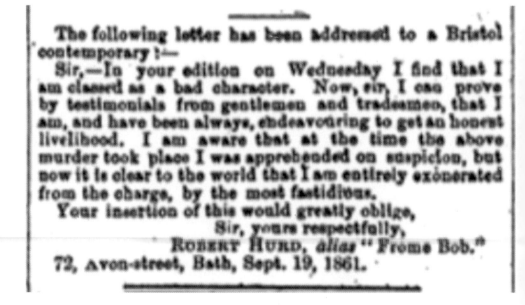

The following letter has been addressed to a Bristol contemporary:—

Sir,—In your edition on Wednesday I find that I am classed as a bad character. Now, sir, I can prove by testimonials from gentlemen and tradesmen, that I am, and have been always, endeavouring to get an honest livelihood. I am aware that at the time the above murder took place I was apprehended on suspicion, but now it is clear to the world that I am entirely exonerated from the charge, by the most fastidious.

Your insertion of this would greatly oblige,

Sir, yours respectfully,

ROBERT HURD, *alias* "Frome Bob."

72, Avon-street, Bath, Sept. 19, 1861.

On cross-examination the witness added the following:

> *I went to Frome market when I left them; Sandy Hill Lane leads down to Hurd's house; it is about a quarter of a mile down the lane; I saw nothing besides on the road; I am sure I saw the prisoners; one had a short "slock" on – that was Sargeant; Hurd had on a sleeve waistcoat; I don't know how the others were dressed.*

The defence then changed tack and put the witness's own past in the spotlight, to throw doubt upon his credibility.

> *"It is true that in a previous employ you were dismissed over the theft of cutlery?"*

Watts, momentarily taken aback by the question, swiftly composed himself and answered:

> *"I once worked for Lord Cork, and left his employee because some silver spoons were lost."*
> *"Were you not turned away from Lord Cork's for stealing these silver spoons?"*
> *"They said I had stolen the silver spoons but I hadn't."*
> *"Did they not, in fact, charge you with stealing them and then turned you away for it?"*
> *"They said I did it."*
> *"And did you not take poison some time ago, and charge it upon your wife?"*
> *"That's nothing to do with this matter."*
> *"And that's your answer?"*
> *"Yes, that's my answer."*
> *"Thank you Mr Watts, you have been most helpful. No more questions, m'lord."*

The toll-collector at the Marston turnpike gate, 64-year-old Richard Babey, was called next. He too had given his disposition the previous October.

> *In September last I kept the Marston gate: on the 24th of September I saw four men in the Tytherington Lane; I could not say whether they were the prisoners or not; they were standing near the bar under a hedge and were there about ten minutes; two of them went on through the gate towards Frome; the taller man [Hurd] beckoned to the others, who remained near the gate, and they followed him; Watts passed through the gate about the same time, and overtook them; this was just after my*

dinner hour, which is about one o'clock; a carriage went by at
the same time; one of the men had a smock frock on.

When cross-examined, he added: 'I had never seen the prisoners before; there was only one other man I had seen that day with a smock frock on, like one of the prisoners'.

As in the magistrates' court, Sarah Cox was called forward to testify as to what time the nearby Rectory bell was rung. This had been heard by all concerned – or at least Watts and Hurd had previously mentioned hearing it – which could at least pinpoint one time accurately, even if there were any contradictions between other testimonies:

> *I was in service of the Reverend Richard Boyle, of Marston Rectory, in September; it was my duty to ring the dinner bell, usually at half past twelve and a quarter to two; it was rung a little earlier on the 24th of September – twenty minutes to two. My master's carriage came home that day about half past one.*

Further sightings of Maggs, Sparrow and Hurd on the day of the murder, and within the crucial time period, were now put forward by prosecution witnesses that placed the trio even nearer to the Watts' farm; although doubt over timings and, indeed, their very authenticity, would be raised by the defence counsel.

The first of these witnesses to take the stand was 20-year-old Henry Hillier:

> *I live at Ridgway; in September I was working at Tytherington as a mason, I worked for Roger Burge; on the 24th I saw the prisoners Hurd and Maggs; I had known them three years; one had a smock frock on, and the other had a coat on; one had a high crowned hat, and the other a Jim Crow; they were coming from Vinney Lane which leads to Tytherington Road* (Battle Farm was located around a ten minute medium-paced walk from this 'junction').

Edwards, confident after his cross-examination of Joseph Watts, took a similar confrontational stance with Hillier:

> *"So when exactly did this sighting take place?"*
> *"It was before I had my dinner, which might have been about two o'clock."*
> *"Mr Hillier, have you never said it was between ten and eleven?"*

Hillier hesitated for a few moments, but then answered:
"No, I haven't."

"Will you swear you did not tell John Jones it was between ten and eleven?"

"I don't mean to say anything about it."

"Mr Hillier, will you please state for the satisfaction of myself, the jury and the rest of this court, which of the prisoners is William Maggs?"

Most likely unbeknownst to Edwards beforehand, this proved to be an ace up his sleeve. A visibly shaken Hillier now turned his attention towards the three prisoners standing at the bar. There was an uncomfortable silence in court as he looked from one to another. He eventually half-pointed towards Sparrow, but immediately doubted himself and withdrew his hand.

"Mr Hillier. I ask once again if you can point out for the satisfaction of this court my client, William Maggs?"

The witness remained silent, unable to answer. After more hesitation though, he finally pointed to the right prisoner.

"Ah, at last, now do you swear that this is William Maggs?"

The witness did not answer, although Edwards did not press him; his point, he believed, had been well and truly made. Somewhat laconically he merely said:

"Thank you Mr Hillier, your appearance on the witness stand this morning has been most enlightening. No more questions, my lord."

Hillier stood down and left the courtroom immediately, his head down and his attention firmly on getting out of there as quickly as he could. The prosecution could only look on helpless and wonder what had gone wrong: was Hillier's motivation for coming forward purely down to possible financial gain and had he been so desperate for the reward money as to fabricate his 'evidence', or at the very least change it to fit the crucial period? The prosecution could only hope the next witness would be more assured:

My name is Henry Lambton and I was working at Robert Burge's house on the 24th of September; his house is at Tytherington; Titmarsh [Farm] is about a quarter of a mile from it; I don't know the prisoners, but I saw them come out of the Bruton road, down the fields; when I first saw them

they were in the Tytherington Road; there were two of them;
they had come out of Vinney lane, which passes Tytherington
road; one had a coat on, and the other a smock; one a high
crowned and the other a low crowned hat; this was before
I had dinner; a boy called Allard was working with me, in
Mr Chedzey's barton; he had gone away at that time for Mr
Chedzey's dinner.

The 'boy called Allard' referred to was, of course, Alfred Allard,
who had earlier testified as to having seen Sarah Watts about one
o'clock, as he was on his way back with Mr Chedzey's dinner, to
where Lambton and Hillier were working.

The defence counsel now rose for the cross-examination:

"Can you state for this court, the relationship between your-
self and the previous witness, Henry Hillier, and what exactly
passed between the two of you?"

"The last witness is my master," replied Lambton. *"He*
[Hillier] *said, when they went 'that's Maggs and that's*
Sparrow.' I only saw them then; other men went down the road,
but master did not say who they were; master never said, to my
knowledge, it was between ten and eleven that the prisoners
went down; I was in Frome on Wednesday, and went to a public
house with master; I went into one room and he to another, so
that I did not hear what he said."

Edwards, seemingly talking to himself but obviously for the jury's
sake, then said: 'So this was between ten and eleven the prisoners
went down.' He then turned back and addressed the witness once
more. 'Thank you Mr Lambton, there is nothing more I wish to
ask you.'

It was now the turn of another 'new' witness, whose chilling
testimony it seemed, concerned an actual sighting of the supposed
murderer. The witness took the stand and swore his oath. He then
began:

My name is Robert Walter and on the 24th of September I
was going from Frome to Maiden Bradley; I knew the house
occupied by John Watts; I could see it from the turnpike road. I
saw someone coming from the house up towards Bull's Bridge;
he had a dirty smock frock on; I did not see what hat; he was
going at a sort of shuffling run; he had something under his
arm; this was from half past two to quarter to three o'clock,
as nearly as I can say; I only had a sight of him about two
minutes.

The defence counsel, Edwards, was immediately on his feet and focused on the fact this evidence had not been presented before at the magistrates' court. He asked the witness why:

> *I have been before the magistrate in this case, or somewhere,* replied Walter. *I was examined by somebody, I don't know who; the prisoners were not there; I heard of the murder within a week of the time it happened; I have been in ill health for some time.*

Seemingly satisfied by this answer, the defence then asked Walter if he could add anything more.

> *The man appeared to have a smock frock on, but that is all I can say about him; I had been into Frome, but am sure it was not as I was returning that I saw the prisoners.*

Once the defence had finished, Mr Moody, the prosecutor, stood and asked Robert Walter if he was aware of the fact that John Watts often went to town. 'I knew Mr Watts was in the habit of attending Frome market,' he said.

If Robert Walter had indeed seen the murderer going from the farm, then it lent weight to there being a lone perpetrator. This did not eliminate any of the three prisoners, of course, and the next few witnesses were called to establish Maggs and Sparrow's movements after the specific time Walter had given: between two-thirty and a quarter to three.

> *My name is Joseph Noble and on the 24th of September I was in a field near the road that leads to the Mount from Feltham; I saw [the] prisoners, Maggs and Sparrow, in the field near the Mount; they were coming from Felton, and were going towards Frome; this was between three and four o'clock; they had dark coats on; neither had a frock on.*

Cross-examined, Noble then said:

> *I think they had the same coats on as they now have. They were going on quietly; they came along close by me; I had not often seen Maggs before. They did not appear hurried.*

Harriet Morgan, the following witness, stated that she knew Maggs and Sparrow and...

> *saw them on the 24th of September, between three and four on the road leading from Blatchbridge, They were between*

Mrs Moss's cottage and my house; and in the direction of Frome; they were not far from the Mount when I first saw them ... [cross-examined] ... neither had a smock frock on; Sparrow had the same blue coat that he has now; nothing in their manner attracted my attention; I don't know that ever I saw Maggs in any other and dark clothes; I never saw him in a white smock frock, though I have known him many years.

Further witnesses with other sightings and clothing descriptions of the accused were called in quick succession. Henry Keane, who knew the prisoners, testified that:

on the 24th of September I saw Maggs and Hurd; they were going down towards the Asylum from Lower Keyford on the hill; this was at about half past two; I saw Maggs put his hand in his pocket, take out something, and give it to Hurd. I was not near enough to see what it was. ... [cross-examined] ... they were going along very slowly; Maggs had on a dark coat.

Alexander Barber, a gardener at Frome, and 'new' witness, testified to having seen Hurd and Maggs on the day of the murder at around 4 o'clock at the Frome market:

There were three others with them, he said. *Maggs had a dark coat on; the two I did not know had on Jim Crow hats – a dark one and a light one – as I was passing by I heard Hurd say, 'a watch, and no tin'.* On cross-examination, Barber added: *I don't know that I have ever spoken to Hurd, though I have long known him; I was passing by them when I heard the expression, 'a watch, and no tin'. I never went before the magistrates of my own accord; I was first examined more than a week ago; I was sent for first, and then formerly examined; I am not certain how long it was ago, but I think it will be three weeks next Thursday; there was a great many men standing in market; I know a man called Whimpey – he was there with Hurd and the others.*

Now outside the crucial time-period of 4 o'clock, when the Watts returned and found their daughter, the landlord of the Crown Inn, in Keyford, seemingly corroborated Sparrow's statement that he, Maggs, Hurd, and Sargeant, had gone to his public house:

My name is Joseph Singer and I keep the Crown Inn, at Keyford; on the 24th of September the prisoners came to my house with a man of the name of Sargent; they were there at about four o'clock; they were not there about one and two; they remained together in one room till nearly seven; I think Hurd went out a little time, but came back again [this was most likely the time Hurd met John Watts and took him for a beer at the Woolpack] *they went away one after another.*

Joseph Singer was then cross-examined by the defence:

I had not seen them at any other time in my house, Singer said. *There was nothing peculiar in their manner; they were talking and laughing in the ordinary way; Sparrow was at my house the Sunday after; I can't say if he had anything the matter with his hand or not; I don't know what their dress was; I don't know that I ever saw Maggs in any other than dark clothes.*

Taken together, the testimonies of the witnesses who had sworn on their oath to the sightings of the prisoners on the day of the murder, seemed to provide a solid base of evidence that placed at least one, if not all, of the suspects near or in the vicinity of the farm at West Woodlands just before or not long after the time Sarah Watts had been murdered. And yet, there also seemed to be contradiction, hesitation, and even possible fabrication amongst several of the witnesses; which the defence counsel was only too quick to highlight. The prosecution therefore needed to get back onto an even keel and with a shift of location and focus on just one of the prisoners it seemed they might achieve this.

21

North Bradley

The emphasis of the prosecution's case now focused on North Bradley and the fair which had taken place the week after the murder. Sparrow had attended the three day event – he would be arrested on the day after it finished – and during his stay there had possibly as good as 'confessed' to the murder; as certain details he claimed to know were not thought to be public knowledge at the time. It would be up to the jury to make up their own mind as to whether this was just part of the prisoner's imagination, having merely repeated, but then added to, what others had said, or if he was the lone perpetrator Robert Walter had witnessed shuffling away from the murder scene? Another crucial aspect of the evidence the prosecution wanted to present, and highlight, was exactly when the wound to Sparrow's thumb had been inflicted.

The first witness was Martha Watson, daughter of the landlord who kept the public house where Sparrow stayed during the fair:

My father keeps the New Ring of Bells at North Bradley; the fair was on Monday the 29th of September; I saw Sparrow there, but did not observe if he had anything the matter with his hand; on the day after I saw him show that he had a bad thumb; He said he had been fighting on Monday night; I saw it also on the 1st of October; he held it up for me to see; it appeared to me to be very bad; there was matter escaping from the nail; he said he had hurt it in a fight.

My father asked him if it was true there was a murder committed at Frome; he replied that there was, and that he had seen the girl; I asked if he really had seen her, and he said he had – that he saw her on the following morning; he said she had had a blow in the head, and after that was put into the whey; he said there were ten constables there when he was; father asked if there was any suspicion, and [the] prisoner said he did not know; he said there had been four people taken up, and set at liberty again; he said she had a blow in her face; I asked him which he thought caused her death; the blow or the whey? And he said he didn't know; he had told us she had a blow in the head; he said she was lying in the back kitchen, and her clothes were over her head; I understood that he himself saw her in the back kitchen;

He said her uncle had been suspected and taken up on suspicion, but he was set at liberty again, and he said that the uncle had no more done it than he. He said he thought it would never be found out, for he thought there was only one person concerned in it.

Watson was cross-examined by the defence and was not only questioned about when she had been asked for her testimony, and who had been in the room at the time, but whether she could swear she had repeated Sparrow's words exactly. 'I was asked for this on Wednesday, October the 6th,' she replied.

I then told the policeman about it; on the 10th of October I went before the magistrates; I don't pretend to give the exact words used by Sparrow; there was no one there besides father and mother; I have heard many different reports about the murder. I have given his words as nearly as possible.

John Jackson was then called:

I was at Bradley on the 29th of September until October the 1st; the fair is on three days; Sparrow was there and I saw him at a public house on Wednesday; understanding he was from Frome, I asked if he knew anything of the murder; he said two or three had been taken up but they could make nothing out of them; I asked him if he thought it would be found out? He said he did not think it would; he said there was only one man that did it, and he'd never tell; he said the girl was first beat about the head with a stick, then put into a whey-tub, and then taken out and thrown on the floor; I asked if he knew the Watts; he answered, 'yes, very well.'

I heard someone say, [after] Sparrow's neckerchief had worked around under his neck 'Are you going to be hung?' Sparrow replied, 'Well I s'pose it won't be long first;' I saw that his hand was injured, and he said it had been hurt the day before; I thought it was an old wound, I saw his thumb [and] it appeared to have a whitish sort of matter under it. [Cross-examined] 'I went before the magistrates three times; about the knotted handkerchief, I won't swear that Sparrow was laughing and making fun about the handkerchief when he so answered; this was in the public tap-room. I never heard him say that he hoped the parties would be found out.'

Hannah Watts now took the witness stand to give evidence regarding the day after the murder, when Sparrow was supposed to have seen Sarah's body at the farm:

My name is Hannah Watts and I was at Mr Watts's house on the 25th; I was there all day; I am a relation; the body was upstairs all that day; strangers were not upstairs that day; I saw Sparrow for the first time before the magistrates; I'm sure he was not at the house on the 25th; there were not more than two or three constables there.

I went away at 11 at night, and was in the house all day, replied Hannah, when asked about her movements on that day, during cross-examination. *I was in the milk-house sometimes, but not staying there; some magistrates were there, and constables, with neighbours; I knew most of them, but perhaps not all, but Sparrow was not there; some went up and saw the body, and then went out; I did not know Sparrow before I saw him in the magistrates' office; the post-mortem examination took place upstairs. I will not swear that there were not fifty people there that I did not know. I can't say how many men whom I did not know went up to see the child.*

The prosecutor, Moody, now stepped forward and asked Hannah Watts which persons were allowed upstairs on that day. 'Those who were allowed to go upstairs were persons connected with the family,' she replied.

I am the father of Martha Watson and keep the Ring of Bells at Bradley, stated Charles Watson, after he replaced Hannah Watts on the stand. *I saw Sparrow there on the Monday; on the Wednesday I* [also] *saw him, and having heard of the murder at Frome, I asked him about it; he said he lived at Blatchbridge, near where the murder was committed; he said the girl was murdered by a blow in the head, and then put into the whey, and, that the blood stained the whey; he said three or four had been taken up, but had been discharged for want of evidence; he said she had been found on the dairy floor, with her clothes over her head.*

The defence then asked Charles Watson who had brought up the subject of the murder. He answered that he had. He then stepped down. Samuel Tanner took his place:

My name is Samuel Tanner and I live at North Bradley, and was at the fair on the 29th of September; I saw Sparrow there in the afternoon shooting for nuts; his left hand was either tied up, or he had something in it; I saw him again next day, at Watson's [The New Ring of Bells]. *I noticed him particularly because he pretended to be tipsy.'* [Cross-examined]: *'I saw him in the fair; I won't say it was not his handkerchief in his hand: I have not been before the magistrates to give evidence; I was not called on till about a fortnight ago.*

The final 'North Bradley fair' witness was called. This was an employee of the New Ring of Bells, where Sparrow had stayed, called Thomas Harding.

I am a waiter at the New Ring of Bells, North Bradley; this is the house kept by Watson. Sparrow was there on the 29th of September about dinner-time, and again in the evening in the club room; there had been a fight in the kitchen between 9 and 10, but Sparrow was not in it; he was in another room; I saw him in the clubroom after the fight, and he said he would fight anyone for a sovereign; A man jumped up to fight him, I jumped up and parted them, there was no more fighting there. A person accepted his challenge, but I prevented them from fighting.

I saw Sparrow next day and he told me there was something the matter with his thumb; he said, 'Look here, how they served me last night, they bit my thumb'; there was a matter on it. The wound on the thumb did not look as though it had been freshly done. I did not observe his hand on Monday. [Cross-examined]: There were several persons there drinking – sometimes as many as twenty; the fight was between nine and ten o'clock; I said it was a bad bite when he showed me his thumb; I did not tell him he was not in it, because he was a stranger to me, and I thought it no business of mine to do so.

The focus then moved briefly back to Frome and the Crown Inn in Keyford. The three accused, along with William Sargeant, had been drinking there on the afternoon of the murder, but the next witness had evidence about a later date:

My name is Robert Singer and I am in the employ of the landlord of the Crown Inn; on [Sunday] 28th of September Sparrow was there, and I saw that his hand was bad. I saw a piece of rag around his finger. When cross-examined, Singer added: *Sparrow had a pint of beer and a ha'porth of tobacco; but it was not the tobacco paper that he had around his thumb; I am a waiter at the inn.*

He was then re-examined:

I had seen the thing round his thumb after he had the tobacco, but I don't know if it was the paper or not. I did not see what he did with the paper round the tobacco.

The police officer who had arrested Sparrow after the fair was now called to give his testimony:

> *I am* [William Staples] *one of the constables for Wiltshire; on the 1st* [sic] *of October Sparrow was in my charge, for stealing a watch on the 24th of September; he said he had bought the watch at the Victoria public house, off Robert Hurd, and that Maggs was present;* [but] *not having enough money Maggs and he went home; he said Maggs owed him 10 or 12 days work, and that he had not money enough to pay for it; he pawned his jacket & waistcoat to make up the money; he first said he'd given 37s. for it, and then he said 27s.; I observed his thumb to be in a bad state, and he had a mark on his knuckle; the top of his thumbnail was nearly off; I asked how he had hurt his hand; he said 'I hardly know, but I think some Southwick chaps bit it at Bradley fair on the Monday;' Maggs came to Westbury on the 6th, with some linen and a handkerchief for Sparrow. The watch was afterwards examined on the third of October by Mr. Shorland. Sparrow had no handkerchief when he was taken into custody.* [Cross-examined]: *It was this watch which was supposed to have been stolen from Mr Watts; in consequence these parties were taken up; that was the first thing that gave rise to suspicion against them; I have made every effort to trace an owner for it, but have failed; Maggs said he was going down to give evidence for Sparrow, but he did not make his appearance in time; I had told him the time. I have never found out that the watch was stolen although I have enquired in every direction.*

Judge Erle then asked the constable a question about his method, to which the police officer replied: 'I tried to get at the murder through the watch.'

The man who had examined Sparrow's thumb at the Westbury police station, surgeon George Shorland, now replaced his police colleague and took the stand. His testimony would prove to be the most damning of all, in terms of Sparrow's possible guilt and it would be nigh on impossible for the defence to discredit it.

> *I am a surgeon and examined the prisoner Sparrow on Friday, the 3rd of October at Westbury; I found some blood on the front of his shirt; he said he had a bad hand, and that some matter which was on his shirt had got there by his putting his hand into his pocket; There were* [also] *stains of blood in the pocket corresponding with stains on the shirt; I looked at the wound on the hand; it was of several days' standing; the nail was nearly*

off and there was suppuration under the root of the nail that might be caused by a bite. It could not have been in this state if it had been produced by a bite on Monday night, matter would not be formed until the third or fourth day; incrustations would not appear for several days; some of the stains on his clothes were old. [Cross-examined]: *The thumb must have been in a very painful state for some days; I should think the injury had been received nine or ten days ago* [the latter being the day of the murder] *the pain of such would be intense; on the second knuckle of the forefinger there was a mark or bruise. The nail was bitten through. I pledge my professional reputation that a wound would not begin to fester in 24 hours.*

22

Final Witnesses

My name is James Hoddinott and I am a constable at Frome; on the 24th I went to the house of the deceased; there was blood on the floor; there was a silk handkerchief on the table which I gave to Smith; it has been in my possession nearly ever since; I now produce it; I went into the milk house and observed a spot of blood there, as if a man's thumb had been pressed against the wall; there was more than one mark; but I did not observe them till next morning; it appeared as if the person pressed down his fingers afterwards. It appeared that some part of the whey in the trendle had been thrown on the floor; there was blood under the trendle. The trendle was half full of whey and it appeared as though it were bloody. I did not mention that to anyone until next morning. I mentioned it to Mr. Newport. [Cross-examined]: *I saw Maggs on that day in the marketplace at about half past 11 o'clock; Sparrow was with him; he was not dressed as he is now; he had a dark coat on; Sparrow wore a green Jim Crow; I* [also] *saw Maggs, Hurd, and Sparrow as I was going into Cornish's beer shop, with another man. I was at Watts' house about three hours* [on the evening of the first day]. *When I took up the handkerchief there was only Mrs Watts and another woman there. I asked whose it was and they said it did not belong to either of them. Sparrow was not there while I was there.*

With constable James Hoddinott's testimony, the focus of the prosecution was now well and truly on the handkerchief found at the Battle Farm, on the day of the murder, which they wanted to prove belonged to Sparrow. Elizabeth Hillier took constable Hoddinott's place in the witness stand.

I keep the Bunns Lane turnpike gate, leading from Bradley to Frome; I know the prisoner Sparrow; I recollect his coming to my house on the 12th of September; he came to light his pipe; I saw in his hand a dark red and white silk handkerchief; there was near one corner a slit, and not far from it another; I can't say the handkerchief produced by Mr Hoddinott is the one, but it is like it. I saw the handkerchief twice, both inside and outside my house.

Hillier was followed by Mary Francis:

> *I am* [Mary Francis the] *wife of Henry Francis, who keeps the Horse and Groom public-house at* [East] *Woodlands; I knew prisoner Sparrow; he was at my house on the 15th of September; I observed a handkerchief; he was also there on the 20th; I then again saw the handkerchief on his hand and on his knee; he went out and left the handkerchief on the settle; it was very ragged and broken, and had 'slents' in the corner; and was very dirty; the handkerchief produced is like it; I would rather swear that it is the same than that it is not; the marks and slents are like those in Sparrow's. I heard the handkerchief talked of in the tap room in connection with the murder and I came forward to give evidence.* Mrs Francis was then cross-examined by the defence. *It was on the 13th that the pocket handkerchief was left on the settle, I had it in my hand; I have not said it was on the 20th; there were several other persons also present in the tap, John Watts the brewer was present and several men I can't say how many and they may have looked at it; I recognised the handkerchief immediately when before the magistrates; I had not seen it from the 20th till then, but I was still able to recognise it.*

Mr Moody asked the witness if she had seen the handkerchief whilst it was in the constable's possession. Francis replied that 'Mr Hoddinott did not at any time show that handkerchief.'

At this stage in the proceedings, Joseph Noble was recalled. He had been in a field on the day of the murder and had sighted Maggs and Sparrow on their way back up Feltham Lane to the Mount, between 3 and 4 o'clock. The defence counsel, Edwards, asked the first question, to which Noble replied: 'I was not at Mrs Francis on the 13th or the 20th.'

The prosecution now put forward a question, to which the witness said: 'I don't remember seeing a handkerchief then.'

A further witness was called to give testimony, regarding the handkerchief, although he too could not be certain that it was the one produced in court:

> *My name is Robert Brinton and in June last I mowed for Major Trevelyan and Mr Steed. Sparrow was also employed by him; he lent me a silk handkerchief to put some bread in; the one produced is something after the same pattern, but I can't swear to it.*

Constable Edward Newport, who had accompanied Detective Sergeant Smith in his investigation, now gave his evidence:

I am a constable residing at Frome [and] I was present when the examination of Hurd and Maggs was taken at my house; I was at Watts's house the morning after the murder was committed; I have been engaged in tracing it; I produce a Jim Crow hat which I had from Maggs house where he lodged. I saw Sparrow and Maggs in the marketplace on the day of the murder; the hat he wore in the marketplace is a similar hat; when I produced the hat before the magistrate, Sparrow said it was the same Maggs wore; I took him [Sparrow] into custody on the 27th of October, and he said Francis had sworn falsely about the handkerchief, as he had not had a silk handkerchief for seven years; he said that at least half a dozen times; except the one round his neck. On the 25th [September] I was three times at Watts's house but I did not see him; there were about 10 or 12 persons there in the morning. Newport was then cross-examined: I was not there on either occasion more than half an hour; I saw [the] prisoners on the 24th of September; I can't say whether I was then with Payne. When I saw Maggs in the Market Place I think he had a top coat on but I am not certain.

The father of the victim was briefly recalled and stated that he and his wife were in the habit of attending Frome Market; she went regularly, he occasionally. The next person in the stand would prove to be one of the most controversial of all the prosecution's witnesses. His name was Robert Hilliar and he had quite a tale to tell; although for those in attendance at the magistrates' court the previous October, they had already heard it. Whether they believed it, was another matter.

On the 2nd October I was employed to break stones on the road from Blatchbridge to Woodlands; on leaving work at 6 in the evening I passed on the road through Woodlands, and on to Blatchbridge Hill. While there on my way home I saw Maggs coming out of the lane; he went on to Blatchbridge Hill and crossed the road, and went into another lane, behind Oak Cottages that leads up to Keyford; I went into the field close to the lane, where there is a 'stave-gate'; and passed up the hedge. While Maggs was in the lane, a man met Maggs, but I don't know who it was; when Maggs met this man he asked whether he had heard anything afresh today, and the man said he had; Maggs said 'what did 'ee hear;' he said 'I hear that the officer has been to Bill Sparrow's house', and said, 'Oh, my good fellow, it is good it is not thee that done this murder, you'll have a pardon and £50;' [Maggs then] said 'He won't have a

pardon nor £50, [because] he's the man that killed her;' that
was all I heard them say. I have known Maggs a long time and
I am sure he was the man. I could see over the hedge that was
between us but I could not see who the other man was.

The defence, unsurprisingly, cross-examined Hilliar intensely, but
he answered all the questions unflustered. The first was about the
time of the 'sighting', which was then followed by several others:

This took place at nearly 7 o'clock; I had sat down and rested
myself on my way home; It was not dark at this time ... On
the 24th of September I was working at Woodlands within 100
yards of Mr. Watts ... I did not say to Hester Hurd on the sec-
ond of October that I did not know Maggs, nor ask her what
sort of man he was ... I know William Burge; I did not say
to him on the day Hurd's house was searched that those three
persons knew no more who did the murder than I did, or that
I believed the murderer was not far from the house ... I heard
of the reward for the discovery of the murderers [but] I had no
dispute with my wife about getting the reward that was offered;
I will swear that a hundred thousand times ... I have not said
that the murder was done by someone within 100 yards of the
house ... I did not tell Burge that I met Maggs in the lane, and
that Hurd also met him and began to talk about the murder;
I never had any conversation with him about Hurd; I did not
tell the same person that it was Sparrow that met Maggs ...
when I went to be examined before the magistrates my wife did
not ask me whether I knew Maggs ... I did not say I did not,
nor ask what sort of a man he was; she did not tell me that I
was to go to Shepton and wait to see the prisoners, and then I
should know Maggs ... I was never in gaol for stealing; I was
once in gaol 14 days for some turnips that my girl took; that is
the only time I have ever been in gaol; I never gave orders to
a young woman living with me to go and steal one of Farmer
Taylor's sheep ... I did not go before the magistrates earlier
because I was afraid to go; the men were not all in gaol; I had
a long way to go to my work, and in the dark, and I was afraid
that I might get an injury; I was afraid of these men ... I heard
my evidence read over to me yesterday.

After such a mauling of his crucial witness, prosecutor Moody felt
he needed Hilliar to explain a few things for the jury's benefit. The
first 'fact' he attested to was that he had been attacked by the son
of the woman he lived with – he had been accompanied by Hurd's
sister – due to his decision to give his evidence.

In fact, several witnesses, in the period from committal to trial, had faced intimidation of one kind or another, whether it was verbal abuse, threats against their families, smashed windows or, in the case of Hilliar, physical bodily harm.

> *William Burge is my wife's son; I live close by Hurd; I was attacked the day that Maggs and Hurd were committed; I had given my evidence and was attacked by Burge and Hester Hurd; after I got home they came into my house; I was knocked down by somebody; I saw them come in the room, and the lights were put out; the windows were also beaten in on another occasion; I have since left the place.*

Another witness, William Butler, attested to the fact Hilliar was working where he said he had been, although why the prosecution felt this was necessary, is not known. 'I know [the] last witness Robert Hilliar; on the second [of] October, I saw him at work on the Maiden Bradley Road about 4 miles from Frome.'

The final witness for the prosecution now entered the witness stand to deliver her testimony. This was Sarah Battle; her family owned Battle Farm, where the murder had taken place. She lived elsewhere in West Woodlands.

> 'On the 24th September I was at the house of Mr Watts; I once lived there, and I knew Sparrow; he worked with farmer Hoddinott at Hyde Croft Farm; Sparrow sometimes came there; Maggs lived in a house not a quarter of a mile from the house.' When asked by the defence how long this had been, Sarah Battle replied: 'That would have been 16 or 17 years ago.'

After Sarah Battle had stepped down, the prosecution stated that its case had concluded. As it was now 8.30 in the evening, the judge adjourned the court until the following morning and the court rose. The jury were delivered into the custody of the bailiffs, who shut them up for the night in an apartment provided for them; in the meantime, Maggs, Sparrow, and Hurd, were taken back to their temporary cells and locked up. The next day it would be the turn of the defence to present their case and in doing so hope to prove to the twelve jurors the innocence of the three suspects.

23

Defence: Preliminary Address

The following day, Wednesday 7 April 1852, the prisoners were brought back to court once more. This time it would be the turn of the defence, Mr Edwards and Mr Cole, to outline their case. As soon as the court was ready, the former rose and addressed the jury:

Members of the jury, with the case for the prosecution now closed, it becomes my duty to offer you some observations on behalf of the prisoners at the bar. In doing so, however, I feel anxious lest, by any observation I should make, I should give any sort of importance to the evidence which has been brought before you; because I declare to you that in the whole course of my life, never have I heard so severe a charge preferred against a person supported by more unsatisfactory evidence than that which has been brought before you on this occasion.

I am not at all surprised that unsatisfactory evidence should be offered for the purpose of convicting these men of the crime: under the circumstances it would be next to impossible that the evidence should not be suspicious. There was this poor girl, in the middle of the day, and almost in the midst of the town of Frome, surrounded by houses in all directions, brutally treated and murdered, under circumstances which, thank God, are very unusual in this country. The utmost excitement prevailed immediately all round the neighbourhood. Reports were spread in all directions and everyone was most anxiously concerned, and very properly concerned, to find out who were the perpetrators. One after another was brought up for examination, and it seemed that one person, whose name I will not mention, was brought up, who was discharged. This I allude to because it shows that in the excitement of the moment, and under the influences which I have been describing, persons against whom not a breath of evidence could be brought were suspected of the crime.

It appears that Mr Watts had lost a watch and it was ascertained that Hurd sold Sparrow a watch on that day. Immediately a report was spread that the murderers were detected and that the watch was discovered. Now, if this was really the case – if the stolen property was found on the men

– it would be good evidence that they had committed this most horrible crime. They were taken up on suspicion and as to the story of that watch, it turned out that it was not Mr Watts's and there was not the slightest reason to suppose that the watch was obtained in an improper manner.

Circumstances had, in fact, given rise to suspicions which were perfectly ill founded. The neighbourhood was greatly excited, and you know that when this is the case, imagination might often exert more influence than reason; and a suspicion will often arise, where there is no evidence at all. And may you remember another circumstance: a reward of £100 was very properly offered for the purpose of discovering the criminals; so that while on the one hand you have the people in an excited state of mind, on the other there is a reward offered which might excite the cupidity of persons desirous to obtain it.

Judging of the matter from these circumstances, I should expect that when the case came before you the evidence would have been found to be just as it had proved. I have to complain, on the part of the prisoners, that when before the magistrates they were refused an attorney to assist them. Accused of so serious a charge, unacquainted with the forms of a court of law and with the laws of evidence, they were refused the assistance of an attorney to cross-examine the witnesses that appeared against them; and not only that, but the magistrates on more than one occasion refused to hear witnesses who came to give evidence for them. Now that is just the state of things that might be expected where prejudices had been excited; but the prisoners are now before you – a jury of twelve perfectly unprejudiced persons – and I trust that you sit there determined to weigh every particle of evidence given against these men, and are determined to carry out even-handed justice, whatever might be the result, to return a verdict such as you might justly return on the evidence before you.

There is another thing that I have to complain of: Smith the policeman comes down, pounces on three men at a moment's notice, and asks them to make a statement. My learned friend has mentioned to you that the judge who presides over this court, and for whom I entertain the highest respect, has expressed an opinion that this was a proper course for a policeman to adopt. Now, if this was a matter of law, I should feel myself bound to take his Lordship's decision; but as it is a mere point of prudence, I think I am bound, with the most perfect deference to his Lordship, to say that in a case of this sort, if constables are allowed to put prisoners on their examination, and elicit statements from them, it might be attended with the most fearful consequences, and more especially as this is the opinion of almost every learned Judge that sits on the bench. I say that they should not be allowed thus to examine them and then bring their own statements against them in evidence.

The prisoners, when brought before the magistrate, made statements which they had duly considered, and they applied for permission to bring witnesses to prove these statements; but that was refused. You, the jury, however, are not here to trap these men, and when I have gone through the evidence, you will find that there is not the slightest piece against Hurd or Maggs.

I will now call your attention to the evidence; and as there is the least against Hurd, I will commence with him. My learned friend, in opening his case, admitted that it was the one most difficult to prove. The spirit of his remarks was that he could bring no satisfactory evidence to show [Hurd was] *implicated, but nevertheless asked you, members of the jury, whether you were convinced or not, to have the kindness to convict* [him]. *Now I should like to see that turned into a syllogism, for I cannot at all understand, in this instance, my learned friend's logic. It appeared that the father of this girl, who had told* [him] *the story – a most melancholy one it was – came home and found the poor girl murdered, and naturally the desire at once arose to obtain justice. As soon as he had composed himself, the first thing he did was to go to the constable and tell him what had occurred.*

The news spread as quickly as possible, and everybody was soon talking about it. He comes out from the constable's and meets Hurd. Among all the population, all feeling the utmost possible concern, Hurd only expresses his sympathy, and, without knowing him before, in the overflowing of his heart, asks him to go to a public house and take a glass of beer. Is this the conduct of a murderer? If this man had gone to that house and committed that offence, his conscience would surely have condemned him. He would have seen a hand where no one else did, and heard a voice where to others all was silent. If he had perpetrated that offence, the father would be the last person he would dare to approach; but perfectly unconscious of suspicion, and knowing his innocence, he goes, and there before all the people expresses his opinion that the perpetrator ought to be drawn and quartered for the offence committed.

Mr Smith comes down from London and, of course, creates quite a sensation. Everybody expects Mr Smith, whose detective powers are so well known, will unravel the mystery that surrounds this crime. The story of the watch gets told to him; and what does he do but go to Newport, and Newport sends to Hurd to come to his shop. Was Hurd at all afraid to meet the officers of the law? Did he skulk away? No: he goes to Newport and finds him with the constable. The constable asks him where he was on 24th of September – proof that there was some suspicion attached to him. Did he hesitate for a single moment? He at once gave them a relation of where he was – though one, perhaps, in some respects wrong. But I ask you, if you should be asked where you were ten days ago, if one of you could at once tell? It would only be by thinking it over and over, that you would be able to call it to your memory. Doubtless, the man told them where, at the time he believed he was.

What was the next thing against him? There he was with the charge made, but free; and was he taken up and secured? Not at all. He was free five days; and I ask you, do you think that any murderer would have remained so one single moment? I admit it would have been extremely difficult to escape under the circumstances; but, depend upon it, if guilt had been preying upon the heart of that man, the voice of that guilt would prove stronger than the suggestions of prudence, and he would have attempted to fly from justice.

And then, on the 6th October he is going down as a witness for Sparrow, and accompanies Smith for the purpose of explaining whose the watch was, and thus clear the man from the charge; and then, in the face of the magistrate, Smith, says to him, 'You are my prisoner; I apprehend you.' 'Why?' says Hurd in surprise; 'What for?' 'I apprehend you for the murder of Sarah Watts.' The man supposed he was joking, and could scarcely believe it was the case; and he said, 'You are joking; that is not the charge.' He could not believe it possible that he was charged with that offence and thought it must be some other. Was this the conduct of the guilty man, or was it not that of a man perfectly conscious of his innocence? There is one witness that has been found in the purlieus of Frome, and brought before you, who told you that on the 24th September he was in the marketplace at Frome, and heard Hurd say, 'a watch and no tin'. Is this a reason why you should suppose that these three men had committed a murder that day? If Hurd had perpetrated that horrible crime, would he have gone into the public market, and with two other persons talk over it, and the circumstances attending it?

It might be said, perhaps, these were companions. Thank God that there is this one circumstance attending crime.

An honest and good man might be a faithful friend; but vice alters the character in that respect, and when persons are guilty together, every one fears his fellow; and so it is quite impossible that they would be talking the matter over. If there was any dependence to be placed on this story, there can be no doubt that the man had sold the watch, and he might have been talking about it. It appears that Maggs had sent to get the money to pay for the watch. As for the places where the prisoners had been seen – if my learned friend's statement is true, they must have been gifted with ubiquity, and been in several places at the same time!

You have been told that Hurd was seen at the Marston turn-pike-gate, but that was in going down to his house. It was also said that Hurd was seen at three or four o'clock in the afternoon. I ask you whether this is evidence which shows there could be even a reasonable suspicion against the man who now stands at the bar. Watts spoke of the time as half past one and another witness saw him between twelve and one. But I shall call a sergeant of Marines who will prove that he was in Hurd's company, in a public house, and that he remained there till two o'clock. Mr Watts, no doubt, might have seen Hurd and the other men sometime or other during the day, and they might have been confounded with the men that passed through the Turnpike gate; but if this sergeant can be believed, he was at the time at a distance.

If this is the case in regard to time, it shows you, the jury, the responsible situation you hold this day and, having the lives of three men in your hands, how much caution you ought to observe the evidence brought before you. I submit, however, that not the slightest evidence of a conclusive kind can be adduced.

Now I come to Maggs; no doubt the evidence for the prosecution is a little stronger against him, in as much as this, that it has been stated he was seen at a greater number of places; but only in that. Respecting the statement that Maggs made, I will again observe that it must have been almost impossible to him to state at once what he did on the 24th, ten days after. Smith had been making inquiries of him and he must have known that suspicion existed against him; but did he run away? Like Hurd, he remained, perfectly conscious of his innocence; and on the sixth of October he was apprehended.

It appears that Maggs and Sparrow were seen with Hurd at 11 o'clock, and between 11 and 12 they were seen by Newport in the marketplace. According to the story urged for the prosecution though, they were seen at a quarter before 12 o'clock at

Marston Gate; so being in two places at the same moment. My learned friend has informed you that there is a variation in the time of the clocks, but that is not shown in evidence. One said he saw Maggs and Sparrow come out by the turnpike gate, while Bailey said he saw them, at precisely the same moment, at the Asylum. Not the slightest reliance therefore, can be placed on the time. Let you not, then, come to the conclusion that because the thing is difficult to prove you must be contented with unsatisfactory evidence; and if the evidence does not point out the circumstances clearly, you should not take it upon your consciences to convict the prisoners.

Then Hillier came before you and I must say I never saw such a scene in any criminal court in all my life, as when he was asked to point out which was Maggs. He looked upon one, and then another, as if trying to see whether there was any- thing in the expression of their countenance to show which was which; and when asked whether he could swear that that was Maggs, he could not. And feeling he had committed himself, immediately walked down. His boy then comes up and pledges his oath that on the day in question his master said to him, when some men passed, 'that's Maggs, and that's Sparrow.'

The men were also seen at a public house in the evening, and there was then nothing remarkable in their appearance. They were drinking, joking, and talking, just as others might; but could you, members of the jury, for a moment suppose that three men having committed such a crime, would then go to a public house to amuse themselves?

One other matter brought before you as evidence was a declaration; but according to the law that can be no evidence against Sparrow, and it can be no evidence against Maggs either, except that he knew Sparrow had committed the murder.

It is important to see what the story is about. It was told to you by the man Hilliar, who represented that he had been working on the road on the second October, and left work at six o'clock. But after working from six in the morning to six at night, is it probable that he would remain until seven for no earthly purpose? Well, he told you that, and that on returning he saw Maggs; he then went over a gate and walked along by the hedge. Another man met Maggs, and so he placed himself between two trees and came up and he overheard their conver- sation. A more improbable story was never heard. And what was the conversation that took place? Maggs asks the other man whether he had heard anything further. This man says that a policeman had been down to Sparrow, and said to him

'My good man, I am glad you did not commit the murder, for you'll have a pardon and £50', to which Maggs then said, *'He'll not have the pardon nor the £50, for Sparrow was the man that killed her.'* Is it to be supposed that men would thus go and talk over the matter on a public road? Now, I shall call a witness to show that on that day, from five or six o'clock till night, Maggs was in his own house, and that this man was refused to be heard before the magistrates.

As to the case against Sparrow, had the statement of my learned friend been borne out, I would certainly have had much difficulty in meeting it; but never has evidence more signally failed as in the present case. The first thing against him is that he was seen at different times in company with Maggs.

The next thing against him, and which is to be the strongest and convincing proof, can not be made out. A handkerchief was found in the cottage, supposedly belonging to the murderer, and that handkerchief, my learned friend said, would be proved to belong to Sparrow. I contend, however, the handkerchief might not have been left by the person who committed the crime, and even if it was, that handkerchief was not marked by the name Sparrow; and people do not carry about pocket handkerchiefs marked with other person's names. And if it was obtained by improper means, then surely would not every effort be used to render it impossible to identify it. The evidence it belongs to Sparrow has utterly failed. The first witness said it was like the pocket handkerchief Sparrow had, but then so are hundreds and thousands of others like it.

The next witness on this point stated what was clearly false, for when asked the question: *'Did you see the handkerchief from the 30th up to the time you went before the magistrates,'* she said, *'Never.'* My learned friend then said, *'Did Hoddinott ever show you the handkerchief?'* *'No;'* but this was clearly contradicted by Mr Hoddinott. The only evidence, in addition to this, was that of the man who was called to show that six months ago Sparrow lent him a handkerchief, and which, he said, was something after the same pattern. Then it was stated the man had said he never had any silk handkerchief at all; but it appears he said he only had one that he wore about his neck.

The next thing, as alleged in the case, is one which I must complain has not been fairly referenced to the prisoner. My learned friend has stated, as part of the case, that Sparrow had related circumstances which could only be known to the man that committed the offence. He stated that the poor girl was knocked on the head and then thrown into the whey, and *taken out upon the floor. But you have been told in evidence that on that very night the news of the murder was known all over Frome, and that there was blood in the whey.*

We all know how these things spread, and that they lose nothing in their spreading; and naturally enough the statement went a little beyond the truth, for he said that there were clots of blood in the whey, which was not the case. Supposing he does appear to know a good deal of the matter, you should not attach the slightest importance to it. My learned friend also said Sparrow had stated there were ten constables at the house, and it appears there were a great number; but what is more natural than to make the matter more horrifying, and to make it appear he was well acquainted with the circumstances, exaggerations of this sort should be made? Do you suppose that if these men actually committed the offence they would be desirous of talking about it? They would have said nothing about being near the house.

Another piece of evidence is that somebody, seeing Sparrow's neckerchief had slipped round, asked whether he was going to be hanged, and he said he might be soon. I asked the witness who made that statement whether it was said in joke, and the answer was that he could not swear it was not. The man's conduct and manner, then, shows that he could not be the guilty party.

Now we come to the last part of the case – that of the marks on the wall. My learned friend first supposed that these were made by the murderers, but there was not the least evidence of that; and I am satisfied that all the probabilities are against it. It has been put to you that the man must have injured his thumb against an iron staple, but it appears that there is no iron staple there at all, only a wooden one. It appears that the murderers lifted the deceased up; and what is more probable than that, there being a great quantity of blood about, one of them touched the wall with it. I will argue that Sparrow's wounded thumb was occasioned at a fight at a fair, and that Sparrow, like the others, has never shown the slightest sign of guilt, but from the first to last has declared his innocence and expressed his most earnest wish that the guilty party be brought to justice.

I have now gone through the circumstances of this distressing case, but before I sit down, let me ask your consideration of this fact – that there is no evidence whatever connecting the prisoners, or even showing a probability they committed the offence.

A man was seen running away from the house with something, and most probably this was the murderer; but I will put it to you that if, in the face of evidence as clearly in favour of the prisoners as it could possibly be, you convict them, will you not have failed in your duty to your country, to your God, and to the three men at the bar?

I thank you for the attention you have paid and with his honour's leave I will call the first witness.

24

Witnesses

The first witness to be called for the defence, Peter Mortimer, was a recruiting sergeant for the marines who had been at the Victoria Inn on the day of the murder. He had gone to give evidence before the magistrates, but had been refused, although, as pointed out elsewhere, this was common practice and not as biased as the defence counsel had tried to make out. Mr Cole, the other defence barrister, took Mortimer through his testimony and evidence:

> I am a sergeant in the Royal Marines, and was recruiting at Frome in September; on the 24th I was at the Victoria beer-house there recruiting; I saw a man named Whimpey there about 12 o'clock [and] I saw Hurd at about 12 o'clock, he had a dead goose with him under his arm; I also saw Maggs and Sparrow a few minutes after; they remained in my company up to about two o'clock. I heard Hurd offer a watch for sale at that time; I went before the magistrate, but they would not hear the evidence. I have often seen Whimpey with these men; the offer of the watch was generally made to those present. I did not state to Sergeant Smith that the prisoners left at half past one.

The following witness was John Thorne, an agricultural labourer who worked at Feltham Farm, which was close by Maggs's house in Feltham Lane.

> On the day of the murder I saw Maggs and another man with him; I can't say if it was Sparrow or not; I saw them about five minutes before or after three, and they were on Feltham Hill; they were going towards Maggs house, and walking along quietly; Maggs spoke to me as he passed. I can't say to be sure when my attention was drawn to this circumstance. My master, James Allard, drew my attention to this.

If the man seen running away by witness Robert Walter, between 2.30 and 2.45, on the afternoon of the murder was Sparrow (or even Maggs), it meant that they had somewhere between ten minutes at the least, and thirty-five minutes at most, to get from Battle Farm to Feltham Farm, a distance of less than a mile and a half, as the crow flies, but considerably longer if taking a route that the 'shuffling man' seemed to be taking. This route would most likely have taken them up Tytherington Lane, before they turned right into Vinney Lane and at the end, left briefly up Blatchbridge Road, and then right again into Birchill Lane. At the far end of this, they would have joined Feltham Lane and headed down to Maggs's house. Although not impossible, it was a tall order and Thorn would no doubt have remembered if one or other had been out of breath; which they almost certainly would have been had they covered that distance in that time.

The next witness was more precise and placed the two of them together coming from the other direction, which tied in with the prisoners drinking in the Victoria before returning home, as Vicarage Street is the road that runs into the town centre, behind that public house.

> *My name is Sarah Stephens and I live with my father at the Butts, near Blatchbridge: on the 24th of September I was at my aunt's, in Vicarage Street; on returning I passed by Bellows lane, and heard the clock strike three; I saw Maggs and Sparrow going up Bellows Lane in the direction of Maggs's house; they stopped and talked to a man for about five minutes in Mr Allard's field.*

The defence briefly focused on a different day, that of Thursday 2 October, and the evidence of Robert Hilliar. This was related to the supposed conversation he heard Maggs having with another man regarding Sparrow and Smith. This witness was the father of the previous one, and if his testimony was true, then it literally obliterated that of Hilliar's:

> *My name is Charles Stephens and I am a mason, living at the Butts, at Blatchbridge; on the 2nd of October I went to Maggs's house, setting a grate about five, and left at about eight o'clock; he* [Maggs] *was there all the time, holding the candle.*

Charles Stephens's place on the stand was taken by one of Maggs's daughters, 16-year-old Ruth, who still lived with her parents:

> *I am the daughter of the prisoner Maggs; I remember* [on] *the day of the murder my father and Sparrow came home, at about quarter past three; my father sent me up stairs to get his purse; they did not remain long; I used to wash Sparrow's clothes, he has a silk handkerchief which he wears around his neck. I don't remember his thumb being bad.*

Ruth Maggs was then cross-examined by one of the prosecution barristers, Mr Moody. He asked several questions, including one concerning Sergeant Smith's visit and one about Sparrow's handkerchief.

> *I remember Smith coming to the house and to my mother for Sparrow's handkerchief; Sparrow lived at my father's house; I did not see my mother give Smith anything; I did not give him anything; I know young Burge, he does not keep company with me intimately; I never saw any other silk handkerchief of Sparrow's in the house and if he had one there I must have seen it; I don't remember Smith examining me and taking down what I said.* Mr Moody repeated the question and she replied, *He did examine me and he took down my answers. Mr Smith asked me some questions about Sparrow and my father; I didn't know that he took them into custody; I told him that I was told on the 24th of September of the murder, and neither Sparrow, Sargeant nor Hurd came to my father's house that day; that was true.*

Maggs was now re-examined, somewhat confusingly it seemed, by Edwards:

> *I did not say that my father or Sparrow had not come, but that neither Hurd nor Sargeant came; I did not say that my father and Sparrow did come; I misunderstood the question of the learned counsel; I did not feel afraid when the policeman asked me those questions; on Saturday afternoon there was nothing the matter with Sparrow's thumb, nor on Sunday or Monday morning; I first saw it when he came home from the fair.*

This was, of course, a blatant lie, as Sparrow had not come back to the Maggs' home after the fair. He had been arrested over there and remained in the gaol at Westbury police station until brought to the guardhouse in Frome and then, after being charged with the murder, taken straight to Shepton gaol. Nevertheless, this was not challenged, and the prosecution merely asked if she had been in gaol herself. 'I have not been in gaol,' she answered. This was true for the time being.

The judge asked her to clarify the interaction with Smith, regarding Sparrow's handkerchief: 'I went upstairs with Smith for Sparrow's handkerchiefs. I did no give them to him. I did not see my mother give them to him; I did not see him take them.'

Ruth Maggs stood down and her place on the witness stand was taken by the Chief Constable of Frome at the time of the murder, Thomas Ivey. Once called, he testified that 'on the 24th of September I saw Maggs and Sparrow together in the marketplace at about 11 o'clock; Hurd came also over the bridge.'

The focus of the defence now switched to Sparrow's injured thumb, with the next witness having met the prisoner at the fair:

My name is James Allen and I am a baker, residing at North Bradley; I was there at the fair on the 29th of September; I saw Sparrow with a gun in his hand shooting for nuts; I saw his hands, but did not observe anything the matter with either of them; I did not observe that either hand was tied up; I saw him again in the evening and he challenged me to shoot, I saw nothing the matter with his hand. I saw him next day, and he showed me his thumb; it was very bad. It was very sore and bleeding.

On being cross-examined by the prosecution, Allen added:

The next morning he drew my attention to his thumb and said "See how they have bit me last night" I did not look minutely at the hand on the 29th, to see whether it was hurt.

Richard Grist, who owned the grocery shop in Keyford next to the Crown Inn, and was the constable John Watts had first informed of the murder, was called next. He remembered the day of the murder, he said, and that he had seen Hurd with a dead goose in his hand about 3 o'clock in the afternoon. Like Peter Mortimer though, he also had gone to the magistrates' meeting at Frome to give evidence for the prisoners, but was not examined.

Elizabeth Payne corroborated James Allen's testimony that there was nothing wrong with Sparrow's thumb before the Monday night of the fair:

I saw Sparrow on the Sunday evening after the murder, at his uncle's,' she said. *'I was in his company about ten minutes; I saw his thumb, and there was nothing the matter with either of his hands on that occasion.*

Edwards then rose and announced the defence's case was concluded. It would now be up to the judge to sum up and the jury to deliberate and deliver their verdict.

The Verdict

Before Judge Erle delivered his summation of the case, the prosecutor, Moody, rose to redress several points he felt were needed, regarding the defence's case. To begin with, he said that he was most unwillingly called upon to perform a duty which had been seldom cast on him; but he felt it his obligation to address them (the jury) calmly and to confine his remarks to the facts of the case. With regard to Hurd, he had not said he was concerned in the murder. The evidence rendered it probable he had plotted the robbery, and if the judge should decide against him on a point of law, they might have to discharge him. He also had not contended that Maggs was the person who committed the murder, but that he was present when the crime was committed, and that Sparrow was the man who committed the offence.

The prosecutor also thought it necessary to remark on the proceedings at the investigation before the magistrates at Frome. The course of refusing an attorney to be present in such cases was not unusual, and there had been an Act of Parliament recently passed by which magistrates were almost prohibited from admitting them. The course complained of had, he admitted, been taken. The magistrates did refuse the prisoners an attorney or witnesses but they did so for the purpose of justice, because they could not tell what use might be made of the facts then arrived at. The witnesses who had deposed to these facts might be tampered with and it was, therefore, sometimes found necessary to hold what was called a 'close examination'. Mr Moody concluded by remarking that Sparrow and Maggs, being proved to be together both before and after the murder, would mean that if Sparrow was guilty and had committed the deed, then it would go far towards implicating Maggs. With respect to Hurd, his Lordship had expressed to him an opinion in law that the fact of Hurd planning the robbery would not prove him to be an accessory before the fact, and he should therefore not press the case against him.

Judge Erle now delivered his summing up to the jury, in a very lucid manner, according to a subsequent account in one newspaper:

> I caution you to bring to the inquiry a mind unprejudiced by anything you might have heard, and also unprejudiced by the

complaint made by the learned counsel for the defence, and which appears to be unfounded. As to the complaint made, that the officers of police enquired of the persons apprehended and tried to obtain information from them, I consider that that is no grievance. If no inquiries are made, crimes will not be discovered; although opportunities ought to be afforded prisoners to make their own statements. If they were honest to the police, they would clear themselves from guilt; while false statements might operate against them and confirm their guilt. The public has no reason to complain of innocence being cleared, and guilt being brought forward.

With respect to the magistrates, I think they are quite justified in the course they have taken. I have known important cases where the magistrate has used their discretion, and discharged parties whom he should not have discharged; and I therefore think it quite proper that with important cases the magistrate should decline to try persons themselves, and commit them on the charge.

It would appear that three modes of producing death has been used: first, by giving a blow on the head, then by throwing the body into the whey, and then by holding the windpipe and producing suffocation.

There are two matters which are most important in your consideration, and which are attested by respectable witnesses. One is that a mark of the left hand had been left on the wall, from which it is concluded that the hand was bleeding when the impression was made; and the other is that when Mrs Watts returned there is a handkerchief on the table, which was not there when she went out.

At one o'clock the girl is seen and at about half past two the murder must have been committed; and it is, most probably, one of the murderers that was seen running out of the house, in a smock frock, and carrying something. The question for you is, whether both or either of the prisoners, Sparrow and Maggs, committed the crime?

The case for the prosecution premised that a robbery had been planned, and the charge against Hurd is that he counselled that robbery. I might state that where a robbery is planned, and in executing it a murder takes place, then all engaged in the robbery are responsible for that murder. The law is that where persons are concerned in committing a robbery, whatever one did, all are responsible for; but if a man is not present and only counselled a robbery, he is only responsible to that which he has counselled. There is nothing to show that murder had been counselled in this case.

Sometimes a burglar goes and breaks into a house at night, and arms himself for the purpose; but it does not appear that any arms were used in this present occasion, and it appears to me that Hurd is entitled to be acquitted. The learned counsel has very properly withdrawn the case against him. The evidence of Hillier has been remarked on by the learned counsel for the defence and certainly he seemed to be quite at a loss for some time, and very unwilling to commit himself by identifying Maggs.

If the handkerchief could be traced to Sparrow, it would be a strong fact against him, and it is important to consider whether it has been satisfactorily proved to be his property. The circumstances of there being a wound in the thumb, taken with that of blood being found on the wall, must also be taken into consideration.

If you think that there is no reasonable doubt over Sparrow's guilt, it is your duty to convict him; if there is, you must give him the benefit of the doubt. With respect to Maggs's guilt there is no such circumstance as that of the handkerchief. The statements made by him might be considered to fix guilt on him, if there were other strong evidences of it. The great thing against Maggs is the evidence of Hilliar, and you must consider whether or not you can place reliance on this ... I now ask you to consider whether both or either of the prisoners are guilty.

After deliberating for a few minutes inside the courtroom, the foreman of the jury asked permission for them to retire and so they were escorted to the Grand Jury room. All those who remained in court could do was to wait for the jury to return with their verdict, however long this would be. In the end, they were gone only twenty minutes before they re-entered, ready to deliver their verdict.

All eyes were now fixed on the foreman as he stood up and stepped forward.

"Have you reached a verdict upon which you are all agreed?"
"Yes m'lord."
"How do you find the defendants?"

The moment the foreman delivered the verdict, the three prisoners were on their feet, protesting their innocence.

"My Lord, we are all innocent," exclaimed Hurd, regarding his co-accused, *"Providence has done this."*
"I declare to God we are innocent," shouted Maggs.
"We were not within a mile of the spot. God has done it," echoed Sparrow.

Hurd, now a little more composed, added, *"My Lord, it will all be found out within a month; it will be seen that we are all as innocent as lambs. Let me speak to Mr Smith."*

The others joined Hurd in unison: 'Let us see Mr Smith,' they cried in despair. Their desperate pleas, however, although not necessarily in vain, were not required, as they had in fact misheard the verdict: all three had been found 'not guilty' and acquitted of all charges. They were free to go.

PART FOUR

(8 April 1852 – 16 September 1861)

26

'Frome Bob'

For men like Bob Hurd, Will Maggs, and Bill Sparrow the six months spent in Shepton Mallet gaol, between their appearance at the magistrates' court in Frome and acquittal at the Taunton assizes, would normally be seen as an occupational hazard; but as they had been found 'not guilty' of the Sarah Watts murder by a jury, it was more of a 'rum deal', as Hurd called it.

As soon as they were freed, they all returned to their old ways and Frome was once more 'blighted' not only by the nocturnal activities of the Maggs-Sparrow gang but also the fiery temper of Robert 'Frome Bob' Hurd. Witnesses who had given testimony against the trio had already put up with intimidation, smashed windows and even physical violence before the trial, mainly from confederates of the three. On his return to Frome though, Hurd now decided that a few scores needed to be settled personally and on the Saturday night after his acquittal, he paid a visit to several public houses in his locale: these were no social visits.

The first pub he entered was The Crown Inn, in Keyford, run by Joseph Singer. This was the pub that he had been standing outside when John Watts came out of Constable Grist's shop next door. The landlord had, in Hurd's eyes, testified against him and the others, stating that, along with William Sargeant, they had been drinking in his hostelry between 4 and 7 o'clock on the day of the murder. Even if it was not true (and the prisoners had confirmed they were there at that time), it was a sighting that occurred outside the critical time, between 1 and 3 o'clock. Nevertheless, 'burning with malice and revenge' as one news report read: 'Hurd went to The Crown at Keyford and abused the landlord Joseph Singer in the most infamous manner, threatening his life and spitting on his person.' He then went out and followed the route he had taken with John Watts and entered the Woolpack Inn. The beer house run by Benjamin and Sophia Cornish had been the focus of attention when the landlord and landlady testified that Hurd and the others had been outside on the morning of the murder as the Watts passed by. Again, Hurd attacked the landlord and threatened his life in 'the foulest language', smashing a table with cups and glasses on it. After he had gone, Benjamin Cornish informed the local authorities and a special warrant was then drawn up for Hurd's arrest.

A number of constables went around immediately to the cottage in Mount Lane, where Hurd was staying with his parents, with the intention of arresting him. When they arrived, they found Hurd was expecting them. The door was strongly barricaded and Hurd shouted that he would kill the first man who entered. As the day was drawing to a close, the constables called on W.H. Sheppard Esq. – one of the magistrates who had presided over the committal trial the previous October and who lived not far along the road at Keyford House – to ask his advice. Wisely, he suggested they leave it until Monday to let things cool down, and so they withdrew, thankfully, to their homes.

When Monday arrived, a large body of well-armed constables returned to the cottage. They found it just as well guarded as before, but now with Bill Sparrow inside, as well. 'The ruffian then appeared at a chamber window with a large bludgeon,' the *Bath Chronicle* dramatically reported, 'swearing he would never be taken alive and again threatening to murder the first man who broke open the door.' When Sheppard the magistrate appeared, he went up to the door and 'remonstrated' with Hurd, who for once saw sense and quietly surrendered. Perhaps the sight of the six barrelled revolving pistol brandished by one of the constables, helped 'his bravado to forsake him'.

The following morning Hurd appeared before the magistrates, who required him to find the huge sum of £200, plus two separate sureties of £100 each, or serve a year inside in default. He could not (rather than would not) pay and so Robert 'Frome Bob' Hurd was back behind the walls of Shepton Mallet gaol less than a week after he had left. He must have had a good idea this would happen if he took 'revenge' on witnesses, but he had a reputation to uphold: he was 'Frome Bob', after all, not just some petty criminal. Despite this dire situation, his cockiness and dark humour remained in abundance:

On his way to the prison, wrote one newspaper, *Hurd boasted to the officers of some of his exploits at races, fairs etc. and told them that he had made up his mind to three things – viz, never to commit murder, rape, or to rob a poor man, but he considered it no harm whatever to rob anyone who had plenty.*

It was also reported:

On entering the gaol the impudent fellow said to Mr West, the man in charge, 'Well Governor, you and I went on very well in the last six months. I hope we shall agree quite as well for the next twelve months; but how often shall I be able to write

home?' Mr West replied, 'Once a quarter.' Hurd, with his usual
effrontery, then said, 'Oh! That won't do for me. I shall write to
a higher authority, remember I am not here for a felony.'

Prison seemed to hold no terrors for 'Frome Bob', the moniker by
which he was increasingly known to friend, foe, and newspaper,
alike. It emerged that whilst awaiting the trial in the Watts case,
he had written several letters to the secretary of state complaining
about the way the magistrates and others had presented the case
against him. However, he did this stretch of time without any complaint. Although many in his position would have reflected on their
situation and realised the futility of their actions and resolved, if
not to go completely straight, then at least to learn from the consequences of their past actions; not so Hurd. As with so many villains
past and present their chosen way of life was not all about the
money, it was about kudos, reputation and social standing amongst
their fellow criminals, or 'respect' as it might be called today.

When the doors of Shepton gaol swung open in front of him
twelve months later, on Wednesday 20 April 1853, he immediately
made his way back to Frome once more, as he felt there was still
unfinished business. His destination: The Woolpack.

On Saturday evening last about nine o'clock he [Hurd] *again*
visited Mr Cornish and carried a jar of beer into the tap room,
sat down and called Mr Cornish to give him a pint of beer. Mr
C. refused and advised him to leave the house. This he would
not do and took a cup down from the shelf, and poured his
beer out of his bottle and drank it. He then became very vio-
lent, making use of very dreadful expressions and threatened
Mr. C. for which offence a warrant was [again] *issued for his*
apprehension.

Hurd was arrested and brought before the magistrates. However,
when in court a strange thing happened. While giving his testimony, Benjamin Cornish stated Hurd had made him a promise
that he would never molest him again and would leave town if
he (Cornish) would look it over this time. At this moment, Hurd
himself interposed: 'Gentlemen, it is my intention immediately to
go to London; I should not have interrupted Mr Cornish if I had
not had a drop of beer: I will leave town if you will look it over this
once.' Surprisingly the magistrates agreed; gave him a reprimand
and discharged him.

If Hurd did as he had promised – and there is no reason to think
that he did not leave immediately – he was certainly not gone for
long. In August 1853, he was drinking in The Lamb, in Frome,

according to the *Bath Chronicle*, when a dispute arose over a shilling. Hurd 'took the affair up' and as part of the argument, a man named John Wheeler threatened to 'tell something that he had heard about the murder at the Woodlands'. Hurd then punched him on the nose and was later charged with assault. He was fined 6d and 6s 10d costs or seven days imprisonment. The fine was paid and this time Hurd left town for good.

27

'Bill' Sparrow

When exactly Maggs and Sparrow recommenced their nocturnal activities, after their release in April 1852, is not known – although Sparrow was obviously with Hurd in his dramatic stand-off a few days later. At around midnight on Friday 5 June 1852 though, the pair were seen by farm employee Charles Wheeler in a field of cows belonging to James Allard. Allard lived at Feltham Farm, not much more than a stone's throw from Maggs's house. Maggs was seen holding a cow's head to keep it quiet, while Sparrow took care of the other end, milking the cow into a large brown pitcher. Having finished with one cow, they moved on to another. Wheeler was obviously fascinated by these goings-on, as he continued to watch as they moved on down the lane to a field at Marsh Farm, owned by the Hoddinott brothers but rented to their sister Sarah. That evening she had taken her twelve cows into the field and locked the gate for the night. As the pair was milking one of these, Wheeler plucked up enough courage to act and approached them.

> *I made a move and Sparrow jumped up and got close to Maggs and they both walked off close together,* Wheeler later explained. *I followed them into another field and I saw Maggs take a bludgeon out from under his coat and give it to William Sparrow. The bludgeon had a string at one end with a cord through it which Sparrow put over his hand, the bludgeon was about a foot and a half long and thick at one end. Maggs took the pitcher and went on.*

Wheeler's intention was to take the two thieves into custody, but when they threatened to 'beat his brains out' he came around to their point of view and went home. He kept quiet about the incident, for the time being at least, as the milk theft did not come to light until later, when Sparrow was arrested for another crime that took place a few days after.

On the night of 12 June – a Saturday – Maggs and Sparrow decided to break into a grocery shop in Stony Street, Frome, just off the Market Place, which was owned by John Plaister. Unfortunately for them, a Mr White, who lived nearby, was spending the night watching his potatoes, as some had been stolen the previous night – possibly down to the notorious burglars as well, or members of their gang – and at two in the morning he saw two men walk down the lane and jump over the wall of Thomas Bunn's garden in Monmouth House, Cork Street. White ran off to get the assistance of three other men and when the quartet returned they apprehended the robbers – who White now recognised as Maggs and Sparrow – coming out of Plaister's shop and laden down with a large cheese (weighing, as it transpired, between 30–40lbs). A struggle ensued and although the bag containing the cheese was dropped, Maggs and Sparrow managed to get away. The pair also left behind a couple of the 'tools' of their trade; two caps which had been altered to act as a disguise for their faces.

The following day, White and the other men, along with help from a constable, were able to track the thieves' route into the shop. They had climbed over a wall, across a large garden, up and over another wall about 10ft high, across the roofs of two outhouses and finally to the door of the cheese room. The door to the grocery shop was still locked, just as the owner had left it, so it meant that the thieves had used a key to obtain their booty.

An extensive search for the culprits was carried out, including a raid on Maggs's house. When the constables arrived though, they were confronted by Mrs Maggs, whom they would later describe as a 'complete virago', pointing a gun at them and swearing that she would shoot them if they didn't leave. One of the constables managed to wrestle it from her and the cottage was searched. Inside they found 'about twelve pounds in weight of skeleton keys' – about 130 in number, in seven bags – along with a large quantity of string and cotton, which was discovered under the floorboards. When a wall partition was torn away, they also found a large amount of sandpaper and other property that Plaister would later identify as having come from his shop. It showed that Maggs, at least, had let himself into the shop before.

Meanwhile, the two perpetrators had decided not to hang around to get caught and had taken flight. As it turned out, they had both gone into the nearby woods – as bandits, criminals and refugees from the law had done for centuries before them. The fugitives stayed together during their time on the run, but Sparrow's luck ran out within Bidcombe Wood on 24 June 1852, a couple of miles south of Warminster, in Wiltshire – almost two weeks after the robbery – and word soon reached Frome that he had been captured.

As the *Taunton Courier* reported:

> *About fifteen constables and others immediately hastened off*
> *and when they got within a mile of the spot where he was*

captured they were met by about two hundred of the villagers of the neighbourhood, who stated that Sparrow was taken off to Warminster by the police and that a young man had caught him in the wood.

Maggs had also been spotted in the wood 'but was not taken. Some inducement was then thrown out to encourage the party,' the newspaper report continued:

and they all returned and staid out the whole of the night in search of Maggs, but we have not yet heard whether they have been successful [Maggs, in fact, had managed to evade capture for the time being] *Sparrow was brought before the magistrates and remanded for a week. There is another charge against them for milking cows.*

Sparrow appeared before the magistrates on the day of his capture and was charged with three offences. Two of these were for simple larceny (the theft of personal property, unattended by acts of violence) which was the stealing of milk with Maggs and one for the cheese burglary. Sparrow, however, was not a happy man; one of the local papers reported that '[d]uring the whole of the examination he behaved in a most violent manner, swearing at the magistrates and witnesses furiously.'

On the following day, he was committed for trial at the next Quarter Sessions, for 'feloniously milking cows belonging to Sarah Hoddinott [at Marsh Farm] to the value of three pence' and for a similar offence against James Allard on the same night to the value of four pence. On the more serious charge of burglary he was remanded to the next assizes and an order was made for him to be legally represented and paid for out of public funds.

The Quarter Sessions took place at Wells on 5 July 1852 and Sparrow was convicted of stealing the milk. The charges were fully proved and the Chairman (Colonel Luttrell) passed a sentence of fifteen years transportation. Presumably the sentence was so harsh because this was his second conviction for an offence serious enough to warrant transportation. Nonetheless, he seemed to have recovered from his fury at being captured and had regained some of his cocky insolence, possibly learned from Hurd, as one newspaper reported that '[t]hroughout the trial he behaved with great effrontery and impudence,' and after he had been sentenced "[t]he ruffian said to the Rev. Mr Rous, who was on the bench beside the chairman, 'I hope, Mr Rous, you will sit there till I come back, and I'll bring you a ring tailed monkey to play with.'" The reporter from the *Bath Chronicle* was less impressed though: 'This piece of bravado, however, is merely second hand, the very same words having been used by a prisoner who received sentence at an assize some time ago.'

Sparrow was taken to Wilton gaol – where he had spent time some eight years previously – and on his arrival, 8 July, his details were again entered into the Description Book. He was now 33 years old, with a height recorded as being 5ft 6ins (meaning he had grown an inch since the last time!). His complexion was now 'sallow' rather than fair, but his eyes were still hazel, his hair brown, and he was still unmarried. He had picked up a few distinguishing marks since his last time inside, including two scars on the palm of his left hand and a bruise on the back of right hand. It was also noted his 'left arm is or was broken'. His occupation was given as 'labourer', while his medical condition was described as 'delicate' and his behaviour listed as 'very good'.

A few weeks later, on the 4 August 1852, Sparrow was back in court once more; this time at the Summer assizes held in Taunton – where he had stood trial for murder a mere four months earlier. This was for the cheese robbery in Frome, back in June. One newspaper reported the proceedings and noted the difference between his two appearances, four months apart, at the assizes:

> *Sparrow, who when on trial for his life at Taunton, wore his best clothes with the air of a decent mechanic, now stood before the court in his true character as a cunning, hardened, determined villain. His hair had been closely cropped, and he looked an undoubted 'jail bird'. The prisoner cross examined the witnesses with considerable tact and with the appearance of great rustic bashfulness pretended that he couldn't address the jury as he ought to do, and that he wished his lordship would let him have some gentlemen* [presumably this referred to legal representation]. *He was found guilty, on which he changed his tone and whined for mercy.*

The judge, however, was in no mood to be lenient. 'Oh! You're a very desperate character,' he told Sparrow. 'I must inflict a sentence upon you that will rid the country of you for a very long time. The sentence upon you is that you be transported for ten years.' The judge was then informed of Sparrow's conviction at the recent Wells Session – and the resultant sentence of fifteen years transportation – and so he added that the 'present sentence must take effect on the expiration of the former sentence. The country is, therefore rid of this pest for twenty five years.'

Although seemingly resigned to his fate as he continued with his reported 'very good' behaviour, 'this pest' was not going to be banished from the country of his birth that easily! While he waited to be sent back to Wilton gaol, from which he had every expectation of being transported to Australia, Sparrow, along with another convict, dramatically broke out of prison.

At the time of this escape he was housed at Wells gaol; a temporary holding place at the back of the Town Hall. On being admitted, after the assizes, he had been put into a room with thirteen other criminals. A newspaper report would later say of this 'cell', where the prisoners had been confined, that 'a more disgusting place could not be imagined, a dirty stable would have been far preferable.'

During the evening of Monday 9 August 1852, the prisoners had their legs put into irons, as was the normal procedure, and they were then left in the room to sleep. Their 'beds' were sacking suspended as hammocks, on which the prisoners slept in their clothes, as there was neither bed nor covering. At about 10 o'clock, as was his practice, the governor made his rounds to ensure all was 'right' and two hours later, at midnight, a guard had been sent to check everything was still well and reported it was indeed 'quiet'; however, at 4 o'clock in the morning, in an act severely lacking in the criminal's code of 'honour among thieves', one of the inmates alerted the guards to the fact Sparrow and another prisoner – the aptly named Bird – had 'flown the nest'. William Bird had also been convicted of burglary and like his fellow escapee, the sentence had been transportation.

Once aware of the prisoners' escape, the guards dashed into the room and quickly worked out the sequence of events. A pair of tongs, normally chained to a fireplace there, had been broken off and used to make a hole in one of the cell walls. Their escape made national headlines.

> *The prisoners were both heavily ironed on both legs,* The Times reported. *The first man must have got out legs first and then dropped about 9 or 10 feet into a shallow stream of water. He could then easily help his fellow out. Having got out of the water, they were in the yard of an inn which was shut up by high gates and there were traces of the irons on the paint made as the men were getting over the gates. They were then in the open country with thick woods and standing corn and beans.*

The authorities, however, were swift in ensuring the prisoners would not enjoy their freedom for long. A number of special constables were sworn in, to help the regular police force, and the majority began to search the nearby woods and fields. On the authorities' side was the fact that '[t]he great difficulty the convicts will have will be the removal of the irons as they are steel hardened [and] from the weight of the irons it would be impossible for them to go faster than 2 miles an hour.' A handbill was printed giving a description of the prisoners and offering a £20 reward for information leading to their capture.

In the end, Sparrow and Bird's flight of freedom did not last long, even though they somehow managed to rid themselves of their shackles. On the Tuesday afternoon, less than twelve hours after their breakout, a farmer named Stevens met two men on the road between Shepton Mallet and Glastonbury. He had seen one of the handbills and engaged them in conversation. Convinced that they were the two escaped convicts, but realising he could not capture them on his own, he bade them farewell and supposedly went on his way. Sparrow went into a field and Bird stayed in the road, but Stevens kept them under observation from a distance, until an old man happened along and was sent to get assistance.

Once help had arrived Stevens traced the fugitives to a wheat field, at the top of which the prisoners were discovered lying down. Stevens immediately pounced on Sparrow, while another man grabbed Bird. The pair offered no resistance as they were brought back down the field, but on reaching the gate Sparrow turned on his captor and began to violently beat him. Stevens somehow managed to keep hold of him until further assistance arrived.

The prisoners were taken to nearby Shepton Mallet gaol, where Sparrow had spent the previous winter along with Maggs and Hurd, awaiting their fate in the murder trial at the Lent assizes (Hurd was, of course, already back inside as well, serving his year long sentence for the 'revenge' attacks on the Frome pub landlords). With this final roll of the dice over, it seemed there was now nothing standing between Sparrow and his transportation to the other side of the world.

28

'Will' Maggs

With Sparrow recaptured and Hurd already serving time, Will Maggs was the only one now still at liberty and the search for him continued unabated. He had evaded capture for more than three months – since the night of 12 June 1852 – when he and Sparrow had gone on the run after escaping capture during the Stony Street burglary. There were reports he had been sighted 'prowling about in the woods', and near his house on the outskirts of Frome but to the great embarrassment of the authorities he was still at large.

There were also various rumours of him sneaking back home in female attire and eventually these reached the ears of the law. The magistrates decided to act and on the night of Tuesday 21 September, at around midnight, Chief Constable Nicholls and half a dozen of his men surrounded Maggs's house in Feltham Lane. Hearing voices from within they decided, somewhat bizarrely perhaps, to knock on the door – with predictable results. They heard a noise 'like someone trying to escape', upon which three of the assembled constables broke down the door and rushed upstairs to the bedrooms. The constables remaining outside saw the top half of the fugitive appear out of the building's thatched roof and despite this somewhat comical picture, one of them threatened to shoot him if he did not surrender. Meanwhile, the constables inside the house had climbed up to the loft and, in the light from their lantern, saw the lower part of Maggs's body dangling down through the thatch and dragged him back in by his legs. He was handcuffed and brought to Frome at three in the morning, where he was secured in the guardhouse to await an appearance at the magistrates' office after it opened eight hours later. When 11 o'clock finally rolled around, Maggs was remanded to Shepton Mallet for a week. For a brief period, the three prisoners – Maggs, Sparrow, and Hurd – were reunited in the same prison they had left a few months earlier.

On Tuesday last, [28 September], according to one newspaper, *the notorious Maggs was brought before a bench of magistrates, consisting of Lord Dungarvan, WH Sheppard, Dr Harrison and J. Sinkins for further examination on two*

*charges of burglary. The occurrence created considerable excite-
ment in the town, and the streets were lined with people in the
same manner as when Maggs and his companions Sparrow
& Hurd were in custody on suspicion of being the murderers
of the little girl Watts at Keyford. The prisoner appeared very
much dejected.*

*The evidence against him was similar to that upon which
Sparrow and Hurd have already been transported* [This
was of course wrong, as Hurd was only in for a year and
Sparrow was still waiting his turn]. *In the case of the robbery
of Mr Plaister's warehouse, it was proved by a man named
White who [while] watching his garden to prevent depredations
on the night of the 12th of June last, saw Maggs and Sparrow
get over a wall and go to the door of the warehouse. White ran
and got the assistance of 3 other men, and on returning caught
Maggs and Sparrow coming out laden with a bag containing
cheese; a struggle ensued, but though the goods were captured,
the thieves got away.*

*Two caps belonging to Maggs & Sparrow were also found;
they were so made as to form a disguise for the face. Newport
the constable captured the prisoner at his house last week just
as he was in the act of disappearing through the thatch; and
now deposed that on searching the premises he discovered seven
bags of skeleton keys containing 130 altogether concealed under
a floor in a loft and that lying with them a pair of knitted socks
such as housebreakers wear over their shoes to prevent noise;
they were wet and the fresh grass upon them clearly showed
that they had been recently worn.*

*The prisoner frequently, during his examination, declared his
innocence and said 'There was a just God above who would see
him have justice and that he didn't expect it here'. He also said
there were a hundred worse characters in Frome than he; that
the keys* [belonged to] *a man named Norton and that there is
another* [set of keys] *now in Frome. He appealed to the magistrates after his examination was closed for them to intercede in
sending over his wife and family to him when he is abroad. He
was fully committed to take his trial upon both charges.*

Although not yet sentenced, Maggs request to the magistrates
obviously meant he realised the 'game was up'. He would have
seen the fate of his companion-in-crime Sparrow, and realised that
there was nothing between him and the long voyage to Australia,
apart from months or perhaps years in one of the rotting hulks
used for the temporary storage of convicts.

On Monday 25 October 1852, Will Maggs appeared at the Somerset Adjourned Michaelmas Sessions at Wells to stand trial for stealing milk and the burglary at Frome. Maggs had one last throw of the dice and produced Zachariah Starr, a shoemaker who swore that he had shared a double-bedded room with the accused at the Red Lion Inn, in Trowbridge on 5 June; the night the milk was stolen from Allard's cows. Starr also claimed he had not met Maggs before that night, which was surprising as they were near neighbours and Starr had lived in Frome all his life. As it turned out Zachariah wasn't much of a 'star' after all and a local policeman was able to prove that there was no such place in Trowbridge. Having perjured himself, Starr stood trial himself the following April and although he explained to the court that what he had meant to say was he had 'slept at Trowbridge and they told me that it was a person named Maggs, and I thought it was the Red Lion,' the bench was unimpressed and not surprisingly he received six months for perjury.

Meanwhile, with months at sea and subsequent years of hard labour in a hot barren country staring him in the face, Maggs tried another course of action. He handed his trial counsel a letter for the learned judge:

> *Kind sir I hope that I ham Not in truding two much on your valluble time but as you have my case in hand so that I shall not be a lowed to speask i therefore shall carrey a clear counchauce to my grave as the child un born of my innocency of this charge and I ham given to understand that my enemy have given me such a ill character on the paper that I ham not deserven for the ixpress purpose of poisoning the minds of the gentlemen in court against me I was employed by 7 well none respectable gentlemen in frome for nearly 30 years and bore a good character of them all and this I can say by a clear counchance that the man is a waiting to swear for spite the thing that he never saw this I am sorry to say by the contrivance of a woman and a rach of a man who is Now transported they had by contrivonce agot false keys planted in my house unknone to me which will make the gentlemen in court think I am connected as envy have given me such a character therefore I beg you will move this question to the court for me the keys have Nothing to do with this charge sir I beg to subscribe my self your most umble and obedient servant William Maggs.*

It was all to no avail; with his witness arrested for perjury the judge had few doubts and Maggs was given one month with hard labour in Wilton gaol for the milk theft, followed by a sentence of fifteen years transportation for the cheese robbery. Like Sparrow, Maggs was to be removed involuntarily from his country of birth, and like his fellow convict, he had no intention of going quietly.

Along with the two consecutive sentences for hard labour and transportation Maggs had already received, there with still other charges he had to face and so it was doubtful he would ever see his family again. With nothing else to lose, and while in Wilton gaol awaiting the further court appearances, Maggs hatched yet another plot to escape his fate. He teamed up with a John Wilson, who had been sentenced to ten years transportation the previous January (while Maggs and the others were still in Shepton awaiting the Lent assizes). Wilson was only 16 and described as 5ft in height, fair complexion, hazel eyes and brown hair – almost the exact description, coincidentally, of Sparrow when he was at Wilton the first time, although the latter was five inches taller). Despite Wilson's young age, he was recorded as being adept at villainy. Maggs, on the other hand, was described as 46 years old with a sallow complexion and grey hair. It was also recorded he had a downcast look, seemingly resigned to his fate. This was probably, like Sparrow's 'very good behaviour,' a front for what he had in mind.

> *These criminals were as usual, confined in separate cells,* reported the *Bath Chronicle,* 21 March 1853, *but on Monday morning about four o'clock* [coincidentally the same day and time as Sparrow had escaped from Wells gaol the previous August] *by a course of the most ingeniously devised stratagems they succeeded in breaking out of their respective places of confinement, and by means of a rope, which they had curiously knotted in lengths of about three inches to the extent of four yards, the oakum comprising which they had secreted during their daily labours, assisted each other over the prison wall, a shute or gutter, connected with which affording some facility for this purpose.*

The similarities between the escapes continued with the authorities adopting, after this second gaol-break had been discovered, 'very prompt and energetic measures' and again handbills were distributed that offered a £20 reward.

Maggs was probably contemplating his last escape and the three months of freedom that he had gained the previous summer. Maybe he was going over in his mind the events that led to his capture last time and was determined not to repeat those mistakes. Whatever he was thinking there was one thing that he had not taken into account: the weather. Possibly desperation made him make the attempt whatever the circumstances but it was doomed to failure. At 9 o'clock on the same day as their escape, Maggs and Wilson were captured in a field, not far from Taunton.

The severe weather, as reported by the newspapers, had indeed played its part.

> It appears that the prisoners, when they left the gaol, had no other clothing than their shirts; the morning was exceedingly cold and snow had fallen in the night. In this state and with a small portion only of bread, they had concealed themselves until half past four in the afternoon, when a labourer at Fitzroy Farm observed them emerging from a wet ditch in which they had lain, probably from the early part of the morning ... [with] immediate information being given, Brown & Jarvis [the two men who captured them] with other assistance easily secured their prisoners and safely lodged them in their old quarters.

Another report stated that:

> When captured they were greatly exhausted from the exposure they had undergone to the most piercing weather we have experienced this winter. Both criminals were brought back on a cart and about nine o'clock when we understand that a warm bed and supper was provided for them at the request of the prison surgeon.

Although the actual escape attempt had failed, the ingenuity of its conception generated belated admiration from several newspapers. The *Taunton Courier*, for example, waxed lyrical in its report:

> The dexterity with which Maggs and his companion contrived their escape was of the most outstanding nature, involving a degree of ingenuity and labour unsurpassed by the most successfully daring efforts in the annals of crime. The slight portions of the prison of which they availed themselves had not altogether escaped the attention of the magistrates in their occasional inspection of it; but the possibility of mischief arising there from did not appear sufficiently imperative to require more than the exercise of that ordinary circumspection which is so eminently assigned to the interior regulation of that prison.

The *Wells Journal*, a little later, was even more glowing in its admiration as further details emerged:

> They were confined in cells which adjoined but did not communicate; it is therefore inexplicable how each became acquainted

with the others intention, though it may be that Maggs got out of his cell and then assisted Wilson. Both prisoners escaped through the crown of the brick cells in which they were confined which it is assumed must have been reached by means of their bedsteads, their only instruments, it is believed being a spoon and fork. Having removed some of the bricks from the crown of the cell and drawn themselves through the apertures they let themselves down between thirty and forty feet, and made their way to the airing yard. They then got access to the prison kitchen and got out upon the furnace making a hole through the roof upon which they got out and by mean of the rope which had already so much aided them they managed to scale the wall and drop themselves into the street and succeeded in getting clear off.

The mystery of the affair consists in this, that a patrol was stationed in the corridor leading to the cells and that another patrol was on duty in the yard all night. Both corridor and yard are lighted with gas and yet neither officer seems to have seen or heard anything of the operations of the convicts. Their escape was not discovered until six o'clock in the morning. They escaped in their shirts only, the clothes of each prisoner being removed from his cell every night.

On the same day as the glowing report of his escape attempt in the *Wells Journal*, 26 March 1853, William Maggs was once more in court, at Taunton, to face a further charge of burglary. He was up in front of William Erle, the judge who had presided over the Sarah Watts murder case the previous year and had summed up sympathetically during that trial. This time, however, His Honour was not so sympathetic and although Maggs at first denied this new burglary charge, he eventually changed his plea to 'guilty'.

Like Sparrow before him, the initial sentence for transportation was increased, but this time the fifteen-year tariff Maggs had already received was increased to transportation for the rest of his natural life.

William Maggs was now resigned to never seeing his family again.

29

Battle Farm

On 25 October 1852, the day Maggs was sentenced to transportation for fifteen years, John Watts, father of Sarah, died at Battle Farm. He was 63 years old. The cause of death was 'disease of the heart' but perhaps unsurprisingly, the newspapers, with poetic licence, said he had died of a 'broken' one. The previous thirteen months had certainly put him under a great deal of stress, from the time he had found his daughter's body, to having to recall the details and relive them, again and again throughout the inquest, magistrates' court and then ultimately the assizes and then to see the men accused of brutally raping and murdering her walk free from court; leaving the crime unsolved.

It is possible that John Watts may have died with more peace of mind than he had known for the past year and a month. With Maggs sentenced to fifteen years transportation, Sparrow already earmarked for twenty-five, and Hurd still only half-way through his year long sentence, perhaps the bereaved father thought at last some justice for his daughter, however indirectly, had now been served.

John Watts was buried six days later on the 31 October 1852, at Trudoxhill Congregational Church and so joined his father (David Watts, who had been the pastor there at the start of the nineteenth century) and his murdered daughter, Sarah, who had only been laid to rest there the year before.

After the death of her husband, Leah Watts seems to have remained at Battle Farm, at least for the rest of the decade and a little beyond (her name appeared there on the 1861 census). Her son, Thomas, moved back to the farm and took over the duties formerly discharged by his deceased father, but he had not been there long before another dramatic turn of events took place, although of a completely different nature.

The railways had come to Frome exactly two years earlier, in October 1850. An Act of Parliament in 1845 had given rise to the Wilts, Somerset & Weymouth Railway Company, whose ambition was to open lines from: Thingley Junction near Corsham to Salisbury; Frome to Radstock; and from Westbury (via Frome) to Weymouth. Isambard Kingdom Brunel was appointed engineer of the line and construction began soon after the 1845 Act had been passed.

By 1848, however, an economic depression had arrived. Loans, for the most part, were no longer available and calls on shares went unpaid. This affected many of the numerous railway schemes, including the WS&W who had only completed fourteen miles of track before it ran out of money. This stretch, from Thingley to Westbury, opened in September 1848. All other work on the line was suspended for the foreseeable future, due to the bleak financial forecast. Much of the land that had been earmarked by the company was now re-let to its previous owners, while the countryside that the route would have traversed was left scarred for many miles, punctuated throughout with stretches of half-constructed bridges and immense earthworks. It was decided that only the section between Westbury and Frome should be continued at that time. With the WS&W having run out of money, it was up to the Great Western Railway (GWR) to step in and finance its completion.

The Wilts, Somerset and Weymouth Railway Company, although independent, was really part of the GWR, having been set up with the hope that a local sounding concern would attract more subscriptions. With this façade shed, the parent company took over construction of the Westbury to Frome section in March 1850. The WS&W was no more and would eventually be dissolved.

The financial outlook remained unsettled, but with the much larger company possessing greater resources, the Great Western was soon able to begin work on the line once more and had given it top priority in the hope that a lucrative trade would be forthcoming from the nearby Somerset coalfields.

Once this section had been given the go-ahead, land had to be repurchased and new lands acquired. One of the men from Frome who sold land to the railway company was local magistrate and businessman John Sinkins. As magistrate, he had been present at all four magisterial sessions which had seen Maggs, Sparrow, and Hurd, committed to trial for the Sarah Watts murder, while as the latter and owner of numerous acres in the Wallbridge and surrounding area, he also knew a good deal when he saw one. With the coming of the railways, the route chosen went through much of his land and so from autumn 1846 he had been selling it; first to the Wilts, Somerset & Weymouth and then later to the Great Western. In November 1846, he had received £1,800 for five acres, while two days later, another 4¾ acres had been sold for the same amount (Sinkins had originally purchased the land for only £90 per acre). Three years later, in March 1849, he was given a cheque for £3,342, for a further eight acres and work began on the section that ran through this land almost immediately.

Sinkins also owned the land on which Frome station was to be built and once this had been purchased, construction work began at the start of August 1850. Such was the GWR's desire to open the line as soon as possible, that the station had been virtually completed by the end of that month. Although the section between Westbury and Frome had been set for a double track, resources dictated that only a single line was laid between them.

The line between the towns of Westbury and Frome was finally opened on 7 October 1850. The weather for the ceremony was, according to one eyewitness: 'fine but blowing,' and at 7 o'clock in the morning, a special excursion train to Oxford (with a ticket cost of 3s 6d) marked the official opening. Less than a hundred passengers travelled on this special Oxford train – which bore the name *Wolf* – and although the entire day was deemed a public holiday, there were no celebrations or bands playing at the station to see the train off. A report in the *The Times* contained a scathing account of this fact:

> *Our reporter was dispatched to Frome to chronicle the usual rejoicings and public demonstrations which occur when a line first connects a town with railway communication. But our reporter returns with a blank note book. Frome is an exception to his experience of similar occasions. There was no enthusiasm in the place to be recorded ... no officials welcomed the commencement of a mode of communication undoubtedly calculated to exercise considerable influence on the trade and commerce of the town. The bells of the parish church were silent, no flags were hoisted, no cannon discharged, the work people of the town who had been granted a holiday, had no other occupation than wandering to and from the station to watch the arrival and departure of the trains. The whole population, by their listlessness and apathy, seemed to exemplify the truth of the saying: A want of occupation is not rest, the mind that's vacant is a mind distressed.*

There was a dinner in the evening, at the Crown Hotel – where future King Edward VII would stay incognito three years later – an ancient inn in the town centre, which was presided over by Mr Miller (John Sinkins's solicitor, who had handled negotiations with the railway companies), but again the event seemed to be imbued with more gloom than celebration. Many of the fifty invited guests failed to turn up and those that did expressed in a rather plaintive manner, their dissatisfaction with the slowness of the railway company in reaching the town. John Sinkins though, in an after dinner speech, injected a laconic and acerbic note when he mused that 'They (GWR) have been calling "Wolf" for so long with regard to the railway coming to Frome, but at last it has come.'

The excursion train to Oxford had been followed later that day by four regular trains to Chippenham. This number of trains, both ways, between the two towns became the daily service for the next six years, until the section of line between Frome to Yeovil was completed, in September 1856, and the service increased to five trains each way daily, plus two on Sundays.

At the time the line between Westbury and Frome opened, talk of extending it from Frome had all but ceased. In 1852 though, another Act of Parliament was obtained by the Great Western giving the impetus to take the line all the way to Weymouth. Once more, the GWR believed a more local sounding company would fare better at raising funds and so the 'Frome, Yeovil and Weymouth Railway' company was born. Sadly, like the WS&W before it, it was unsuccessful and short-lived; the GWR having to take back the reins and finance the line itself, while the subsidiary company, was dissolved in all but name.

When work finally began on the section of line immediately beyond Frome, the route it was to take ran right through the middle of Battle Farm (or rather the eighteen acres of land, not the farmhouse itself). The owners of the land on which the farm stood, and was named after them – the Battle family – readily agreed to the terms the railway laid down and so this piece of land was now added to the rest which ran from Frome station, out through Blatchbridge and Feltham and on through West Woodlands.

Work on the section of track which was to pass through Battle Farm began sometime in 1854, the same year the eight-mile long mineral branch line from Frome to Radstock was opened; this latter event being on 14 November 1854. Early the following year the GWR raised more capital: £1,325,000 worth. This was to complete certain of the works, including the sections which had been the remit of the old Wilts, Somerset and Weymouth. In January 1856, the GWR shareholders learnt that £1,433,000 had already been spent on the WS&W, of which £750,000 had been used on purchasing land (including Battle Farm) and works to unfinished parts of line beyond Frome (and Warminster).

After the disruptive construction work had finished, which must have very inconvenient in terms of the daily running of the farm, the first train went over the embanked section that ran through Battle Farm on 1 September 1856. This was part of the twenty-six mile section between Frome and Yeovil, with stations in between at Witham, Bruton, Castle Cary, Sparkford and Marston. As with the

Westbury to Frome section, this was a single line. To begin with, there were five trains a day, in each direction.

Another coincidence, or perhaps more of a rather bizarre incident, occurred on the railway less than a year after the line that ran through Battle Farm opened. On Thursday evening, 13 August 1857, George Taylor, the driver of the *Leopold* steam engine fell from his train and was fatally injured. During the inquest it transpired that he had been trying to 'worm' his way into the carriage of a female passenger, but after a refusal had been attempting to return to his cab when he had fallen off the side of the carriage. The jury returned a verdict of accidental death. When the guard gave his testimony he said:

> *When we were about a mile from Witham, towards Frome, I saw the deceased fall from the tender against a wall and rebound against the carriage I was sitting in, which broke the panel of the door. I was leaning on the window of the carriage. I endeavoured to stop the train as soon as possible, by blowing my whistle, and went along the tender and told the stoker. We went back and found the deceased by the side of Bull's Bridge, where he had fallen, he was sensible, he made no remark how the accident had happened.*

Bull's Bridge was, of course, directly outside Battle Farm and so once again death and tragedy had come to that place.

30

The Maggs Family

With William Maggs, husband, father, and head of the household, sentenced to transportation for life, the future might have seemed very bleak for the large family he left behind. But Maria, his wife, *de facto* head, and her brood were made of sterner stuff. They were by now used to him not being there as he had only been at liberty for six months out of the previous eighteen (from the time of his murder arrest in October 1851 to his 'transportation for life' sentence in March 1853); and even then, three of these 'liberty' months had been spent 'on the run' with only sporadic visits to see them.

As the family had already notched up numerous convictions throughout the previous decade, it seemed more than likely it would become a case of 'business as usual' and for a short while after William Maggs's final incarceration this was the case. Maria had, of course, spent time in gaol in 1843 – four months hard labour in Shepton Mallet – while the year before that, 1842, Sarah and Mark, her eldest daughter and son respectively, were handed custodial sentences for the theft of cheese (15-year-old Sarah received two months, while 11-year-old Mark had three months hard labour and was ordered to be whipped). Two years later, after being caught stealing potatoes, Mark Maggs had been sentenced to transportation for seven years.

Of the couple's twelve children, two other daughters, Rosetta and Mary, had each received four month sentences for stealing from their place of employment, and Emily, although seemingly honest, had seen her husband sentenced to ten years transportation for his part in the Frome vicarage robbery in 1849.

Perhaps the most notorious incident within the annals of the remaining Maggs family's history of crime, however, was one that took place around the time William Maggs received his first sentence of transportation. Not long after their father had been captured in September 1852, following his time on the run, one of his daughters, 14-year-old Laura, decided to follow in his footsteps and formed a little gang of her own. It consisted of herself and two of her younger sisters – 9-year-old Naomi and 6-year-old Fanny! It is not known for how long this juvenile 'gang' was operational and details of any successful heists have been lost in the mists of

The Awful Killing of Sarah Watts

time, but what is certain is a burglary they attempted to carry out
went disastrously wrong and they were arrested. And so, like their
grandfather, uncles, father, mother and several older siblings before
them, the three Maggs girls were brought before the magistrates to
answer for their crime.

Understandably, after the events surrounding their father
during the previous twelve months, their court appearance caused
a sensation in both local and national newspapers, one of which
reported that:

> Three of the daughters of the notorious burglar W. Maggs – have
> been apprehended by the police and charged with attempting to
> break into a farmhouse at Woodlands near Frome. The house
> is not far from the scene of the Frome murder, on suspicion of
> perpetrating which, Maggs and two of his associates were tried
> at the last Somerset Assize but acquitted. It appears that while
> the occupants of the farm were at the market these girls went
> into the garden, lifted up the sash of the window, and, having
> propped it up, the eldest was proceeding to assist her sister to
> get in, when they were discovered. On being taken to the mag-
> istrates and the case gone into the youngest [Fanny] was dis-
> charged, the eldest [Laura] was committed to Shepton Mallet
> house of correction for two months and her sister [Naomi] for
> two months with hard labour attached. Their ages are respec-
> tively six, nine and fourteen years.

Why 9-year-old Naomi should get hard labour added to her two
month sentence, while her older sister, Laura, did not, is not
known; although one assumes the magistrates had a good reason
for doing so at the time.

This seemed to have been the last time that any of the Maggs
children, or their mother, was reported in the newspapers, but
not their last conviction – as shall be shown a little later. Either
they became so adept at their illegal craft they were never again
caught, or once the influence of their father was removed they simply decided 'enough was enough' and chose a more 'straight and
narrow' path for their lives.

In the same report that gave details of the Maggs girls' appearance before the magistrates, the newspaper reflected on the family
and its incarcerated head:

> The family is a most incorrigible one. Maggs has nine or ten
> children [it was, of course twelve] all of whom it is stated, [are]
> as expert at poaching and thieving as their notorious father. He
> himself is partly the victim of a bad example, his own father

having early initiated him into the career of vice and infamy
which he has pursued for so many years. His wife was formerly
convicted of theft and suffered imprisonment and both a son
and son-in-law have been transported, the latter for a burglary
at Frome Vicarage. The gang of which he was the head was for
a long period the terror of Frome and the surrounding district,
but it is hoped that they are now effectively dispersed; and as
to Maggs and his immediate associates, from the amount of
evidence collected against them on various charges, there can
be no doubt of their ultimate fate.

If the newspapers and population of Frome thought they could now breathe a sigh of relief from the Maggs-Sparrow gang, they were wrong. The two men who had given their names to this notorious bunch of criminals and miscreants might have been put behind bars and faced a future in the colonies, but this did not mean that the remaining gang members had stopped their old activities.

John Plaister, owner of the grocery shop from which Maggs and Sparrow had stolen the large cheese that had led to their transportation sentences, could not rest easy. Despite the thieves being behind bars, he remained puzzled over items that seemed to be disappearing overnight, despite finding all his doors and windows securely locked in the mornings. The obvious seemed not to have occurred to him, however, until the discovery of the large number of skeleton keys at Maggs's house. Although these were ordered to be melted down, Maggs had claimed at the time, possibly as a means to invoke leniency, that there was a similar quantity still in the town.

In regard to these 'mysterious' burglaries, the *Bath Chronicle*, in June 1854, reported Maggs 'appears to have spoke the truth for once in his life'. The newspaper continued with the story:

Every exertion was then made to obtain them [the keys]*, but*
the constables were unsuccessful. Mr Plaister from time to time
has missed tea and other articles from his shop. Being unable to
account for its disappearance as he invariably found the doors
locked he at length determined to watch and secreted himself
with another person on the night of Thursday last [25 May]
on which occasion he detected two men in the act of scaling
a wall. He immediately rushed from his hiding place, which
was upstairs, and called to his man to follow him with a pis-
tol. Instead of obeying his master he hastened to the window
and called out Thieves! Thieves! The men who were getting over
the wall with their booty dropped it and made off. Mr Plaister

followed them and fired at them, and on his getting over a wall he fell thereby giving the thieves time to escape. The bags left behind contained tea, tobacco and other grocery to the value of upwards of £5.

The robbery must have been effected by means of skeleton keys as the doors were left locked and in the same state as they were over night. They always took things not likely to be missed, as they left on the counter a sovereign and some silver which had been placed there on a bill. One man is now in custody on the charge; his name is Daniel Lusty and he was a companion of Maggs and his gang.

When Mr Lusty, a 25-year-old labourer from York Street in Frome appeared before the assize court the following month, he was surprisingly acquitted of the charge, but he did not take it as a sign to change his ways and in 1857, he received four years for a similar offence.

The Maggs girls might have kept out of the papers but at least one of them kept the magistrates busy for a while. At the start of October 1857, at the age of 20, Ruth Maggs was arrested for being a 'Rogue and vagabond [who] did behave in a riotous and indecent manner at Frome on the 3rd of October 1857' and was brought up before magistrate Harrison, who gave her one month's hard labour in Shepton gaol. This was her first offence but was swiftly followed by a second; the details of which explain her activities a little more clearly. In May 1858 she was arrested for '[b]eing a common prostitute [who] did unlawfully wander in a certain public street and behave in so riotous and indecent manner at Frome on the 19th May 1858.' She was given another month's hard labour, again by Dr Harrison, although this time assisted by W.H. Sheppard: both of whom would well remember her father's acquittal some six years before.

Five months later Ruth Maggs was at it again and charged with the same offence as before, but this time it was magistrate Sheppard alone who dealt with her. He gave her only twenty-one days this time, possibly the circumstances were different or he was less cold-hearted than his colleague; either way this was her last appearance before the magistrates, although what she would do next added yet another dimension and twist to this story.

31

Frome Post Office Robbery

T he Maggs family, although notorious and at times down-right prolific in their thieving, did not have a monopoly on criminal activity in Frome. There were many other individuals, families or small groups involved in a variety of nefarious activities: the majority, if not the entirety, against the law.

One such crime occurred in autumn 1855 and at first glance seemed not to bear any relationship to the Sarah Watts murder four years earlier. Nevertheless, its relevance to that case would grow in the years to come and be vividly recalled in Frome; if only because the main perpetrator was herself called Sarah Watts and after she had been caught, tried, and sentenced to transportation, was alleged to have told the authorities that she would tell what she knew about the West Woodlands murder in exchange for being let off.

On 3 September 1855, Sarah Watts a 21-year-old domestic servant, employed at Frome post office in Vicarage Street, was brought up before local magistrates Dr Harrison and John Sinkins (both of whom had presided over the committal proceedings of Maggs, Sparrow, and Hurd, back in October 1851) and charged with having stolen a registered letter containing upwards of £100 (worth approximately a hundred times that today).

Accused along with her was Charles Druce, a butcher aged 25, who was said to have received one of the notes knowing it to have been stolen. Only around half of the total amount stolen had been recovered by the time of this magistrates appearance and the constable in charge, James Nicholls – who had helped to capture Maggs in 1852, after the fugitive's three-month woodland escapade – asked that the two be remanded in custody while he made further enquiries.

At their next appearance on 7 September 1855, the case became clearer. The registered packet had contained the grand sum of £101 13s, which was made up of eighteen bank notes and a number of cheques belonging to the Trowbridge Branch of the Wilts and Dorset Bank. The money had been placed in a bag and sealed with sealing wax, before being sent by coach to the Bath post office and then on to Frome, where it arrived on the morning of 30 August 1855.

Opening and checking such bags was the duty of Mary Ann Payne, a post office assistant who normally came downstairs about

6 o'clock in the morning to carry out this task. On 30 August she found the bags outside the locked office, as usual, and lying on the passageway floor. The outside door was shut. After she unlocked the office and carried the bag inside, she noticed that although the wax seal was unbroken, the string seemed to have been tampered with. Opening the packet, she found two registered letters inside and looked for the bill which would give details of what the bag should contain. This was missing.

Payne explained further that she had also noticed that the string on the bag had been cut and re-tied two or three weeks before, but as it was 'so firmly tied' she had not reported it to Mr John Stevens Jones the postmaster until now, when the letter list was missing.

The prisoner Sarah Watts had been employed as Mr Jones's servant since the previous December and one of her duties was to rise before Mary Payne and take delivery of the post, which normally arrived between 4.30 and 5 am. This meant that there was a period of time of at least an hour when she would be alone with the bags. At the same time, nothing had been missed before her employment, but since she had arrived, registered letters had gone missing on three previous occasions.

Constable Nicholls took the witness stand and gave evidence that on 1 September he had accompanied the clerk of the magistrates to Frome post office, remaining outside while the clerk went in. Whilst there, he saw Watts go from her employ to a house directly opposite, where the Druce family lived and then return almost immediately. Shortly after this, he was called into the office and asked to arrest Watts on a charge of having stolen a registered letter. When questioned Watts told him that the 'things' were over the road at Druce's, and Nicholls made his way there. He was greeted by Mrs Druce senior and, on going upstairs, she showed the constable a box belonging to the prisoner, which Nicholls took back across to the post office. The box was locked and Watts claimed that Mrs Druce had the key, but as it was not forthcoming, he broke it open and found six bank notes, a quantity of cash, some jewellery, and various other 'important articles'.

James Gough of Stuckey's Bank in Frome then gave evidence that Watts had come to the bank on 31 August (the day before Nicholls had gone to the post office) and presented a cheque for £9 14s, which he cashed for her. He did not find this unusual, as he knew her to be employed by the post office and she often cashed cheques for Mr Jones.

After being apprehended by Constable Nicholls, Watts claimed she had been shopping in town with Amelia Druce, Charles's wife, and had given her the remaining notes to look after; therefore if any were missing, Amelia must know about them. Nicholls was having none of this, however, and arrested Watts. On their way to the guardhouse next to the Blue Boar – where Maggs, Sparrow, and Hurd, had once been detained – Sarah Watts said she would tell 'all about it' if she could be forgiven; a forlorn hope given the amount of money involved and the fact that it was obvious what she had been doing.

With his suspect safely secured, Nicholls carried out a further search of the Druce house and found various newly bought items, including an accordion, a small workbox, two shawls, and two bibles. Also, amongst the haul, Nicholls stated, were 'earrings which I produce [that] were taken out of Amelia Druce's ears, and given up to me on my asking her for the [said] earrings, which were bought by the prisoner in her presence, at Mr. Wells, a jewellers, in Cheap St'.

The bedroom of Amelia's parents and an attic was now also searched and more goods found, including three new bonnets, a child's hat, and a quantity of new drapery. A search of Watts's bedroom at the post office produced some 'wearing apparel' gold ear drops, and four brooches.

Arthur Hillman, the regular driver of the mail coach, now gave evidence to the magistrates, to say he had been asked by Watts to tap on the window of the house opposite with his whip, when he had delivered the early morning mail, and he had done this several times at her request and received a response from a man or woman calling out 'Hollo, all right?' The window in question was the bedroom window of Mr and Mrs Druce, the in-laws of Amelia. When asked about this they claimed that upon this signal they called Amelia, a dressmaker, who they supposed was having dresses delivered. Mrs Druce did admit going shopping with Watts though, and being bought a gold ring and a shawl.

Charlotte Short who worked in the shop of Mr May a draper in the town knew Sarah Watts and remembered her coming into the shop and buying a quantity of fabric with a £5 note, while on previous occasions had made purchases accompanied by Amelia Druce.

Susanna Joyce, wife of Henry Joyce the landlord of the Waggon & Horses Inn in Gentle Street, gave evidence that Charles Druce had come into the pub on the 31 August (the day Gough had cashed the cheque for Watts) and had consumed three glasses of whiskey, paid for with a £5 note. When he heard this, Constable Nicholls went looking for Druce, who gave himself up voluntarily, saying that he had 'picked the note up'. Further evidence was given of Druce drinking at The Angel, in the town centre, run by a Mr Harris, and getting so tipsy that he slept there.

There was little that could be said in their defence. For Charles Druce, it was claimed that he was consistent in his story of having picked up the note, though this was hardly true, as he had also told Mrs Joyce he had been left some money by one of his wife's friends and was thinking of going into business.

Frome-based solicitor, William Dunn, in representing Sarah Watts, said that she had 'yielded to temptation improperly put in her way by the very negligent conduct of her master'. This was, of course, no excuse, but there might have been some truth in it, as it seemed nothing had been done about the registered letters missing on the previous three occasions since the beginning of Sarah Watts's employment. And if postmaster Jones himself was negligent then surely his assistant, Mary Ann Payne, should have seen it as her duty to report the matter, unless small gifts were coming her way, as well.

In regard to the rest of the Druce family, there seemed plenty of evidence for a charge of aiding and abetting, or at least having received stolen goods, but the local police seemed content with the two they already had and both were remanded in custody at Shepton Mallet gaol to await trial at the next assizes – where they were found guilty on all charges and sentenced to transportation for fourteen years.

Not long after, it was rumoured in Frome, and thereafter passed into local 'folklore', that in one last desperate measure to escape justice, Sarah Watts had offered the authorities another deal: if her sentence was negated and she was set free, she would tell them the truth about the murder of her namesake, four years earlier. Like her previous attempt with Constable Nicholls, however, her offer was declined and her sentence stood.

32

William Maggs – Resolution

W hile Maggs's former cronies were still up to their old tricks back in Frome, at least for the time being, their one time leader, after all his trials and tribulations, seemed to have resigned himself to the fact he would spend the remainder of his natural life behind bars. He was 47 years of age and unlikely to come out of this able to continue his old ways – if he came out alive.

After his brief spell at Wells gaol and the dramatic break out from there, Maggs was sent to Millbank Prison, in London, which he entered on the 7 May 1853. The prison book, on his entry, described him as: 'Convict 25290 aged 47 married with 6 children [he had actually fathered twelve] convicted at Taunton and sentenced to life for burglary after a previous conviction.' The description, in regard to previous form, added: 'Before transported, once convicted, & once acquitted of murder;' the first part, being a reference to the sentence of fifteen years transportation Maggs had received shortly before.

Milbank was a massive gaol that was said to have cost half a million pounds to build. In Peter Cunningham's *Handbook of London*, published in 1850, the author described Millbank as:

> *A mass of brickwork equal to a fortress, on the left bank of the Thames, close to Vauxhall Bridge; erected on ground bought in 1799 of the Marquis of Salisbury … The external walls form an irregular octagon, and enclose upwards of sixteen acres of land. Its ground-plan resembles a wheel, the governor's house occupying a circle in the centre, from which radiate six piles of building, terminating externally in towers. The ground on which it stands is raised but little above the river, and was at one time considered unhealthy.*

Millbank had originally been called 'The Penitentiary' or 'Penitentiary House for London and Middlesex' and was the largest prison in London. Every convict – male and female – sentenced to transportation was sent first to Millbank, to await the sentence being carried out. Here they remained for about three months under the close supervision of the prison inspectors. At the end of this time-period the inspectors (there were normally three of them) reported to the Home Secretary, and recommended the place of transportation. According to Cunningham, '[t]he number of persons in Great Britain and Ireland condemned to transportation every year amounts to about 4000'.

Convicts awaiting transportation had been kept in solitary confinement and in silence for the first six months of their sentence, but by the time Maggs was there, this 'silent' system had gradually been abolished and so he may not have been subjected to it. At the same time, large-scale transportation ended in 1853 and many of those marked for exile to Australia ended up serving their sentences in gaols in this country, with Millbank itself eventually being turned into an ordinary local prison.

Mayhew and Binny, in their monumental work *The Criminal Prisons of London*, published a few years later, described the routine that would have existed when Maggs was serving his time there:

> On the arrival of the prisoners at Millbank, the governor informed us, they are examined by the surgeon, when, if pronounced free from contagious disease, they are placed in the reception ward, and afterwards distributed throughout the prison according to circumstances, having been previously bathed and examined, naked, as at Pentonville.
>
> 'If a prisoner be ordered to be placed in association on medical grounds,' added the governor, 'the order is entered in the book in red ink, otherwise he is located in one of the various pentagons for six months, to undergo confinement in a separate cell. On entering his cell, each prisoner's hair is cut, and the rules of the prison are read over to him, the latter process being repeated every week, and the hair cut as often as required.'

The penitentiary consisted of five pentagons – hence the name – and Mayhew goes on to describe each one and what went on within it:

> Pentagon 1 contains the reception-ward, in which the prisoners are all confined separately. In Pentagon 2 the prisoners work at various trades in separate cells. Pentagon 3 is devoted to the women, who are for the most part in separation. In pentagon 4 both the separate and associated systems are pursued. This pentagon contains the infirmary. Pentagon 5, besides its cells for separate confinement, contains the general ward, which consists of four cells knocked into one. This ward is looked upon with a favourable eye by the 'old hands,' who are well acquainted with the prison habits, and endeavour to gain admission to it for the

sake of the conversation which takes place there, and which, in
spite of the 'silent system' can never be altogether put a stop to.
   There are three floors in each of these pentagons, and four
wards on each floor. There is an officer to every two wards,
and each ward contains thirty cells, one of which is a store cell.
Every floor has its instructing officer, but the instructing officers
appointed by the prison authorities teach nothing but tailoring,
and prisoners who are anxious to learn some other trade, must
obtain permission to enter a ward in which there is some pris-
oner capable of giving them the desired instruction.

In the end, Maggs did not stay long at Millbank. He was removed
from there on 9 June 1854, after serving a little over a year, and
transferred to the next stage of the transportation process: a prison
hulk. Late in the eighteenth century, with exile to America no
longer a possibility, prisons within England began to become overcrowded. Someone had the idea of using rotting hulks of decom-
missioned ships as temporary storage for this surplus population,
until their passage to the new colonies in Australia, or other fate,
could be determined. By the January of 1841 there were more than
3,500 convicts housed in this way.

   The hulks were intended as a 'makeshift under pressing circumstances', but continued for more than half a century, despite being
condemned by all those concerned with prison administration and
conditions. The majority of prisoners from Somerset were sent to
hulks in Plymouth or Woolwich, although it depended on where
space was available; Maggs was initially sent to Portsmouth and to
the prison hulk, *Stirling Castle*, moored there.

   On arrival, Maggs would have been bathed, de-loused, issued
with a coarse uniform and placed in leg irons. The convicts would
be sent ashore during the day to carry out heavy labouring work and
other menial tasks, mainly stacking timber, loading and unloading
vessels or scraping rust. To what degree Maggs took part in this is
not known, as his medical condition on reception to the hulk was
described as 'invalided'.

   Gone now were the 'cosy' cells and quiet atmosphere of
Millbank and here were 'messes', with forty or fifty hammocks in a
line, like rows of canvas boats, where the prisoners were expected
to sleep every night.

   In the early days of the prison hulks, those to be transported
would be held on board until there was room on the next ship to
Australia. As the decade wore on, however, it seemed fewer prisoners were being sent abroad and Maggs remained in the prison ships
in England. His next appearance in the prison records was in June

1857, when he was listed as prisoner number 47 and recorded as being confined on the *Defence,* another prison hulk, but this time moored at Woolwich. The register book recorded him as still being 47 (although this might have been a simple human error, substituting his prisoner number for his age). Maggs was, in fact, 51 years old and according to the prison surgeon's report 'very ill'. His behaviour during the previous quarter had been recorded as being 'very good', although this might have had something to do with his illness limiting his ability to doing anything 'bad'.

Mayhew, in his *The Criminal Prisons of London,* spent more than twenty pages describing in detail the daily life on board the *Defence,* and so we can get an intimate picture of Maggs's life during his time on board this hulk. In all there were more than 500 convicts packed into three decks. The lowest deck contained newly arrived prisoners, those serving long sentences to life, and those whose character and conduct were bad. If the behaviour of the latter group improved, and the former deemed to have 'done their time', they could expect to be raised to the next level up – the middle deck – after three months. A further twelve months could see a prisoner raised to the third and upper deck. Here, it was much drier, further from the river, and more exposed to the sun. Once on this level, the expectation was that the prisoner would serve out their time in England.

Maggs, along with all his fellow convicts, would be woken at 5.30 am. They would then get dressed into their rusty–brown red-striped suits, roll up their hammocks, and have breakfast; this normally consisted of 12oz of bread and a pint of cocoa. Dinner would be 6oz of bread, 1lb of potatoes and 9oz of bread, while supper was one pint of gruel and 6oz of bread. After breakfast, a large number of prisoners were rowed ashore and formed into gangs for work.

Unlike several of the other hulks around the coast, Woolwich was the home of the Royal Arsenal and of the 500 or so men aboard the *Defence,* more than 300 of them were engaged in cleaning guns, excavating ground for the engineers department, polishing shot, or stacking timber. Those left on board – and if Maggs was 'very ill' then this would probably have included him – were busy washing and cleaning or attending to whatever trade they had when free men (Maggs had, of course, listed various occupations including 'handle setter', 'agricultural labourer' and 'clog & patten maker'). At 5.15 pm, the convicts were returned to their 'ship' and after supper – which consisted of bread and gruel – could rest until chapel at 8 pm. They returned to their hammocks at 9 pm.

Convicts were allowed visits from relatives once every three months, or could write home after a similar period. There are no records, however, to say whether Maggs ever received any family visits or sent letters back to Feltham Lane.

This, then, would be the pattern of Maggs's life for the foreseeable future. His health seems to have been poor since the beginning of his sentence and this may have played a large part in him remaining in the country for so long; deaths on board transport ships in transit were a topic of hot debate amongst the authorities and could result in penalties for the shipping lines.

At some point in the fifth year of Maggs's life sentence, his health must have deteriorated even further, as he was transferred to Lewes Invalid Convict Establishment on the Sussex coast. This was not necessarily the positive move it might have seemed, because by all accounts this coastal institution was grossly inadequate, overcrowded, and soon to be replaced by a new building in Woking.

On 22 April 1858, William Maggs, scourge of Frome, habitual criminal, convicted felon, suspected murderer, and all-round incorrigible burglar and thief, died of *Phthisis* – otherwise known as consumption – a wasting disease of the lungs. He had served a little over five years of the life sentence and was 52 years old.

PART FIVE

(16 September 1861 – 20 October 1861)

33

September 1861

The approach of autumn in 1861 brought with it the tenth anniversary of Sarah Watts's murder. For those directly affected by it, or who had lived in Frome and its outlying parishes at the time, the events which surrounded that dreadful day in September would have felt as fresh as if they had happened the day before. In the nation's consciousness, however, the murder seemed to be largely forgotten, or at least put out of mind. The passage of time obviously played its part in this, but another killing, just as brutal, shocking, and sensational, which occurred the previous year, had held the country in its grip ever since.

At some point during the early hours of Saturday June 30 1860, 3-year-old Francis Saville Kent was gently lifted from his cot, still wrapped in a blanket, carried quietly downstairs and taken out into the grounds of the three-storey Georgian house where he lived with his family in the village of Road; four miles east of Frome. Once outside, his throat was cut. The wound was so deep that he was almost decapitated. The perpetrator then took his lifeless body to an outdoor privy, where it was dumped unceremoniously on a wooden splashboard located 2ft under the toilet seat. Here it remained until discovered later that day.

Once its gruesome details became known, the nature of this awful and horrific crime appalled and enthralled Victorian society in equal measures, although ultimately, it left ordinary men and women the length and breadth of the country deeply shocked. Not because of the barbarity of the crime, awful as it was, but because it quickly became apparent that despite the child having been taken from the house, all the doors and windows were still locked from the inside the following morning; this meant that the murderer of little Francis Saville Kent was someone from within the household. And if it could happen there, or so the assumption went, it could happen in any middle-class home in the country.

The Wiltshire Constabulary, who policed the county in which Road Hill House was located, immediately launched an investigation, led by Superintendent John Foley. Within a fortnight, Foley and his police force had been put mercilessly under the press spotlight and found wanting. The local magistrates were not happy at how the enquiry was proceeding either and appealed to the Home

Secretary to provide assistance and, as had happened nine years earlier when Detective Sergeant Smith had been sent to Frome, the request was answered by sending another 'intelligent officer' from the Metropolitan Detective Branch. This time the person tasked with the job was one of Sergeant Smith's long-standing colleagues: Detective Inspector Whicher.

Jonathan Whicher and Henry Smith began their police careers as constables in the same year, 1837, and within the same division – E for Holborn – before the former was seconded to the newly-created Detective Branch in 1842, as one of its eight original members. Smith followed the year after. As Detective Sergeants, they had been involved in many cases together and were also both present when almost the entire detective force was 'interviewed' by Charles Dickens for the series of articles he was planning, to highlight their work. It was mainly because of these, when published in 1850, that the detectives had been thrust into the limelight.

The disappointment of the Sarah Watts trial outcome, two years later, was a slight dent in that standing, but on returning to London afterwards there was no time for Smith to dwell on this result, as he quickly returned to the work that would see him, and his colleagues, involved in many sensational cases throughout the rest of the decade. These included the Great Bullion Robbery in 1854 and, four years later, the investigation of the London connection to the failed assassination attempt of France's Emperor Napoleon III, which had killed eight people and injured 156 more.

Meanwhile, Whicher's reputation had gone from strength to strength since the Dickens articles and in 1856 he was promoted to Inspector and handed joint responsibility of running the department along with Inspector Stephen Thornton. Like Whicher, he was another of the original eight and, like Whicher and Smith, a Holborn veteran. By the summer of 1860, when the Road Hill House murder took place, Whicher had become known as 'The Prince of Detectives' and as he boarded the train at Paddington on a warm July Sunday afternoon and began the same journey Smith had taken nine years earlier, his star could not have shone brighter. However, the case would see his glittering career brought to a shuddering halt and tarnish his and the branch's reputation, and although he would later be vindicated in his suspicions, he never truly recovered from the emotional damage he suffered.

After changing trains at Chippenham – as Smith had done – Whicher travelled along the line towards Salisbury as far as Trowbridge. The following day, he was taken by horse and trap to the tiny village of Road (later altered to Rode) to begin his investigation. Road lay exactly half way between Trowbridge and Frome, in fact part of the village, but not Road Hill House, lay in the county of Somerset, and so members of both police forces had been involved from the start. James Watt, a Frome Police Sergeant had found a blood-stained shift (a type of female linen undergarment) on the afternoon of the murder, but after handing it to his superior, Superintendent Foley, it had subsequently, and negligently, become lost (or possibly recovered by its owner, the probable murderer).

Sergeant James Watts belonged to the Frome Police Force, which had come into existence in 1856, as part of the also newly formed Somerset Constabulary. An Act of Parliament that year had made it compulsory for every county to have its own police force (Wiltshire had voluntarily instigated one in 1839) and although Somerset had resisted the creation of its own for so long, despite nearly twice the population as its neighbour, its town leaders were already in the process of doing so when the bill passed through Parliament on its way to becoming law. On 21 November 1856, a huge crowd assembled at Frome Railway Station to welcome the first contingent of police officers – a Superintendent, two sergeants and eighteen constables – to the place they had been sent to protect.

Whicher and Foley did not work well together, the latter feeling threatened by this London 'big-shot', and unlike Smith's investigation in Frome, there would be no silver watch with gold case and dedicated inscription. This was something Whicher was used to – indeed, it was he and Smith who had been reprimanded for not showing sufficient respect to their uniformed superiors back in 1845 – but after he accused Constance Kent, the murdered boy's half-sister, of the crime and brought her to court with suspicions, rather than any concrete evidence, the press turned against him as well. The sight of three hardened, habitual criminals in the dock, as had resulted from Smith's investigation, was one thing, but to accuse the innocent-looking daughter of a well-to-do professional man, not much older than Sarah Watts at the time of her murder, and a relation to this latest victim to boot, was something else entirely.

From the moment the magistrates decided not to commit Constance Kent to trial, Whicher's reputation was effectively ruined, and after his return to the capital ill health eventually forced him out of the branch. He would, of course, be vindicated in his belief – after Constance Kent later confessed to the crime – but it was no doubt a bittersweet victory. This confession, however, was in the future and in mid-September 1861, with the crime still unsolved, newspapers were full of the latest development or any minor detail they had uncovered surrounding the case.

Back in 1851, residents of Frome and the surrounding areas had no choice but to rely on newspapers from other towns and cities – *Bath Chronicle, Taunton Courier, Wells Journal* – countywide weekly papers – *Somerset and Wilts Journal* – or even national dailies – *The Times, Morning Post* – for details and updates on the Watts murder case, or gleaned information via the local grapevine. By 1861, however, the town could boast its own newspaper, *The Frome Times,* which was then two years old. There had been other attempts to start local publications since the murder, but eighteen months after the inaugural edition of *The Frome Sentinel* in 1854, it was incorporated into the *Somerset and Wilts Journal,* and an even shorter life span had fated *The Illustrated Frome Paper,* which both started and finished in 1859, being replaced not long after by the still extant *Frome Times.*

The *Frome Times* had been highly critical of both Foley and Whicher, stating of the latter that '[a]n officer who can play at hap-hazard with such an awful charge as that of wilful murder, and can promise that which he must have known he could not perform, cannot expect to be looked on otherwise than with distrust.' Nevertheless, one of its reporters had detected a disturbing quality in Constance Kent: that of 'a stifled sexuality or rage', although the newspaper's overall editorial belief, regarding the murderer, was that the blame lay squarely at the door of the boy's nursemaid: Elizabeth Gough.

There had been a confession to the Kent murder in August 1860, the day after the victim, Francis Saville Kent, would have had his fourth birthday – when a London bricklayer by the name of John Edmund Gagg approached a police officer and uttered the words: 'It was I did it,' claiming he had been offered the payment of a sovereign if he killed the boy. After his claim was exposed to be false, he was asked what had driven him to concoct such a lie. He replied: 'I was hard up, and thought it better if I could be hung. I am sick and tired of my life.'

Back in London, with the tenth anniversary of the Watts murder approaching, Detective Sergeant Smith may well have wondered if the crime that he had been unsuccessful in solving would ever see a resolution and if an authentic Gagg-like confession might be forthcoming. One week before the tenth anniversary, that is exactly what happened.

34

Confession

Frome police station, situated on Christchurch Street West, was completed and opened for 'business' in 1857, the year after the Somerset Constabulary had come into existence; the first police officers having arrived in Frome near the end of November 1856. Between these two events, the police's temporary residence was in the former Eagle Inn, on the corner of King Street and Eagle Lane, located near the town centre. The Inn had been run more as an 'off-licence' than a public house for a number of years and after the death of its owner in 1856, it was auctioned off as a 'commodious dwelling house, large and well arranged cellarage for bottled and draught wines, spirits etc. ... large retail shop, back yard, and stabling, being well adapted for an extensive wholesale and retail trade.' The police moved in, literally, and during their short residency, it was reported in the newspaper that it was a place 'where a constable is always on duty, night and day'.

The building in Christchurch Street West was constructed to a design by Major Charles Davis, the city architect for Bath and once finished, also became the new home for the magistrates' court, which moved from Edgell's Lane. There were several cells, making the guardhouse next to the Blue Boar redundant. At the same time, it housed the Superintendent of the Frome Police and his family, and in September 1861 this was Edward Deggan. He had been born in Bristol, of Irish parents, and reached the rank of superintendent before the age of 32. Before arriving in Frome, in October 1860, he had been stationed at Axbridge, located at the other end of the county, towards the coastal towns of Burnham-on-Sea and Weston-super-Mare. He lived permanently at the police station with his wife, his son and two daughters.

Into Frome police station, on Christchurch Street West, during the morning of Tuesday 17 September 1861, walked 31-year-old Joseph Seer. He was Frome born, but had been in the army – the 2nd Battalion of the 4th Regiment King's Own – for several years and had recently been invalided out. He had come to the police station to fill in a remittance form, the completion of which would entitle him to three months back-pay. He had been in town for a few days, before he entered the police station. On announcing his business there, he was shown into the office of Mr Turner,

assistant clerk to the magistrates. As Seer filled in the form, the
official noticed the former soldier looked agitated and unhappy. 'If
you have anything on your mind, you best tell it,' Turner told him,
'and no doubt you will feel more comfortable for the telling.' Seer
replied that he thought he should.

Superintendent Deggan, who happened to be in Turner's office
at the time and trusting a hunch, as he later explained, asked Seer,
'It is the Woodlands murder makes you unhappy?' Seer nodded
and said: 'I murdered Sarah Watts.'

Turner and Deggan escorted Seer to the superintendent's
office, where he was asked if he wanted to make a statement and
for it to be taken down in writing. Seer nodded and as he started to
talk, Turner took out a sheet of paper and began to write:

> I murdered Sarah Watts. I hope the God above will let me live
> to see her again in another world. I have it on my mind a long
> time. I was so unhappy. I hope the God above will wash away
> our sins. I did it for love.
>
> It was on a Market day, I asked her to go up Birchhill Lane
> and pick some water-cresses. She wouldn't go. I asked her to go
> up on a Sunday, and she still wouldn't go. I often played with
> her. It was in August it happened. About three o'clock in the
> afternoon. I went to the house. I thought he [John Watts] was
> worth some money, and she wouldn't tell where it was. I told her
> to tell me where it was and I would marry her and take her to
> America. I was very fond of her and then we would live happy
> together. She said, 'The money don't belong to you', I said, 'If
> you don't tell where it is, I will be the death of you.' I took hold
> of her by the neck. I had a poker in my hand, and I hit her in
> the head with it. I said I should have to suffer from it, either in
> Heaven or in Hell. I struck her in the kitchen, and dragged her
> into the dairy. I caught her hold by the feet and put her head
> first into the milk-pail, and left her in the dairy, dead.
>
> I took two shillings out of a cup on the mantle piece. I went
> upstairs and searched about, I took some clothes and went my
> way and went to sea. I had connection with her in the kitchen
> before I knocked her down. I was blamed for it at the time, and
> I enlisted as a soldier to get out of the way. I have never got it
> off my mind, I killed her for love. I was very fond of her.

Once his statement was completed, Seer signed it. The magistrates'
court, held elsewhere in the building, had been in session while this
confession was being made and at the conclusion of other business,
about 4.30 pm, the prisoner was placed in the dock. It would be

later recorded that he was 'short in stature, and was attired in the uniform of an infantry soldier. His appearance was that of a sullen, pre-occupied man. He was, however, quite composed – exhibiting not the slightest degree of excitement.'

Dr Harrison and John Sinkins were the two magistrates present as Seer was brought before them; both had presided over the Maggs, Sparrow, and Hurd committal proceedings ten years earlier, but now supposedly faced the true murderer. The court had been cleared before the prisoner had been brought in, although a reporter from the *Frome Times* had been allowed to stay.

Turner recounted the events of that morning, leading up to and including the recording of Seer's confession, before reading its contents to the magistrates:

> *I read it over to him and he signed his name at the bottom of it,* said Turner. *Superintendent Deggan was present the whole time. I offered him* [Seer] *no inducement whatever to say anything beyond what I have stated. He did it quite voluntary. After this he said he was out the whole night after and got wet, and that he had a brown billycock or Jim Crow hat on.*

When asked if he had any questions to ask Mr Turner, the prisoner replied no. It was then the turn of Superintendent Deggan to give his evidence. He repeated mostly what Turner had mentioned, about the extraordinary events which had transpired that morning. He then repeated the fact that Seer looked agitated causing him to ask, 'What's the matter, you appear to be very unhappy in your mind?' I then said, 'It is the Woodlands Murder makes you unhappy?'

'What made you say that?' asked Dr Harrison.

'I had heard he was suspected.' replied Deggan. 'I took him to my office, in company with Mr Turner, and he made a voluntary confession in my presence. I then took him into custody.' Deggan applied for the prisoner to be remanded for a week, which was granted. Seer was taken from the station and transported to the Shepton Mallet gaol, where he would be confined until his next appearance.

The *Frome Times,* in its next issue which came out the day after the confession, headlined their report:

> **The Woodlands Murder: Voluntary Confession of the Murderer.** *Although ten years have elapsed since the tragic affair occurred, there are few in this neighbourhood who do not either themselves recollect or have heard of the shocking murder of Sarah Watts, at the Woodlands, near this town, in August*

[sic] *1851. It will be remembered that all that was learnt of the bloody deed was that the unfortunate victim, who was only sixteen years of age* [sic], *was left in the house alone, her father proceeding to Frome Market. When he returned home, he found the mangled body of his daughter in the dairy, and that the house had been ransacked. Subsequent examination showed that the ill-fated girl had been outraged and probably drowned in a milk-pail. Suspicion fell upon many, and three bad characters, named Maggs, Sparrow, and 'Frome Bob', were apprehended, and the evidence against them appeared so strong that they were committed for trial on the capital charge, but a jury acquitted them.*

Suspicion also fell upon a young man named Joseph Seer, who lived near the Woodlands, but shortly after the murder left the neighbourhood, and enlisted into the army. Within the last few days he has returned to Frome, being invalided. On Tuesday (yesterday) morning he went to the police station in order to get his remittance form filled up, and, whilst there, he made a voluntary confession that he was guilty of the crime of murdering Sarah Watts.

The reporter with a tight deadline to make had not checked his facts, which meant the newspaper was guilty of getting the month of the murder wrong, as well as Sarah's age, which it had reported as being 16 rather than 14. What the report achieved, however, was to create a buzz around town which had not existed since the Frome trio – Maggs, Sparrow, and Hurd – had been marched through the Market Place, ten years earlier, to attend their court appearances. The fact that Seer would now draw just as big a crowd on his next visit to Frome was a foregone conclusion.

35

Joseph Seer

The incredible unfolding of events on Tuesday 17 September 1861, when ex-soldier Joseph Seer walked into Frome police station and confessed to the killing of Sarah Watts, had naturally become the talk of the town. It had also made national news again, replacing the Road murder, at least temporarily, in the minds of the newspaper reading, crime-addicted public. It all seemed a bit too good to be true and the next issue of the *Frome Times* intimated as much:

> *The extraordinary self-accusation of the soldier Joseph Sears [sic] – so startling and entirely unexpected – naturally created a profound sensation throughout the neighbourhood. At first the strange confession was reservedly believed. It is so clearly corroborated the main feature of the tragedy, and seemed so terribly earnest and real, that it was generally looked upon as the true revelation of a long hidden crime. In a day or two, however, the entire truth was doubted. When the horrible details of the murder became again fresh in the public mind, it was clear that the story by Sears was not the exact truth.*
>
> *The principal points of disagreement may be briefly described as follows. First of all, the name of the Sears who was at the time suspected of having perpetrated the brutal crime was William and not Joseph. Then it was remembered that the latter had left this neighbourhood and taken to a seafaring life for many years before the commission of the crime, and was not again seen here till the year 1856. It was somewhat strange, too, that in his confession he was incorrect as to the month in which the crime was committed, for it was in September and not in August that the shocking occurrence took place.*
>
> *Again, when it was recollected that the murdered girl was only 14 years of age, the prisoner's expressions of his love for her and of his having offered her marriage were, to say the least, somewhat improbable. In addition to this, there was the inexplicable statement 'that he was blamed for it at the time'. If he had not been seen in the neighbourhood for years before and after the murder, it was impossible that he could be suspected of being the criminal.*

In his confession he also says that he went to sea, and after-wards that he enlisted as a soldier – which was clearly inconsistent. Finally, there was the important fact that the prisoner was discharged from the army as being of unsound mind. These were ample grounds on which to base a disbelief of the entire story.

In the name of unbiased reporting, or so it said, and possibly wishful thinking, the local newspaper retained a certain amount of belief in the confession:

But, on the other hand, several of the circumstances we have named were not entirely incompatible with the prisoner's guilt. The difference in the [fore]name was in itself of little importance, neither could the discrepancy in the date be considered as affecting the matter. That the girl was undoubtedly found outraged would go far to substantiate the prisoner's statement. Moreover, if the prisoner had not been in the neighbourhood for years, how was it that he became so intimately acquainted with the details of the murder? By some it was even affirmed that he was in Frome on leave of absence about the time. On the whole, therefore, it was not impossible that the prisoner's self-accusation could be shown to be substantially true.

Almost as soon as Seer was on his way to Shepton Mallet, Superintendent Deggan had commenced his investigation. His first point of call was a visit to the West Woodlands neighbourhood. Afterwards, he travelled across the county to Shepton Mallet, where he interviewed Seer in his prison cell. With these two elements completed, Superintendent Deggan's enquiries took him to London. He was back in Frome just in time for Seer's next appearance before the magistrates. On 24 September 1861, the prisoner was accompanied from Shepton gaol by Sergeant James Watts, the officer who had discovered the shift at Road Hill House the previous year. At the entrance to the police station, a large crowd awaited his arrival; and the few spaces open to the public in court were soon taken. It may not have dawned on everyone present, but it was now exactly ten years to the day since the murder.

Seer stood in the dock, dressed in the coarse grey waistcoat and jacket of the prison, with the same sullen composed demeanour as on his first examination. There were no observable symptoms of imbecility, although it was reported that he had torn his soldier's coat into shreds during his confinement.

The only witness to give evidence at this session was Superintendent Deggan, who stated briefly the results of his investigation. He had discovered that the prisoner had left the Frome

Union Workhouse in 1844 at the age of 13. The building had been built about 1838, as a result of the New Poor Law Commission a couple of years earlier. It had cost £5,400 and was situated on the south side of Weymouth Road (a little way out of the centre, in the area known as Badcox). It was designed by local architects Scott and Moffat and was based on the Y-shape model. There were spacious walled grounds, a small entrance lodge and as well as pauper accommodation, there was several cells provided for tramps. Each one consisted of a stone bed, stone table, and primitive washing facilities. Like the rest of the workhouses throughout the country it was a grim institutional building designed to house, but at the same time discourage the very poor, the inadequate, and the sick, from entering as anything other than a 'last resort'. It was designed to make life inside more unpleasant than outside.

When Joseph Seer left the workhouse he had gone to London, where his mother was living. After some time he went to sea in the *Malabar*, one of shipping agent Richard Green's boats, leased to the East India Company. According to Seer, he was then in India for many years. The name of the ship's Captain was William Henry Parr. After his discharge in 1856, Seer made his way to Frome and found that his father and mother were dead. In December 1857, he enlisted in the army at Bristol and was discharged from his regiment only a few weeks before arriving back in Frome.

The superintendent stated that he had failed in his attempt to discover anyone who could swear to having seen the prisoner in the neighbourhood during the period intervening between 1844 and 1856. He had learnt all of this information either in West Woodlands or from talking to the prisoner himself. Deggan had then proceeded to London to trace Seer's career at sea. His first visit was to the Destitute Sailors' Asylum, near the London Docks, but on examining the books of that institution from 1844 to 1861, no entry in the name of Joseph Seer could be found. He then went to the Sailors' Home, and his examination of those books met with the same result. His search in the books at Green's Shipping Office and Sailors' Home at Poplar was equally fruitless; and as a last resort, went to the Registrar General's Office in Adelaide Place, London Bridge. In the shipping papers he found that, from the years between 1843 and 1859, the *Malabar* had indeed been commanded by William Henry Parr. In the latter year the vessel had been lost. During those years, the ship had made an annual voyage out to Bombay and then back home. From this discovery and conversations with Seer, it was evident the prisoner was well acquainted with the *Malabar*, although his name could not be found among her crew.

On searching other lists, the superintendent found the entry 'Joseph Sears, ordinary seaman, 24 years old, native of Frome, Somerset', which stated that he had joined the *Rosebud of Newcastle*, in 1855 at Elsinore, in the Baltic. He was discharged from that ship at St Katherine's Dock on the 17 September 1856; his previous ship being a Norwegian vessel also sailing in the Baltic. This was all that the superintendent had been able to trace. He said he thought there could be no doubt the prisoner had joined the *Malabar* under a fictitious name. Deggan then asked for a further remand, which the bench granted.

Despite what the *Frome Times* had highlighted regarding the discrepancies of his story and the mounting evidence, the opinion of the court was that Seer's confession had yet to be contradicted; and they stated that 'if his friends could do so', they had better bring evidence to shew [sic] where he was in 1851.'

Although Superintendent Deggan was the only witness to give evidence in court, there were others there who were called upon to answer certain questions, or give brief statements.

Leah Watts, now widowed for almost nine years, was asked by Dr Harrison whether she knew the prisoner from any previous occasion. She stated that she had never seen him before last Sunday week and knew nothing whatever of him.

An uncle of the prisoner then rose and said his nephew had not been near the neighbourhood from 1844 to 1856 and therefore could know nothing of the murder. In reply to this, Dr Harrison said the prisoner had given very clear evidence against himself, and it was their duty to thoroughly investigate it, repeating the fact that at present the confession of the prisoner had not been contradicted. He also wished it to be clearly understood that no question had in fact been put to the prisoner. What he had stated was quite voluntary and it would not do for people to think that what he had said was in answer to any questioning.

Trying a different line now, Seer's uncle said that he was insane, giving the example of his nephew having lost himself a few days before in a field. This did not wash with the magistrates, however, and they countered the charge by stating that the surgeon at Shepton gaol was of opinion that he was not insane.

The prisoner was removed from the court during these conversations.

Seer's brother, who was also in court, now stepped forward and, in reply to a question from the bench stated:

> 'No-one of the family knew anything of the prisoner from the time he went to sea till 1856.'

They had often wondered where he was but they never heard of him. His brother and his uncle (who was in the omnibus trade in London, but had since died in Australia) could make nothing of him, and he was sent to sea. The Bench then expressed the opinion that if the prisoner knew anything of the murder, and was not the perpetrator, he must have spoken to someone who knew everything concerning it. 'He knows nothing of it but what we told him,' retorted the uncle.

'But you could not tell him what he says of it,' came a rebuke from Harrison, '[as] he has spoken of circumstances which no one but the actual murderer could know; and I am of the opinion that if he himself was absent at the time, he has somewhere met with the actual murderer.'

At the suggestion of the Bench, the brother was admitted to an interview with the prisoner, in the presence of the superintendent, but away from the court. After this had finished, Joseph Seer was conveyed back to Shepton gaol during the afternoon.

Meanwhile, with all interest aroused in the case, it was perhaps obvious that the names of the three original suspects would surface, and their less than respectable characters, before and after the trial, scrutinised for public consumption. Maggs, of course, was unable to defend himself – having died back in 1858 – and Sparrow was incarcerated in gaol, but 'Frome Bob', Robert Hurd, was still very much alive and, having left the town of his moniker, was at present living in Bath, albeit at an address within the most notorious area of the city. Hurd addressed the following correspondence to a Bristol newspaper that had carried a report about the sensational events taking place back in Frome. It read:

> Sir, – In your edition on Wednesday I find that I am classed as a bad character. Now, sir, I can prove by testimonials from gentlemen and tradesmen that I am, and have been always, endeavouring to get an honest livelihood. I am aware that at the time the above murder took place I was apprehended on suspicion, but now it is clear to the world that I am entirely exonerated from the charge. Your insertion of this would greatly oblige, Sir, yours respectively, ROBERT HURD, alias 'Frome Bob'. 72 Avon Street, Bath, Sept. 19, 1861.

It wasn't just the trial from 1851 and the three main suspects that were now in the minds, and on the tongues, of Frome's population; there was another event, from a few years later that also became a talking point and which would attract Superintendent Deggan's attention.

36

The Other Sarah Watts

After Joseph Seer's second appearance before the magistrates, on 24 September 1861, exactly ten years to the day of the actual murder, Superintendent Deggan continued his investigation. There were a lot of questions to be answered, including one surrounding Deggan himself from the morning of the confession. On that day, as he recalled in his evidence before the magistrates, he had remembered Joseph Seer's name being 'in the frame' for the murder at the time, and yet the superintendent wouldn't move to Frome for another nine years, so how could he have known? Even if he had read it in a newspaper, it would be a phenomenal feat to recall a specific name, a decade on, particularly one which had not been mentioned in court and so would not have been in any reporter's notebook. But the answer to this question would not be forthcoming although others soon would.

After Deggan had knocked on the doors of several houses at West Woodlands and talked to their inhabitants, two things became abundantly clear: first, none of the people in that area had any personal knowledge of the prisoner until he had stepped into the clerk's office a fortnight previously, and second, a name kept recurring as someone who might know the identity of the murderer. Initially, Deggan must have thought he was the butt of a cruel joke, or that the people he was talking to were raving mad, as the name of the person being mentioned was that of Sarah Watts!

As Deggan had not been in Frome six years earlier in 1855, but rather at the other end of the county, it would have been surprising if he had known anything about the Frome post office robbery of that year. After he did find out though, he may well have been bemused by the coincidence. The name of the main perpetrator of the robbery, as many people in Frome knew, had also been Sarah Watts. It had been a kind of oral tradition within the town, as Deggan discovered, that when found guilty at the assize court, this Sarah Watts had offered to 'tell all about the Woodlands Murder if she were let free.' The offer had been politely declined and so her sentence of fourteen years transportation had stood.

This supposed knowledge of the murder had become 'much talked about since Seer's extraordinary confession,' reported the

Frome Times: it was just a shame she was no longer in the country. On investigating further though, Superintendent Deggan found information that revealed the convicted Sarah Watts had not been deported after all, but had remained in the country to serve out her time. This had become a more regular occurrence by the mid-1850s, as transportation was increasingly seen as inhumane on one hand, while on the other, the increasing respectability of Australian society meant they no longer wanted any more of what was deemed to be Britain's underclass. This had been the case with Maggs who, despite his sentence, had not been transported before he died, and Sparrow, who was currently serving the remainder of his sentence in Dartmoor Prison.

With this new information and by magistrates' decree, Deggan headed again to London. Sarah Watts's last known whereabouts was at Millbank Prison – where Maggs and Sparrow had previously spent time. On his arrival he discovered that she had been moved to an institution in Brixton and from there to a place called The Refuge, located in Fulham, a reformatory set up to house women thought capable of being lead away from a life of crime. He finally tracked her down there and interviewed her about her supposed proposition 'to tell all' five years before. She strenuously denied having made such a statement, in regard to the murder, and denied having any knowledge of the prisoner Joseph Seer, stating that she had never seen nor heard of him until Deggan had mentioned him.

In the course of his interview, Deggan told the magistrates, he had found that she was 'cognizant of the details of the murder', and that she suspected one of the three on trial in 1852 of being the murderer but did not have any specific knowledge, as claimed by 'oral tradition'. As well as the coincidence of her name, she had been in service near the spot at the time of the murder, working for farmer Henry Crees at Marston, so it was only natural that she should have retained a lively remembrance of all the circumstances of the tragedy, Deggan concluded. He also reported that on account of her good conduct while in prison, she was to be discharged.

After having recounted the findings of his investigation to the bench and informed them of his failure to find any trace of the prisoner's whereabouts in 1851, he asked for a further remand. The Bench considered this request and as there were one or two aspects they themselves wanted looking into, they agreed and remanded the prisoner once more.

In another coincidence between the two cases – the Sarah Watts murder and the post office robbery – one of the magistrates for the latter case had also been present on the Bench during proceedings of the former: Dr Harrison. For the most part, this was of little significance or consequence to the matter in hand. What was of significance, and bore potentially seismic consequences, was a fact between the two cases not uncovered by Superintendent Deggan. It involved two other people named at the post office robbery trial known to Sarah Watts; namely Charles Druce and his wife, Amelia. Charles had stood alongside Sarah Watts at the trial and had also been sentenced to fourteen years transportation (although like his partner in crime, his sentence had instead been commuted to custody in England). During the trial, his wife, Amelia, was proved to have been a shopping companion to Sarah; going into town with her and while there having presents bought for her – a pair of earrings that a constable had taken from her ears being one example. How the two women – Sarah and Amelia – first struck up their friendship is not known; Charles is the most likely reason, although there is the possibility they had met earlier in life, when Amelia had been living in Lower Woodlands and Sarah was working in service nearby.

Whatever the circumstances behind the origin of the women's amity, Charles and Amelia married in 1850 and moved into a property in Keyford, owned by Amelia's step-mother. Charles's parents, meanwhile, remained in Vicarage Street, in a house exactly opposite to the post office where Sarah found employment and then became directly involved in the crime that transpired through the various ill-gotten gains stored at the address. It seems then that Sarah also lavished presents on Amelia and they became as close as siblings, perhaps sharing secrets, family or otherwise, and keeping confidences, personal or criminal; trusting one another with their darkest thoughts or deepest feelings. They did after all 'share' a man, so to speak, in Charles Druce; whereas he was Amelia's marital partner, he was Sarah's criminal one.

All this leads to the fact that when Superintendent Deggan interviewed Sarah Watts at the Refuge, she declared she had never seen or heard of Joseph Seer. This may of course have been true, but one thing Deggan was not aware of was that Amelia Druce – Sarah's shopping companion and perhaps closest confidante – had the maiden name of Seer, and before Amelia married Charles, she lived with her parents in West Woodlands, in a house just down the road from Battle Farm. She was also Joseph Seer's aunt!

37

Disclosure

When Joseph Seer had been brought to Frome for this third examination at the magistrates' court, the local newspaper reported that: 'The general excitement has now considerably subsided, and the Court-hall afforded ample accommodation for all who desired admittance.' While in court, Seer's demeanour was once more 'perfectly rational, and his appearance exhibited not the slightest trace of insanity. He was again dressed in the prison uniform.' Deggan had given the findings of his investigation, in regard to tracing Sarah Watts and admitted that he still had not yet been able to track Seer's whereabouts in 1851.

However, by the time of Seer's next appearance in Frome, on Tuesday 8 October 1861, news that an important disclosure would be forthcoming ensured that 'considerable excitement was manifested in the town,' and 'long before the arrival of the prisoner, groups lined the road to the station, and the court-room was filled quite an hour before noon.' The prisoner was accompanied once more from Shepton Mallet by a police officer and, once more, it was Sergeant Watts (it had been a Constable Best on the previous occasion); it was reported he 'appeared somewhat paler than on Tuesday last, otherwise there was no alteration in his demeanour.'

The magistrates at this hearing were The Earl of Cork (who acted as chairman), Dr Harrison once again, and local businessman John Sinkins; all three men now having had long associations with the Sarah Watts murder case.

The Chief Constable of the county, Valentine Goold, was present and watched as his subordinate, Superintendent Deggan, took the witness stand. 'Since the first instant,' Deggan began, 'I have made further enquiry into the case, and I am now in a position to produce evidence which will lead to the identification of the prisoner, and to his having been in this town at the time of the murder.'

The first piece of 'evidence' to reinforce Deggan's sensational revelation was an elderly man called James Payne. After he had taken the witness stand and sworn the oath, he said:

> I live in Broad Street, Frome, and am a cooper. I know the prisoner Seer from his childhood. I well remember the murder of Sarah Watts. I knew the prisoner when he was a baby. I knew

him in childhood, and I know him in manhood. I lived near him – a quarter of a mile off. When he was about seven years of age, he lived in a lane called Birchill Lane, in a house built by Samuel King. After he was seven years of age I missed him for some years. I saw him and knew him at different times during his life, but I can't mind when it exactly was.

The last time I saw him before the murder was in Badcox [the area in Frome where the Union Workhouse was located], *where he wished me 'Good Morning'. That was about three weeks before the Woodlands murder took place* [and was] *between the Ship and the Sun. I should not have known him if he hadn't spoken. I looked round and wished him the same. I then said to him 'That's Seer'. I said, 'How are you, Seer?' He said 'I am pretty well; I hope you are the same'.*

I didn't see him again – the murder was done on a Wednesday – till the Saturday week after the murder. I went into the Castle Inn, Frome, that evening, to find my wife. I found my wife there selling some lace – she was a lace-maker by trade. When I found she was there, I saw she was selling some lace to a girl I called Maria Staff. I never knew her [real] *name. At that point Seer came into the room. He brought in a pint of beer. He was quite intoxicated in beer. My wife and Maria Staff were talking about the murder that took place in the Woodlands. Seer then, after hearing this discourse, stood up and said he had done all he could do with the woman and then he murdered her because he should never be found out.*

Well, I should have told of it at the time, but my wife persuaded me that I should be murdered if ever I should tell of it. I said to Seer, 'If ever I should see you in Frome any more, I shall have you taken up if you don't give yourself up'; but he gave himself up before I saw him. My wife has been dead two years coming December. I wish she was living. Immediately after this took place I left the Castle Inn, and told Seer I would go and get a constable. My wife then ran after me, and caught me three or four yards before I came to Mr Nicholl's, who was that time a constable. My wife said, 'If you do tell of it, you will be murdered as sure as you be born'.

The magistrates then asked Payne about the girl who had been buying lace:

I didn't know the girl's name. She travelled about with her mother buying lace. I have seen her [one] *time since. I saw her three years come Christmas. I called her Maria Staff, because she came from Staffordshire. She always stopped at my house when she came to Frome ... I can't mention one in Frome who knew the girl. I didn't think the people at the Castle knew her. My wife was a lace-maker, and used to sale [sic] lace to this girl. There was no one in the room beside this girl, her mother and my wife, Seer and myself. No waiter was there at the time. This was between 6 and 7 o'clock, and the house was not then full. I do not know, I can't say, that any one of my wife's acquaintance knew the girl, for she did not stop at my home more than one night at a time.*

The Earl of Cork, as chairman, then asked Seer if he wanted to ask the witness any questions. The prisoner touched his forelock and replied 'No, sir'.

The chairman now returned his attention towards James Payne: 'You have lived in Frome many years and you knew that three men were tried for this murder?'

'I have lived in Frome 40 years,' replied Payne. 'I told my wife when Frome Bob was taken up that I would tell about it. She told me if I did she would murder me. I never knew Frome Bob was tried for it.' At this juncture, it seemed strange Payne would say he was not aware Hurd had been tried for the murder, given all the press reports surrounding it, but all would become apparent, later.

During the examination of this and other witnesses, the prisoner frequently smiled, the newspapers reported, but made 'no other manifestation'. Next to be called to the witness stand was a woman named Mrs Edgell:

I live at Prospect Buildings, Bath, and remember the time of the Woodlands murder. Some days after the murder – [although] before I heard of it – a man came to my house to ask for assistance. He appeared very agitated. His thumb was scratched and he had a scratch on the left side of forehead. He said he came from Frome, and had been to Bristol to try and get a ship, and was going to London to try and get employment or go for a soldier. He appeared to have been drinking, but was not tipsy. I can't say that the prisoner is the man. The man was stouter, and his hair was lighter, but he was about the same height as the prisoner.

I observed that his thumb was bound up. I asked him what was the matter with it. He seemed in great agitation and said he had hurt it. I don't say the prisoner is not the man. I gave him some relief. I don't exactly remember how he was dressed, but he had on either a dirty white jacket or a smock-frock and a cap. If I had heard of the murder [by then] *I certainly should have had the man taken up on suspicion. We were living then at 13, Friar's Bellevue, Bath. He was about the height of the prisoner, with round features – not unlike the prisoner. It was between 6 and 7 o'clock in the evening, and it was light. The scratch on his forehead was two or three days old, I remember. I am not able to identify the prisoner as the man, but I am not satisfied that he is not.*

Superintendent Deggan then added, for the magistrates' benefit: 'With regard to the thumb. I wish to state [that] at the time of the murder a bloody thumb-mark was found on the wall.'

When asked if he had any questions for this witness from Bath, the prisoner, Joseph Seer, again declined the offer.

Although resident in Bath for the past several years, having lived up to his promise of leaving Frome for good, Robert Hurd, alias 'Frome Bob', was in the public gallery and volunteered to give evidence; the reason for Payne denying knowledge of Hurd being on trial for the murder became clear. If he admitted now that he had known about Seer's confession at the time of the assizes trial back in 1851 and had not gone to the magistrates with his damning information, he was as good as admitting to knowledge that would have had the case against Hurd, Maggs, and Sparrow, thrown out before it reached court. This would, of course, have spared them six months in Shepton, two days at the assizes, and another twelve months for Hurd back in the same prison, for his reprisals against certain of the witnesses.

It can be imagined, given his previous behaviour in various courts, that Hurd fixed him with a tempestuous 'stare', almost daring him to say something bad about him. We shall never know what Hurd wanted to reveal to the court, however, because at the suggestion of the magistrates' clerk, Mr Cruttwell, Hurd was told to report what he had to say to Superintendent Deggan; who merely stated that what had been said to him would not be presented as evidence at the present time, but might lead to important results in the future. Frustratingly, what Hurd said to Deggan has been lost in the mists of time, as the reporters were unable to record it, and there does not seem to have be a 'future' time when it was actually presented in the official proceedings.

Robert Hurd sat back down and the next witness took the stand:

My name is James Vallis and I am a shoemaker, living at Keyford. I know the prisoner. I saw him three weeks ago. I saw him several years ago. I can't say how many – it may be five or more years ago. He spoke to me, and wished to know where his uncle lived. I directed him to Woodlands. Mr Hunt, of Keyford, spoke to him.

Mr Hunt was the third and final witness, but appeared very reluctant to say anything. After some hesitation he took the stand. 'It was five years next December the prisoner came to me. He is distantly related to me. I had not seen him till that time since he was taken to London after his mother ran away and left him.'

As no further evidence was to be produced at that time, Chief Constable Goold applied to the magistrates for a remand and after some consultation, Joseph Seer was remanded until the following Saturday. At the end of the newspaper reports on this session, the editors revealed they had been told, or rather it had been 'suggested', that they should ask their readers to give police any information regarding the identification of the 'lace-girl' from witness Payne's statement. For now though, she remained one more mystery in this increasingly complex case.

38

Resolution

'We have reason to believe that the Superintendent has since succeeded in obtaining information which will probably justify him in applying for the discharge of the prisoner on Saturday.'

So wrote the *Frome Times* in their edition of Wednesday 16 October 1861, in regards to what would be Joseph Seer's sixth and final time before a magisterial bench since confessing to the killing of Sarah Watts. Before that revelation, the newspaper had reported the prisoner's appearance – his fifth – at Frome police station on Saturday 12 October. It seemed that each time, in terms of crowds waiting to catch a glimpse of this former soldier, was different – some had attracted large numbers of people, others had not – but this was reflective of the nature of this extraordinary case, which seemed to have new twists and turns each week.

The appearance on this Saturday – 12 October – was expected to be a mere formality, and so not such a large crowd was expected. Also reflecting its 'low-key' nature, there was only a solitary magistrate present for most of the proceedings: John Sinkins, although he would be joined towards the end of the session by the Earl of Cork, who actually arrived just in time for some legal 'fun and games'.

Once Joseph Seer was placed in the dock, Superintendent Deggan took the stand and addressed the magistrate:

> *Since Tuesday last I have been making enquiries respecting the prisoner, and particularly respecting Maria Staff, the lace girl; but cannot hear of any person in this town who ever knew her, or heard the name. I have also enquired at the whole of the lodging-house, but cannot get any clue whatever.*

Sinkins reminded the superintendent that 'Staff' was not her real name, but rather a nickname that Payne had said he gave her. 'Just so, sir,' replied Deggan.

The superintendent then continued with his findings with the revelation of a letter he had received since the previous court session:

> *Since Tuesday I have* [also] *received a letter from a person who states he formerly was a sergeant in the 32nd Regiment of Foot*

and that in 1847 there was man called 'Seers' in that regiment. That man bore a very bad character, and for some serious offence was tried by a general court-martial and sentenced to a term of imprisonment in Calcutta Gaol. If the prisoner and that man be one and the same, he must have been in Calcutta Gaol at the time the murder was committed. From what has been stated I believe he has been in India, and this letter may give a clue to his whereabouts in 1851. In consequence of receiving that letter, I have written to the Under Secretary of State, at the War Office, London; also to the Adjutant of the 32nd Regiment at the depot, Preston, Lancashire, and also to the sergeant who wrote the letter. If the information contained in the letter applies to the prisoner, it will be in his favour. I expect replies [to my letters] in the course of a few days, and therefore apply for a further remand till this day week.

The magistrate requested the letter from Deggan and after reading it, said: 'It is here stated that Seers was a man 5ft. 7in. in height. The prisoner had better be placed under the standard, and we can then see if the description corresponds.' The prisoner was accordingly measured and was found to be only 5ft 5in.

The request for a further remand was granted until the following Saturday. Just after the removal of the prisoner, a solicitor, Mr Bartrum, entered the court and addressed the magistrate. He had been instructed to defend the prisoner, he said, and asked to be permitted to cross-examine the witnesses James Payne and Superintendent Deggan. Deggan interposed and said that it would be impossible to get Payne to the court now and he (Deggan) was not prepared to be cross-examined that day and so, under the circumstances, Mr Bartrum had better defer his cross-examination until Saturday next.

The magistrate, John Sinkins, then added, in reference to Mr Bartrum, that no witnesses had been examined at that session and the superintendent had only made a statement justifying a remand, which had been granted.

Bartrum was persistent; he was most anxious to be allowed the opportunity of cross-examining the witnesses, he continued, and was sure that in a case of this importance the Bench would not decline to 'accede to so fair a request'. The solicitor added he was there at considerable inconvenience to himself but now he was here, he hoped the magistrate would not render it necessary for him to come again.

> *"It would not be fair to my brother magistrate for myself to go into the case to-day."*

"I am not prepared to go into the case either," added Deggan
'as none of the witnesses are present."
"But surely Payne can be sent for."

As the argument between the three of them continued, Lord Cork
entered and took his seat on the Bench. Mr Bartrum renewed his
application to this arrival. Lord Cork then replied:

"You should remember, Mr Bartrum, that all that has occurred
is in consequence of the prisoner's own confession. He has occa-
sioned very considerable trouble, and he must take the conse-
quences of his own act."

"But your honours; the prisoner is a hopeless lunatic and is
not responsible for his own acts."

"The Surgeon of the Gaol has certified that he can not find
in him any traces of insanity," replied Sinkins.

For the sake of the prisoner and of his friends, he said, the prisoner
should be allowed an opportunity of setting himself right with the
public.

Lord Cork was of the same opinion as his judicial colleague
and told Bartrum that as the opportunity of cross-examining the
old man Payne at the proper time had been neglected, they could
not promise he would be allowed to do so next Saturday either.
John Sinkins then added that the prisoner had been asked if he
desired to ask the witnesses any questions, and he had replied in
the negative.

'I again alert your honours to the fact of my client being a discharged lunatic,' said Bartrum.

'Mr Bartrum,' replied an increasingly exasperated Sinkins, 'you
seem to be contradicting yourself. One moment you are urging
that the prisoner be allowed to set himself right with the public and
then the next, you are insisting your client is a hopeless lunatic.'

The solicitor mumbled his way through a reply to the magistrate's observation, and after some brief consultation the Bench
made its final decision and refused to recall either of the witnesses.
Bartrum then asked if the Bench would allow them to be recalled
on Saturday. This was a matter of life and death, he said, and it was
but fair that every opportunity should be given to the prisoner. This
verbal thrust and parry continued for a little while longer, although
was conducted in a warm manner, according to one newspaper.
The Bench, however, declined to make any promises on the subject
of recalling the witnesses. The solicitor, seeking to salvage something from his otherwise wasted day, changed tack and requested an
interview with his client. Mr Turner, the assistant magistrate's clerk,

who was also present, opposed the application unless the superintendent was present. Again a brief verbal sparring between solicitor and clerk ensured, with the former objecting to interference from the latter, given that he was also a witness for the prosecution.

After this long period of wrangling the proceedings reached a sort of compromise. The magistrates still declined to promise the recall of the witness James Payne, but as Superintendent Deggan would have further evidence to bring forward at the next appearance, he (Bartrum) should be allowed to cross-examine him on the whole of his evidence. Perhaps sensing this was the best deal he could presently hope for, the solicitor applied for permission to do so, which was granted and the proceedings brought to a close.

As it turned out, however, the solicitor would be no more than a bystander, watching as the incredible conclusion to the case unfolded. The news that there was going to be a possible resolution to the Seer's case was announced through the *Frome Times*'s revelation that: '… the Superintendent has since succeeded in obtaining information which will probably justify him in applying for the discharge of the prisoner on Saturday'. And, as expected, with the possibility of the prisoner being set free, huge crowds gathered from early on Saturday 16 October 1861. They stretched along the route that Seer and Sergeant Watts would take into Frome, and crowded outside the police station to watch them enter the court. Some of the gathered masses might even become the 'lucky' ones and manage to get inside to watch the proceedings unfold.

As befitted the occasion, the Bench consisted of six magistrates: Sinkins and Lord Cork, who had been present the previous Saturday, Knatchbull, Harrison, Dickinson, and Duckworth. Valentine Goold, the Chief Constable of the Somerset Constabulary, was also present, as, of course, was defence lawyer, Mr Bartrum.

Joseph Seer was brought in and placed in the dock. Once the court was in session, Superintendent Deggan came forward and approached the magistrates:

> I am now in a position, he began, to present before you documents which will satisfy you that the prisoner was not in this country at the time of the murder. I have been able to trace him from the time he left the Workhouse, in 1843, till the present time.

Deggan then held up one of the letters he had received:

> This is a letter I received from the India Office, in reply to a communication I had addressed to Sir Charles Wood: -
> India Office, S.W.: Oct. 14th, 1861

Sir, – I am directed by the secretary, Sir Charles Wood, to inform you, in reply to your letter dated the 12th instant, that, on reference to the records of this office, it appears that a lad, then 16 years of age, named Joseph Seer, was on the 19th July, 1847, bound [as] an apprentice to the East India Company, to serve in the Indian Navy for seven years; and that he sailed from England in the ship Malabar, *and arrived at Bombay on the 20th Dec., 1847, and was discharged at that place on the 19th July 1854. No particulars as to the return of Joseph Seer to England are known at this office. I am, Sir, your obedient servant. J. Cosmo Melville.*

This seemed to be the final proof Joseph Seer was not guilty of killing Sarah Watts, as he had not even been in the country at the time. Whether he would be charged with wasting police time remained to be seen. Deggan produced another letter he had received; this one was from the office of Mr Green, the shipping agent at Blackwail:

Blackwail, Oct. 14, 1861

'*Sir, – I am requested by Mr Richard Green to reply to your letter of the 12th inst. Respecting a man named Joseph Seers, and I beg to inform you that a boy of that name, aged 16 years, 4 feet 11 inches in height, whose mother was described as a charwoman, living at 2, Gloucester-gardens, near the Great Western Railway, Paddington, was sent out from the Marine Society, Bishopsgate-street, [sic] together with 19 others, by the Hon. East India Company in the ship* Malabar. *The vessel was commanded by William Henry Parr, and sailed from Gravesend on the 2nd of August, 1847; and Mr Horace Fleming was a midshipman at that time on board the said ship. These boys were to a certain extent passengers, and expected to work during their voyage. I shall be happy to give you any further information in my power. – I am, &c.,*

Signed James Farrell.

Superintendent Deggan said he now had no further evidence to offer and so at this point, Chief Constable Goold said that: 'after the evidence which has been given, I must apply for the prisoner's discharge.'

Mr Bartrum, Seer's lawyer from Bath, who had been retained by the prisoner's family at great expense, now had no reason to cross-examine any witnesses, but stated that he would:

give the police credit for the exertions they have made, to find out the whereabouts of the prisoner at the time of the murder. In a moment of insanity, he had made the extraordinary confession, which has led to his apprehension; but it is now quite clear that this unfortunate man knew nothing whatever of the crime. Prison diet and prison solitude had effected a change for the better, and he is now anxious and willing to give every information respecting himself.

Lord Cork, in discharging the prisoner, however, commented on the folly and wickedness of his conduct, which had occasioned so much trouble to the police and Bench, and so great an expense to the county.

Bartrum then made an application for proceedings to be taken against the witness Payne for wilful and corrupt perjury:

It is due to society, as well as to the prisoner and his friends, that such gross perjury as has been committed by Payne should not go unpunished. He has evidently thought he would obtain the reward which has been offered, and has, in consequence, come forward with his trumped up story.

Lord Cork replied the Bench had anticipated that such an application would be made and had decided not to entertain it at present. At a future time, and with necessary legal evidence, they would be quite willing to look into the charge.

The proceedings were concluded and Joseph Seer returned to the status he had enjoyed up until early on that morning of Tuesday 17 September, a little more than a month before, when he stepped through the doors of the Frome police station: that of a free man.

Leaving aside the issue of Payne's perjury charge, and the reason behind Seer's confession, the decade old question now remained unanswered: Who really did murder Sarah Watts?

PART SIX

(Whatever happened to…)

39

Joseph Seer

The early years of Joseph Seer have proved particularly hard to trace and present a somewhat tragic story. Joseph was the son of John Seer, a sloober or worker in the cloth trade and his wife Emily. He was baptised at St. John's Church, Frome as Joseph Stokes Seer on 2 February 1831 and in 1833 he was joined by a baby brother, Archibald. The 'Stokes' name probably came from an earlier family marriage and never seems to have been used again. The little family seem to have lived quietly until 1837 when tragedy struck. His great uncle John was caught 'stealing goods in the process of manufacture' – 46 yards of Kerseymere, a fine twilled woollen cloth from his place of work. Despite being of good character with five children and 58 years of age he was sentenced to be transported to Van Diemen's Land for ten years, a sentence from which he could never hope to return.

The name Seer does not appear amongst the usual list of Frome's habitual criminals and we can only assume that this was a 'one off' by a desperate man. Whether it had any direct bearing on the troubles of the wider family is not known but within a year or so Joseph had been placed in the local workhouse, his mother was living in London with his little brother and his father drops from the record until the census of 1851 when he is living in Huntingdon as a lodger and printer's compositor. Ten years later he has moved to Ashford in Kent and is married to a dress and mantle maker named Sarah who was born in Huntingdon. John Seer died in Ashford at the age of 58 in 1867. It seems that far from it being the case that both his parents had died when Joseph made his brief visit to Frome in 1856, at least one was alive and had made a new life for himself.

Who left whom is something we shall never know. The indication from the trial is that Emily left the family with the two small children – by now their third and final child, Agnes had been born – and went to stay with a brother in London, lodging Joseph in the workhouse before she went. Possibly John had already left as he doesn't seem to have been in Frome to look after Joseph, neither parent wanted the responsibility of him at that time. Possibly he was disruptive and difficult as his later life would indicate.

There is no trace of any family members on the 1841 census in Frome or London. As we know from the trial Emily returned to Frome in 1844 and took Joseph back to London with her. Attempts to fit him into her new life obviously failed and after a few years he was packed off to sea.

One possible connection between the Seer and the Watts family is a small piece in the *Bath Chronicle* during November 1849 when it is reported that William Seer, uncle to Joseph, was fined 6 pence damages and 8 shillings costs or 2 months hard labour in default, for damage to the property of a Joseph Watts. There are no further details and there may have been a lot more to it – an indication that there was some friction between the 2 families which might have given rise to suspicions amongst the early investigators, though this does not seem to have led very far.

The other son of John and Emily, Archibald became a stone mason and married a Mary Ann Whiting in Hackney in 1860 but spent much of his time in Frome as their two children Frederick and Mary where baptised at St John's in 1862 and 1863 respectively. It was almost certainly Archibald who spoke up for his brother during the trial. Unfortunately there was to be no happy ending for the Seer family. Archie died in Westminster in 1867 and his wife died in childbirth three months later. The two children went to live with their uncle Edmund Whiting, a master stonemason, in Paradise Place, Keyford. It was possibly Whiting that gave evidence at the trial and may have offered Joseph work once he was released which enabled him to call himself a stonemason. Whether work and assistance was offered we don't know, but the troubled life of this sad individual was not destined to improve.

According to the *Frome Times*, Joseph Seer left Frome sometime during the morning of Monday 4 November 1861, with the intention of 'seeking employment as a sailor'. When he was discharged from Shepton gaol, his occupation had been given as stonemason, but within days he became a resident at the Frome's Union Workhouse. Having arrived at the Workhouse's Entry Lodge, Seer, classed as a pauper, would have been searched, bathed and his clothing taken away to be fumigated in a sulphurous acid gas. He would then have been issued with a uniform of simple hard cloth.

Although his stay at the workhouse was not strange in itself – Seer had been an inmate there when younger – the fact that none of his relations in Frome were willing to put him up seemed odd; especially as his family had paid for an expensive lawyer from Bath to represent him, while others had acted as witnesses to prove his innocence. Possibly assistance had been offered by Seer's relatives, but he had refused it, or possibly the friends and relatives felt they had done their bit and now just wanted him to go away.

From what can be gleaned from newspaper reports, it seems that Seer did not return to sea, as the next time he is heard about is the following March, 1862, after an incident at Thornbury Union Workhouse in Gloucestershire. A Joseph Seer was reported to have *'Wilfully destroyed his clothes in the Union Workhouse at Thornbury on the 15th of March 1862.'* This act echoes what he did to his soldier's uniform at Shepton Gaol, the previous autumn. For this latter incident, however, he was sentenced to *'be imprisoned and kept to hard labour for one calendar month'*, in the Gloucester County Gaol. At first sight this could be seen as further evidence of mental instability but it seems that the destruction of workhouse uniforms or property was quite common amongst inmates. The conditions there were so bad that prison was preferable – food and bedding were of a much higher standard and many saw this as a way of temporarily improving their lot. Whatever the reason behind this particular piece of *'wilful destruction'*, Seer served his time and was discharged from there on 17 April 1862.

The prison description book has survived and gives the following information, which is useful for future reports, so as to 'anchor' down 'sightings' of Seer. He is recorded as being a 30 year old labourer from Frome, five feet, four and a quarter inches tall, with dark brown hair, hazel eyes and a dark complexion. The most interesting section though is 'Other Marks' and gives details of his tattoos: *'D left side, Cross and 2 arrows left arm, Sailor flag; Sun and anchor left arm, Woman & flags, heart, arrows. JS "Love" & 2 arrows right arm.'* When his time expired, the gaolers recorded in the 'other comments' section: *'Native of Frome, single, has been a soldier in the 4th Regiment of Foot but was discharged about a year ago.'*

On 12 January the following year he became embroiled in trouble again, this time for 'misbehaviour, Union'. No further details are given, but he is described as 'Joseph Sear a seaman aged 31 from Frome in Somerset, measuring five feet, four and a half inches', but still of swarthy complexion with dark brown hair and hazel eyes. This time he was sent to Dorchester gaol. When admitted, another gaoler had an attempt at interpreting his tattoos and distinguishing features:

> *Cut on right eyebrow, Woman under right arm above the elbow. 2 flags, Anchor. JS. Leah with 2 daggers through it. LOVE 2 darts? across front right arm Anchor below the right thumb and forefinger ??? across the palm right hand @ left arm ???? anchor*

under the left arm above the elbow. Star under left arm down to
the wrist under the left arm – Star & Anchor on back and arm.

There was then a gap of five years before he is heard of again. This is in March 1867, when he is arrested for stealing a silver thimble. The first and only crime of dishonesty he seems to have committed. The entry list of prisoners arrested in the Borough of Tewkesbury and incarcerated in Gloucester County Prison, described him as being convicted on 19 March 1867 and sentenced to fourteen days hard labour. He is described as Joseph Seers, aged 36, 5ft 4½ins, dark brown hair, hazel eyes and a sallow complexion. The most interesting aspect though, is it recorded he is 'not known to the police'. Another attempt is made at reading his tattoos: 'Love. J.S. and anchor on right arm, sailor and crucifix on left, D left side'.

Another six years pass and this time Joseph Seer seemed to have returned to his hometown, as he is arrested for being drunk and disorderly in the Trinity area of Frome. Seer is by now 43 years old and recorded as an 'illiterate labourer'. He was taken to Shepton gaol on 24 July 1873 at 6.10 pm. Magistrates Dickinson and Duckworth (both had been on the Bench of his final appearance back in 1861) sentenced him to seven days hard labour for drunken and riotous conduct unless he could pay a fine of 11s 6d plus costs. Unfortunately he couldn't and so was incarcerated until 30 July. The local press gave slightly more detail, stating that PC Maidment found him in Trinity Street drunk and shouting with a crowd round him and waving a knife. He was described as being 'hardly right in his head' and it was also mentioned twelve years before he had been remanded and discharged on a charge of wilful murder.

Seer's final appearance in the local press would seem to be the result of a session at the Mason's Arms at Marston when he was caught 'carousing' with five other people, during prohibited hours on 28 December 1875. Landlord James Austin had his license endorsed and was fined £2 including costs. This merry band of revellers were fined 10s each or imprisonment for fourteen days.

After this, the trail sadly goes cold. There was a Joseph Seers admitted to Lincoln Asylum in September 1878, dying there in February 1899, but no further details are given. Whether this was the same man who had walked into Frome police station thirty-eight years before it is not known. Either way Joseph Seer bows out of this story at this point, leaving the history books with another question beside that of 'who murdered Sarah Watts?' and that is: 'What made him confess to it?'

40

Maggs Family

William Maggs's part in this story had, of course, ended in 1858, when he died in prison, having served five years of a twenty-five year transportation sentence. Following his death there seemed to have been an exodus from Frome to Bath by not only former crime partners, but most of his family as well.

By the census of 1861, his widow, Maria, had moved to Bath and was remarried to William Larcombe, himself a recent widower and listed as a mason's labourer. Her occupation was recorded as a nurse and they lived at 2 Ferry Buildings, in the Widcombe area of the city. With them on census night, 7 April 1861, were Maria's daughters, Elizabeth (20) a weaver, Naomi (18) a dressmaker and Fanny (16) a domestic servant (back in 1852, they had, of course, been known as the 'Woodlands Three' for their unsuccessful attempt of burglary) and son Frederick (10). Also living with them were four of Larcombe's children: two sons and two daughters. This stepfamily seemed to have been an honest one – no convictions in the newspapers – and so whether it was William's influence, or else Maria had decided to stay on the straight and narrow after the three girls' conviction back in 1852 and the permanent incarceration of her first husband, is not known.

The family remained in Bath and Maria died there in 1878, the same year that Joseph Seer was admitted to the asylum. The majority of the Maggs' brood seem to have overcome their traumatic lives in Frome unscathed and gone on to lead relatively normal lives. Although Laura served two months for burglary in 1852, she does not seem to have been in trouble again. According to one source, she married a sailor called Samuel Chard, in Bristol, in 1871. Elizabeth is last heard of as an unmarried weaver living at 2 Ferry Buildings with the family. Naomi never married but had two daughters, both of whom worked as dressmakers in Bath. She died in 1913. Fanny married Charles Birchill, a successful photographer, and the couple moved from Bath to Bristol. They were married for forty years and had eleven children; she died in 1921. Dinah married Samuel Webber, a canal boatman, in Bath; she died in 1916. Frederick became a valet, although later was a lodging-house keeper in Bath. He married a Maria Merratt and died in 1905.

Emily Maggs was last recorded in the Frome census of 1851, after her husband Isaac Ferris was transported to Australia, but nothing more is heard of her after that. Brother Mark is not heard of again, after being transported in 1847, but presumably made a new life out there once he had served his time and perhaps even changed his name. Mary seems to have stayed in Frome and married a William John in 1866, although nothing else is known about her, while Rosetta cannot be found in the official record after her sentence for larceny in 1847. The remaining two daughters, Sarah and Ruth, still had relatively major parts to play within this story and so their stories will be told in subsequent chapters.

41

Robert Hurd

After leaving Frome for good in 1853 (other than the brief attendance during Seer's confessional proceedings eight years later) Robert 'Frome Bob' Hurd continued travelling and prize-fighting – his name making several appearances throughout the 1850s in the sporting periodical *Bells' Life of London*. He seemed to have stayed relatively honest or, more likely, one step ahead of the law. When exactly he moved to Bath is not known, but in the 1861 census he was at number 72 Avon Street, otherwise known as the notorious Duke of York pub. In many ways, Avon Street was Bath's answer to the St Giles district in London, where Hurd had been a decade earlier when the 1851 census recorded him as living in Old Pye Street. Although Avon Street was on a smaller scale, the same levels of poverty, criminality, and degradation existed. The area had not turned out as planned though.

At the beginning of the eighteenth century Queen Anne had visited Bath to take its renowned waters – the minerals in it were heralded to contain properties which could ward off all kind of ailments – and with a royal seal of approval the city began a period of expansion and popularity that turned it from a relatively small medieval city into the 'Las Vegas' of its day.

In practical terms, this meant development outwards from the walled centre in all directions resulting in an architectural explosion which, when completed, produced a city that would be the envy of the rest of Europe. The east saw various parades built, the west gained a number of magnificent squares, and to the north were erected the crowning architectural pinnacles of the King's Circus and the Royal Crescent.

In the south of the city, it was a different story. With its proximity to the river, this area was for all intents and purposes situated on a flood plain; ideally suited for pastoral grazing, for the months the land was not under water, but totally unsuitable for building on. In a climate of unbridled greed and ever increasing demand for accommodation, however, it did not take long before plans were made for elegant and fashionable lodging houses on the land, with only the flimsiest attempt at flood prevention.

Once built, and after the inevitable flooding had taken place, the houses swiftly ceased to be acceptable as dwelling-places to the upper and middle class visitors they were intended to attract. As the buildings became uninhabitable to all but the poorest of occupants, the whole district, named after the largest street in it, Avon Street, became ever more dilapidated and synonymous with the criminal element. Along with the poor, destitute, and the countless Irish immigrants who now flooded in, came thieves, pickpockets, and brothel-keepers, as well as all kinds of other undesirables with nefarious occupations.

It is perhaps not surprising that Robert Hurd, after he came to Bath, ended up in this area. What is surprising though, is that also listed on the 1861 census at the same address as Hurd, is another familiar name in the story: Ruth Maggs. After being in Frome until at least 1858, when she received a month's hard labour for being a 'common prostitute', she had decided, sometime after that, to follow her mother and various siblings to Bath; although how she ended up living with Robert Hurd is another matter (perhaps there was no room at Ferry Buildings, with her mother, step-father and eight children, or otherwise her most recent past was now deemed perhaps too disrespectful). But live with Hurd she did, to the extent that they married in 1863. They were already living together before this, because when they appeared as witnesses at the wedding of one of Hurd's associates in 1862, they were recorded as common-law husband and wife. Whatever the circumstances behind it, the actual marriage was short-lived, as Ruth died of scarlet fever in 1864. As grief-stricken as Hurd might have been, it did not stop him marrying again before the year was out to an Elizabeth Spillman.

By the following census, 1871, Hurd had moved again and changed wives (or living-partner at least) once more; he was now living in Hampshire with an Ann 'Hurd'. He remained with her in the quiet of the countryside for the next twenty years. Sometime after this though, he must have moved back to Bath because in 1895, Robert 'Frome Bob' Hurd died there of bronchial pneumonia. He was 81 years old.

If the three suspects in the 1852 Sarah Watts murder trial – Maggs, Sparrow and Hurd – were guilty of the crime, the latter seemed to have been the least involved in the actual murder and robbery. But throughout the years afterwards, he always hinted that he knew more than he let on. Even at the trial, when thought to have been found guilty, he said the truth would come out within a month. Then there was the man he punched, after he said he knew something of the woodlands murder. He also, of course, had appeared at Seer's 'trial' and tried to give 'important' evidence, but in the end was only (and frustratingly) allowed to talk to Deggan. So, whatever he had to say on the subject, died with him.

42

William Sparrow

The third and final suspect of the Frome trio who stood trial in 1852, William Sparrow, also had a varied life after his acquittal. Sentenced to transportation for twenty-five years, Sparrow, like Maggs before him, did not end up being sent abroad, but instead served his sentence in a variety of prisons.

With his trials and escape attempts behind him, Sparrow settled down to resume life as a 'jail bird' under the prison number 2342. His first few months were spent in Wakefield, Yorkshire, from September 1852 until the beginning of January 1854, when he was received into Dartmoor Prison – and despite his day-to-day behaviour being described in the muster books as 'good' or 'very good', a note on his general character described him as 'Bad in every respect'.

Dartmoor Prison opened in 1809 and had a curious history attached. Initially it was built to house prisoners of war from France and America. Officers were eligible for parole under a system that enabled those of higher rank to live within the community, in designated 'parole towns'. In 1815, many prisoners were shot during a suspected break out and thereafter it remained closed for more than thirty years; before it was reopened in 1850 as a civilian prison for convicts sentenced to long terms of imprisonment, or to hard labour.

Sparrow whiled away his long bleak years on the moor in the company of such 'unfortunates' as Benjamin Revell, who was serving life for 'bestiality with an ass'; lifer David Allman for an 'unnatural offence with a she-ass' (the difference between the two offences is sadly not explained); John Gaskell, given ten years for stealing a table cloth; Charles Liddle, another lifer, whose crime was that of 'maliciously attempting to discharge a loaded gun with intent;' and a whole plethora of thieves, buggers, robbers, rapists, and child molesters.

Finally, on 30 August 1862, prisoner 2342 was released on licence, after almost ten years on the moor; his stated destination being Warminster. He was now 43 years old with most of his adult life having been spent in prison. He seemed to have served the last month of his term back at Taunton, possibly as preparation for release, as there is a brief report on him by Governor William Oakley of Wilton gaol, dated as above:

Read and write imperfectly – moderate intelligence and slightly informed on religious subjects. General character bad. After trial prisoner escaped with George Bird from the place of confinement near the Assize Court by breaking through a stone wall but was re-taken during the day. Ordered by visiting justices of Wilton Gaol to be kept in irons for one month from 14th August inst.

In the margin was written:

To be treated as a Life sentence. Director's remark on Governor of Dartmoor letter of 12 August 1858.

Whilst Sparrow had been living with the Maggs household, back in the late 1840s and early 1850s, there was every possibility he had started a relationship with one of the daughters: Sarah Maggs. When she realised, or at least assumed, that her love, William Sparrow, would either be locked away for life or spend the rest of his days in Australia, she decided, now aged 26, to seek an alternative. On 4 April 1853, Sarah married Alfred Jutsum, a gardener and son of a cordwainer, or shoemaker, in the Parish Church of Widcombe, Bath, a seemingly honest and hardworking man. Their union produced a son William, before Alfred died in 1857. She had a daughter around 1861, which she named Fanny Maria Jutsum, although the father was obviously not her husband.

Then, in 1862, William Sparrow is released from gaol, whereupon he and Sarah are reunited and married later that year, on 10 November 1862. While she is in her mid-30s, a widow, and described as a seamstress, Sparrow is now aged 42 and a mason's labourer. The addresses they gave are interesting – Sarah was then living at 5 Widcombe Parade, while Sparrow gave his address as 2 Ferry Buildings – the same as Maria Larcombe (nee Maggs). Even more incredible is that the witnesses were Robert and Ruth (Maggs) Hurd! This union, of course, now meant that Sparrow and Hurd were brothers-in-law, and their father-in-law, although dead, was William Maggs. At one time 'united' in a criminal court of law, accused of murder, they were now all united under a different law.

By the census of 1871 William had changed his name to Jones, presumably in search of anonymity (there are probably few more anonymous names than that) and a break from his previous life. There is no record of when the name change took place and it may well have been unofficial, but it seems highly likely that it had a lot to do with the events of autumn 1861, when Joseph Seer confessed to the Sarah Watts murder. Suddenly, the names Maggs, Sparrow, and Hurd, were front-page news again – Hurd, in fact, had written to one newspaper complaining about their reporting of his character. However the change came about, he was, by 1871, living in the Widcombe area of Bath working as a mason's labourer and still married to Sarah, now aged 43. His stepchildren, William and Fanny, kept the surname of Jutsum, while he had three daughters of his own: Rosetta Jones (7), Mary Ann Jones (5), and Alice Salina Jones (2).

Sarah (Sparrow) Jones (nee Maggs) is believed to have died in 1880, and in the 1881 census William Jones is a widower aged 61, living with his 15-year-old daughter, Mary Ann, in Waterloo Buildings, Bath. He is recorded as working on the roads as a stone-breaker, which must have brought back memories, if not all fond, of his time in Dartmoor. Despite his age and daily routine of back-breaking work, it seems there was still life in him, as in 1885 he married a 36-year-old widow, Harriet Hatherill Holtham, daughter of a stonemason. A son, Arthur Leonard Sparrow, was born in November of the same year. He emigrated to Canada around the turn of the new century and spent his working life as a stonemason.

In the 1891 census William reverts to the Sparrow surname, but retains Jones as a middle name, and is living with his family at 10 St Georges Place, Bath. Also present were his wife Harriet (42) daughter Elizabeth (12) and sons William (8) and Arthur (5). Now aged 71, he is still described as a mason's labourer.

Finally, in the census of 31 March 1901, William Jones, a widower aged 81, is recorded as living at 1 Henrietta Place, Bath. His occupation is 'navvy, on roads, retired'. He is described as head of the family, but there is no family and he is probably just renting a room and sharing the house with four other people and one visitor. Nothing else has been discovered about him from this time and he does not seem to have returned to crime after his release from Dartmoor, or if he did, became much better at it and never got caught.

On 20 May 1901, William 'Bill' Sparrow (aka Jones) died at the age of 82 in the Union Workhouse, Lyncombe and Widcombe, in Bath. Once he had become too frail to look after himself, and seemingly with no immediate family to care for him, the workhouse would have been his only option; although luckily (for him) it seems that his time there was very short. His 18-year-old stepson William Sparrow was the informant, a soldier in the 11th Hussars based at their army barracks in Canterbury, Kent.

William Sparrow Senior was the last of the Frome trio to die and, in fact, most probably the last of all the men who stood in

the dock accused of Sarah Watts's murder. If it was him who committed the crime, and he was the person seen by Robert Walter
shuffling away on that Wednesday afternoon in September 1851,
then perhaps he always thanked his luck that a jury of his peers had
found him not guilty of it. And if it was him, then his secret went
with him to the grave.

Leah Watts

On Monday 24 September 1866, a little before 9 o'clock in the morning, Leah Watts left her home in West Woodlands. Fifteen years previously, on that date, her destination had been the Frome market, three miles away. The events which occurred on that day had scarred her life ever since. Today, her destination was a little nearer home. Not long after setting off on that autumnal day, back in 1851, she had been joined by her husband John. This morning though, she would complete the journey alone, as she had done on every 24 September following the dreadful murder of her daughter.

Leah Watts had remained at Battle Farm despite the killing of her daughter, the death of her husband, the coming of the railway, and the confession of Joseph Seer. Reminders of that god-forsaken day still surrounded her though, as she continued the back-breaking work of a small farmer throughout the years; albeit helped by her son, Thomas, and other members of her family. As well as having experienced the day of the murder itself, she had sat through the inquests, the magistrates and assizes courts – which saw those awful men accused but let off – and then ten years later, five years ago now, having to relive it with that imbecilic soldier, after he falsely confessed to the crime. All these details would surely remain in her memory for the rest of her life.

After leaving her home this morning in 1866, she turned left and began to walk up Tytherington Lane. Behind her, as she walked, the toll house still stood – this was where her husband had sought assistance after discovering their daughter's body – and where Mrs Court had accompanied him back to the farmhouse. She passed by Bull's Bridge Farm, where the Pickfords lived and from where Mary Wheeler, who had been visiting, rushed over to comfort her.

As she continued up the lane, she imagined what the man Robert Walter had seen; there he was, up ahead, in his white smock-coat, and hat, shuffling away. If only Walter had been able to see his face, as she wished she could see it now, so she could finally find some peace in knowing who the murderer of her daughter had been. But his back was resolutely turned, as he continued onwards. Where did he go though, on that Wednesday afternoon after brutalising her daughter?

Did the killer continue onwards towards the lane's end and then back to his refuge? But where was that? If he had gone to the end of the lane and turned left, it would have been perhaps to Nunney, where she had been born sixty-eight years earlier and had married John Watts seventeen years after that. Or had he gone right, to Marston, where she had spent several years with her husband and growing family, before her sister had died and the legacy she inherited allowed the move to Battle Farm. Sometimes she rued that inheritance. According to the detective who had come down from London the rumour of money was one of the reasons the farmhouse had been robbed that day.

Had the murderer got that far though up the lane, or had he turned down one of the smaller ones that ran off from it? If so, was it Vinney Lane and on into Birchill Lane, ending up in Feltham Lane, in which two of the men who stood trial had lived. Birchill Lane, she remembered was the place it was said where the young confessor had spent time during his childhood. But then she must not think bad of him, he was obviously not quite right in the head and he was, after all, not the murderer; given he was not in the country at the time. Or was it Little Keyford Lane, where the murderer turned off, which eventually came out at the Mount, home of the third of the suspects.

Or could the slayer of her daughter have turned left, as she was now doing, to go down Tuckmarsh Lane. It was along here that Tuckmarsh Farm was located, where the Allards lived, including Little Alfred – not so little now, having his own family – who had seen Sarah, bonnetless, at dinnertime. She smiled to herself, they were always telling her off for not being appropriately dressed when doing chores. At times, she had even wondered if it was Alfred, as she brought her suspicions, at one time or another, to bear on all the men within the area, especially those who had been brought up before the magistrates in the days immediately after. Then she checked herself for being silly, he would have been too young for such a hideous crime. Whoever it was, did they sleep easy?

Leah Watts passed Tuckmarsh Farm and headed on towards her destination: the tiny hamlet village of Trudoxhill and the final resting place of her husband and daughter. Her father in law – who had been the pastor for so many years – was also buried there with a plaque to remember him on the wall inside.

In her life she had given birth to seven children, but had seen two of them die before her: Thomas who had died when only 2 years old, and of course, Sarah, whose grave she now stood beside, in the graveyard of the little Congregational church within the village. She had also outlived her husband and one of the three suspects.

As she stood by the grave, paying her respects to Sarah and John, she knew somewhere inside that this would be the last time she would make the four mile trip. She felt it in her bones, in her blood and in her soul. She was getting old and her body would no longer have the strength to complete even this relatively short distance. She could feel her life slowly ebbing away. Her only wish now, if she was honest, was that she could join them.

After having also paid respects to her father in law, she left and made her way back along Marston Lane, towards her home at Battle Farm. The day was sunny and although she felt heavy hearted, there was some peace in having spent time in their company. She would return to the family that remained at the farm – son Thomas, his wife Ann and her grandson, also named Thomas.

Two months later, on 19 December 1866, Leah Watts died and a few days after that on 23 December, she finally got her wish and was reunited with husband John, and daughter Sarah, when she was buried at Trudoxhill chapel.

Afterword

So you have read the book and may have made up your mind as to who the killer of Sarah Watts was. Despite the brutality of the murder itself, it is a fascinating story, not least because you can still trace the routes and visit many of the places where the events took place.

A number of the public houses in and around Frome that provide the backdrop to this story have long since gone, like the main protagonists and all those with bit parts; but several of the key buildings and sites remain. The turnpike house 'a stone's throw from Battle Farm' still stands and one can walk the 70yds or so, under the railway bridge, to the entrance of what used to be Battle Farm.

The Woolpack Inn closed in 1961, but the building remains and, at the time of writing, is a shop specialising in water filters. It is easy to stand outside its front door and imagine, as you look across the road, a group of four men in conspiratorial mode, huddled together, as John and Leah Watts pass by on that fateful market day, back in September 1851. The Crown still operates as a public house and the authors, near the beginning of their collaboration, held one of their planning meetings there; enjoying a pint in the tap room, near the front window, where Robert Hurd may have been seated as he observed a distraught John Watts go by, on his way to Constable Grist's grocery shop next door which, although long ceased as such, also still stands. The Lamb known in the 1850s has long gone, demolished around 1887 to make room for an extension to the brewery that owned it, and moved to the top of Bath Street, where today it goes under the name of The Cornerhouse. The Unicorn Inn was demolished long ago to make way for housing and the town's fire station, while the Victoria Inn now serves the needs of a completely different clientele – being a pet grooming parlour under the name 'Frome 'N' Groom'!

In the centre of town, The Blue Boar and Angel are still open for business; the latter an up-market hotel and restaurant renamed the Archangel, while the former – where Maggs and later Sargeant, were arrested by Sergeant Smith – is seemingly little changed since those days; the authors ventured in for a celebratory pint to mark the completion of this book. The Ship too is still serving, but renamed The Artisan, as is The Sun, while the nearby Castle – where Joseph Seer allegedly confessed to the crime according to James Payne – closed long ago, although the building remains.

The police station into which Joseph Seer entered and made his confession in 1861 has long since ceased being used for its original purpose and, at the time of writing, doubles up as a dance school and the temporary base for the local radio station: Frome FM. The railway station remains operational and is, in fact, one of only two examples of this type of station – a single line still runs through it. The magistrates' court has long gone and is now a car park servicing both the town and Cheese & Grain entertainment venue. A reminder of its previous purpose as a magistrates' court persists though, as Edgell's Lane was eventually changed to Justice Lane, a name it retains to the present day.

One can still trace a route from Battle Farm to Maggs's house, via the quartet of lanes – Tytherington, Vinney, Birchill, and Feltham, – which still exists today, and it is just possible that in retracing it, you are following the same route the murderer took after having committed that most awful killing.

In Lower Keyford, Mount Lane, where Robert Hurd stayed with his parents is long gone, and the nearby Mount is a large housing estate, but it is still possible to walk up Feltham Lane, in the footsteps of Maggs and Sparrow on those days (and nights, during their nocturnal activities!) they were heading into Frome via the Mount. From here, you can then descend Culver Hill, past The Woolpack, and into Keyford, past Grist's former grocery shop and The Crown, and the sites of The Unicorn and The Lamb; where Hurd conducted his early morning pub-crawl on that September morning.

A market still takes place in the centre of Frome every Wednesday, although livestock is conspicuous by its absence, having moved long ago to nearby Standerwick, and most of the cheese is now packaged.

The main guardhouse, which stood next to The Blue Boar and was where many of those nefarious characters in the story spent at least one night, has long gone and in later life was converted into a public convenience, before being finally and perhaps shamefully demolished in the mid-1960s.

Descendants of Sarah Watts's family – mainly through one of her brothers – still live in the town, as it might be supposed do those of Maggs, Sparrow, and Hurd. It is still possible, despite the changes and the removal of many buildings, to get a sense of that time and events that occurred more than 165 years ago.

Both authors live in Frome, one in Keyford, and one the other side of town, and have followed, on several occasions, the very routes the likes of John Watts, William Maggs, William Sparrow, and Robert Hurd, along with so many others, would have walked. It is hoped, perhaps with this book in hand, that you, the reader will also get the opportunity to revisit these routes and sites, so as to get a fuller sense of the events that occurred in this book; although never forgetting at the very heart of this story is the awful killing of Sarah Watts, which took place on that fateful market day, Wednesday 24 September, back in 1851.

APPENDIX A: Scenarios A–D

So, was it Maggs, Sparrow, or Hurd, – either individually or in combination – who killed Sarah Watts; therefore meaning the jury's verdict was wrong? Like any fascinating murder case, there are plenty of suspects and it is for each person to make up their own mind, having read this book, as to the most likely candidates. There were several men brought before Frome magistrates (and discharged) before the names of Maggs, Sparrow, and Hurd, came into the frame, but sadly their names were not recorded. And, of course, there was Joseph Seer, as well as a number of men capable of committing such a crime that were never questioned at all.

We have included – as far as we are aware – every important detail that has come to light during our research and presented it with the least embellishment as possible from the original transcripts and newspapers reports etc. It should be said, however, that any or all of the witnesses could have been lying or genuinely mistaken. Robert Walter, for example, may have merely seen someone late for an appointment shuffling up the road (if he saw anyone at all). Alfred Allard might have made up his story about seeing Sarah at 1 o'clock, or it might have been 2 o'clock or 12; he was only 11 years old at the time of the 1851 census (although 13 a year later at the time of the trial – which is possible if his birthday was at the start of April). Robert Hilliar's tale is just a bit too convenient to be true and in the opinion of the authors was probably created in the hope of claiming the reward money, as the defence counsel suggested. Newspaper misprints and witnesses' false memory might all have played a part.

The bottom line, then, is: how reliable is the information we possess and if reliable, how can it be used to determine the killer? Taking all the 'evidence' at face value leaves what we believe are four potential scenarios – A, B, C, and D, – to the killer of Sarah Watts: each will be reviewed in the following section with authorial remarks.

Scenario A: Maggs, Sparrow, and Hurd

Taking the prosecutor's 'evidence' and the resultant sequence of events as our foundation, we can imagine events possibly unfolding like this: rumours of there being a substantial amount of money at Battle Farm reaches the ears of one or more of the defendants.

One of the 'quarter days' is due and so there is a fair chance the rent for the farm, to be paid to the Battle family, is in the house, ready to be handed over. It is also known Leah Watts received money from her sister, two years previously and so various amounts, even as high as £250, have been bandied around.

Maggs and Sparrow do not know the Watts family, but Sparrow knows Battle Farm, having visited there when Sarah Battle still farmed it and so they ask Hurd or Sargeant to point the couple out for them, for a cut in the takings, which is why they are opposite the Woolpack. Perhaps they have even done this several Wednesdays before, but with no luck, as only Leah goes to market, leaving John at the farm, but today they strike 'lucky', as they see both pass by. They then agree to meet up later in the pub.

Sometime after, if the testimonies of Allard and Walter are true, it was early afternoon Maggs and Sparrow go to the farm and break in. Maggs goes upstairs and starts to ransack the place looking for valuables. Sparrow keeps lookout downstairs. They are old hands at this, it is what they do, each has a role and they trust each other.

However, Sarah catches them in the act, having come in from the yard; they didn't know about her and by then it is to late to say something along the lines of 'we got lost on the road, sorry to have bothered you'. It is obvious they are robbing the place and with their previous convictions they know capture means transportation for sure, possibly for life. Her presence then, is a complete surprise. Had they known she would be there and were still determined to continue, surely they would have worn the masks found after they later burgled Plaister's shop, and made her show them were the money was. In panic, Sparrow grabs a stick and bashes her on the head before she can cry out. She starts to struggle and fight back, so he grabs her tightly to keep her quiet, while Maggs carries on upstairs. It doesn't take Maggs long to realise there is no money, so he takes several items of clothing (for whatever reason) and a watch, then quickly heads back downstairs. Sparrow says something like, 'you go off with the gear and I'll take care of the girl'. Maggs leaves the farmhouse, in his smock coat, and is the man seen running away.

This leaves Sparrow alone with Sarah, who still struggles. He decides to rape her, putting his hand across her mouth to keep her quiet, but she bites his thumb. After he has perpetrated this evil deed, it is obvious he will have to kill her so, rather awkwardly, he attempts to drown her in the whey tub, bracing himself against the doorway while he holds her head under; thus leaving the thumb print on the doorframe as he does so, and Sarah's shoe imprints

in the wall. He thinks he has drowned her and flings her to the
floor. He takes his handkerchief out of his pocket to wrap around
his bleeding thumb but then sees her begin to come round, so he
grabs her again before she can scream and strangles her. Now he
flees the scene unobserved, although forgetting his handkerchief
on the kitchen table.

Numerous other permutations of the same event are possible, but what doesn't quite fit with the facts as they are known is
the rape of a 14-year-old girl. Maggs was Sparrow's father-in-law
in all but name (becoming legally so posthumously) if Sparrow
was indeed having a relationship with Sarah, the daughter, at the
time and while the murder was probably unavoidable, given the
circumstances, would he tolerate a child rapist living under his
roof? During this period of history, the legal age of consent was
12-years-old, so she may not *legally* have been a child, but even so
it would take a rare type of person not to feel complete revulsion
for someone who had committed such an act. It is possible that
despite their ages, Sparrow was the dominant partner within their
relationship and that Maggs was afraid of him, or they could *both*
have raped her before Maggs left, in which case there would be
no feelings of disgust between the two. Another possibility is that
Sparrow could deny the rape ever took place and tell his acquaintances that the coroner and police were lying to make it worse for
them. We will never know.

The two meet up later and after Maggs learns what Sparrow
has done, decides the stolen items need to be off-loaded as soon
as possible, so they ask Sargeant to look after 'something' for them
until the heat dies down. He initially does so willingly, as probably
they have helped each other out like this often, but when Smith the
detective arrives from London, Sargeant realises what trouble he
could be in – this isn't nicking spuds or cheese, and he has not long
come out of an 18-month stretch – and so he panics and stashes
the bundle in the field.

The view of one of the authors is that this is the most likely scenario. In weighing up the evidence alone, it seems the jury reached
the correct verdict, the prosecution had not proved its case beyond
a reasonable doubt and there was not enough 'evidence' to hang a
man. The guilt or innocence of the three men in the dock is another
matter entirely though, so let's look at the individual evidence in a
little more detail and how it applies to each of them.

Sparrow

The evidence in support of scenario A is quite compelling in
Sparrow's case: his thumb was injured; a handkerchief left at the

crime scene was purportedly his; he was seen near the farmhouse at a critical time during the day of the murder; Maggs was supposedly overheard confirming his guilt; and he made a 'confession' at North Bradley fair. In the opinion of the authors, the key to whether it was Sparrow or not lies solely with the wounded thumb.

The consensus of witnesses – both mere observers and professionals – was that the injury to Sparrow's thumb was older than the fight at North Bradley. The most damning evidence for this, we feel, is that of George Shorland, the police surgeon, which seems to point to a date for its infliction on the day of the murder. This does not prove Sparrow's guilt beyond a reasonable doubt, of course, even with the bloodied marks on the wall; just because there was blood at Battle Farm, it does not mean this came from the wound of the murderer. It could easily have been smeared there from a hand of one of the people who arrived after the discovery of the body and helped move Sarah upstairs. With no forensic science to help – fingerprinting was still half a century away – there is no way of ever knowing whose blood it was. As for the type of injury, in those days it was a well-known tactic for fighting men to bite the thumb of their opponent. Why would he lie about this unless he was covering up his part in the murder? What possible activity would he need to hide that is worse than the rape and murder of a young girl? Some juries might have seen this as proof enough to hang the man – Sarah's testimony from beyond the grave.

If Sparrow was the lone perpetrator seen leaving the scene by Robert Walter, it would mean the Butts Square witness lied, or else got the timing wrong regarding Sparrow visiting William Sargeant. He could have slipped away, after the Victoria Inn sightings, made his way out to Battle Farm, done the deed and headed back to Feltham just before 3 o'clock to meet up, as pre-arranged, with Maggs, thereby giving him an alibi. It seems likely, given three independent witnesses swore to it, Maggs and Sparrow were around the area where they lived about 3 o'clock and that after calling home, the pair went back into Frome, via the Mount, and met up with Hurd and Sargeant at the Crown Inn.

One point in Sparrow's favour is that his clothing throughout that day does not match that of the man seen running from the farm, while Hilliar's sighting and record of Maggs's conversation, we believe, was a fabrication motivated by the hope of a substantial reward. With the other two main points against him we are still on shaky ground. There is the evidence of witnesses that the handkerchief found in the kitchen belonged to him, although it is strange so many people should have taken such an interest in one man's hanky that they are able to describe it in such detail later.

The ownership of the handkerchief is tenuous to say the least. And finally, there is his recounting of the details of the murder in the pub at North Bradley. Everything he said was either reported in the papers or the subject of local gossip. It is odd that he didn't mention the rape though – as this was reported in the newspapers within days – and would have enriched his story to an eager audience. If he was guilty, this might have been the one thing that he was ashamed of and so he left it out, or else he might have been trying to chat up the landlord's daughter with his tale and felt any mention of rape might sour his chances with her.

One possible problem with Sparrow as the prime suspect by Detective Sergeant Smith, as well as the prosecution, is that it blinded them into not putting all the suspects onto a level playing field. They may have been so focused on whether or not it was Sparrow that they overlooked any facts or circumstances which did not fit in with this version of events. It is what the authors have decided to call the 'Wearside Jack' phenomenon. During the hunt in the late 1970s and early 1980s for the 'Yorkshire Ripper', as Peter Sutcliffe became known to history, the police investigating the crimes received a cassette on which a voice confessed to being the person sought. The police, believing the recording to be genuine, focused their efforts on looking for a man with a Geordie accent, as heard on the tape, while ignoring anyone with a different accent (including Yorkshire, as it transpired). The Watts case we suggest suffered in a similar way.

Maggs

With the above in mind we turn to Maggs. At the trial it was acknowledged by the prosecution that there was less evidence against him, but that does not mean he was not the perpetrator. The facts pointing to his guilt are: first that he was seen wearing a white smock coat, the same as Walter's 'shuffling' man, earlier in the day; and second, that he is supposed to have changed it by the time he headed back into Keyford from his house sometime after 3 o'clock.

Burglary was his modus operandi – stealing the very foodstuffs the Watts' discovered missing – and quite possibly, as mentioned with the Maggs-Sparrow combination previously – it was a case of the 'job went wrong', and Maggs had to kill Sarah before she screamed for help. There is nothing in the rest of his criminal 'career' which would suggest this course of action though and certainly not the added element of rape. But he could have left the Victoria Inn, in the same way Sparrow had and headed out alone to Battle Farm and then, after having committed the crime, met up with Sparrow and returned to the Mount and on to the Crown. There are no sightings of Maggs between 2 and 3 o'clock in the official record after all, and so they become conspicuous by their absence. If it was Maggs 'shuffling' away from Battle Farm with the clothing under his arm, it would make sense that Sargeant helped to get rid of them later by placing the bundle in the field (although why he would do so that close to his house is another mystery, unless, as described earlier, he panicked). Therefore in another of the authors' opinions, if it was any of the 'Frome Three', then it was Maggs. And maybe, just maybe, when Sparrow found out what had happened out at Battle Farm, an altercation took place in which Maggs bit Sparrow's thumb; hence the latter's silence on the truth of his injury.

Hurd

As for Robert Hurd, alias Frome Bob, it may well still have been him, but to the authors it seems more than likely he got mixed up in something that got out of hand. At the very worst, he was merely responsible for seeding the idea of the robbery in the minds of the other two. There was also his response at the trial, when he believed himself to have been found guilty, and said the truth would come out within a month. Therefore, if it was any of the 'Frome Three', both authors agree it was most unlikely to have been him.

Scenario B: Joseph Seer

If it wasn't any of the 'Frome Three', then was Joseph Seer, despite the 'proof' to the contrary offered by Superintendent Deggan, really the lone perpetrator as he had confessed to being?

The only way Joseph Seer could even be considered as the murderer, it seems, is if there was a way to show he was in England at that time and not serving his apprenticeship in India or on board the *Malabar*. But the evidence for him being the killer is strong, if not infallible. The *Frome Times*, for example, claimed in an initial report of his confession that: 'By some it was even affirmed that he was in Frome on leave of absence about the time.' Even if this 'some' included James Payne, there were possibly one or more locals who told the reporter they had seen him but did not come forward for the magisterial proceedings; their existence though, means Seer might just have been telling the truth.

Possibly, he had returned to Frome on leave (or was even AWOL) in September 1851, unbeknown to his remaining relations, and perhaps was trying to find the way to his uncle's house

– it was testified that he asked directions to it in 1856 – which stood along the road from Battle Farm. Once out at West Woodlands, he knocked on the door of a farm, but took the opportunity when it availed itself: that of finding a young girl home alone.

There is, of course, James Payne's testimony to reinforce this and although ultimately dismissed as false, it is strange that the magistrates were reluctant to charge him with perjury (in the same way Starr had been several years earlier, when trying to cover for Maggs). There was also the witness from Bath, Mrs Edgell, to take into consideration and although she does not conclusively identify him, there is enough in her testimony to make the whole episode tantalising:

> *Some days after the murder ... a man came to my house to ask for assistance. His thumb was scratched and he had a scratch on the left side of forehead. He said he came from Frome, and had been to Bristol to try and get a ship, and was going to London to try and get employment or go for a soldier ... he was about the same height as the prisoner. I observed that his thumb was bound up ... He seemed in great agitation and said he had hurt it ... he had on either a dirty white jacket or a smock-frock and a cap. If I had heard of the murder ... I certainly should have had the man taken up on suspicion.*

Another aspect of this scenario is Deggan's investigation, and whether there is a chance he could have got at least some elements in it wrong, then throwing doubt on all other parts of it. And the answer is yes, he did. According to the superintendent, during his research in London and the searching of 'ship' lists, he found the entry:

> *Joseph Sear, 24 years old, native of Frome, joined the ship named 'Rosebud' in Newcastle, in 1855 at Elsinore, in the Baltic. He was discharged from that ship at St. Katherine's Dock on the 17th September 1856; his previous ship being a Norwegian vessel also sailing in the Baltic.*

Unfortunately, either Deggan or a subordinate completely misread one of the documents. The name Joseph Sear was correct (although the surname spelling did not match that of the man in the dock) and the age could be made to fit, more or less, but he had misread the place of birth: the entry said 'Troon' in Ayrshire not Frome; the Joseph Seer in the dock had never been near Newcastle, Norway or the Baltic. This mistake went unchallenged and although it was not relevant to the period surrounding Sarah Watts's murder, it does throw doubt on the thoroughness of his other discoveries, especially his conviction that Seer had joined the *Malabar* under a fictitious name in 1847. The official record proved quite easy to trace and shows that a Joseph Seer had in fact joined the *Malabar* under his own name but as an apprentice and not a seaman.

But other records of his family or early years in Frome have not been so easily traced and therefore he remains one of the most intriguing mysteries of the whole case. At the end of the day, it seems more than likely that when he made his confession, Joseph Seer believed himself to be guilty and so he must remain a strong possibility.

Scenario C: Henry Hillier

If it was not Joseph Seer, or any of the 'Frome Three', the murderer was obviously someone else entirely: but who exactly? This returns to the 'Wearside Jack' phenomenon, whereby, the suspect might well have been obvious to anyone not blinded by the Sparrow scenario – as let's not forget, in the case of the 'Yorkshire Ripper', police had Peter Sutcliffe in front of them for questioning on several separate occasions; each time letting him go. Was the murderer one of those brought up before the local magistrates in the days following the murder but discharged? Or was their name told to Sergeant Smith, during his investigation, but he dismissed it. We shall never know.

This brings us to a possible suspect who, although not mentioned in the book by name thus far, his shadow has laid across it all the way through. In 1850, Henry Hillier (not to be confused with his namesake, who gave evidence at the trial) was charged with the brutal murder of 17-year-old Thomas George, in the village of Nunney. The young man's throat had been severely and brutally cut. During the trial, it transpired that Hillier used to borrow his sister's smock-coat and, in her own words, 'bring it back dirty'. She intimated this is what had happened the day after Thomas George was slain. Despite strong evidence – although let down by the delayed post-mortem – he was acquitted.

At the time of the Sarah Watts murder, Hillier lived at Trudoxhill Street in Nunney. Perhaps he had heard the rumours of the large amount of money supposed to have been kept at Battle Farm and on going there to retrieve it was disturbed by, or merely stumbled upon, Sarah, and took an opportunity for sexual gratification that had come his way; dispatching her afterwards in the same cold-blooded manner he had done to George. To distract attention away from himself, he enlisted several of his relations or acquaintances, including the other Henry Hiller and Robert Hilliar – who lived next door to Hurd – to concoct their testimony not only to collect the reward, to compensate for the fact there had been no money at the farm, but also to rid the town for good of Maggs, Sparrow, and Hurd – three men Hillier despised with a vengeance.

Scenario D: The Maggs-Sparrow Gang and – everyone else!

The murders committed by Jack the Ripper in Whitechapel are some of the great unsolved crimes in the annals of criminal history. Countless names have been put forward as suspects and numerous books published, with many more to come. It is a profitable and expanding industry, but if all these 'ripperologists' could be assembled in one place and the Ripper's identity revealed without the slightest doubt, it is quite possible that they would all respond with one word: '*WHO!!?*'

It is therefore possible that the rape and murder of Sarah Watts was committed by an opportunist travelling through the area, who saw a lone girl and seized his chance to rape and rob, and whose name will always remain unknown (although the abandonment of the clothes is always a sticking point). It is known that other men were considered before Smith's investigations – including uncles of both Joseph Seer and Sarah Watts herself, for example – who were interviewed but released. There are also the men associated with Maggs, Sparrow, and Hurd, on that day – it is possible one of these could have perpetrated the murder?

Charles Whimpey

Charles Whimpey was described in the 1841 census as living in Milk Street, Frome, the son of Edward, a weaver, and his wife, Elisabeth. Charles was 16 at the time and also a weaver. His first conviction was in May 1849, when he was sentenced to two months for trespassing in search of game; while in the spring 1851 he received a four-month sentence with hard labour, for theft and was released not long before the murder. The year after this, Whimpey was committed for trial and described as a well-known thief and confederate of Hurd, Maggs, and Sparrow. The burglary, it emerged, took place the previous May, and Whimpey had been trying to sell the cloth at the Young Fox pub in Bath without success. In his defence he claimed he had bought the item from a hawker for a watch and five shillings. He was found guilty and received a sentence of twelve-months hard labour in Shepton; quite possibly being incarcerated there at the same time as the 'Frome Three'. In 1853, he was convicted of assault and awarded two months hard labour, and two years after that, in 1855, he was acquitted of stealing a watch from the person. In 1863 he was fined 5s plus costs, or another three months, for hunting game with dogs at Nunney, and a year later he was caught with others doing the same thing. This time, as he had so much previous form, he was fined 40s and was able to pay the money, so he must have had a good year! The final mention of him comes in August 1865 when he is fined 16s 6d for assaulting a man in the Bird in Hand beer house in Frome.

So with a number of convictions for assault, he was certainly no stranger to violence – as, no doubt, were most criminals at the time – but would he dare to escalate it to rape and murder?

William Sargeant

According to the 1841 census Sargeant was aged 35 and living at Blatchbridge with wife Maria, 33, and son Thomas, 15. He was arrested in January 1844 for being involved with a fight between Francis Daniell and Ferdinand Candy, in which Candy died. He was charged with manslaughter but as he was only one of the 'seconds' and had already served three months, his sentence was one of fourteen days, two of them in solitary confinement. In the description book at Wilton gaol he is described as aged 38, married, 5ft 11½ins, with a sallow complexion, hazel eyes, brown hair, and scars over his right eye and on his upper lip.

Convicted with George Browning, a labourer, of assaulting 'several constables' while attempting to rescue Robert Hurd at the Unicorn in March 1850, they were both given eighteen months in Shepton Mallet gaol. Sargeant was released in June 1851 and so was in the gaol at the time of the census of 1851, aged 46. He was described in the prison census as an 'edge tool maker', which was quite a skilled job.

He was, of course, arrested in connection with the Sarah Watts murder in 1851, on seemingly little or no evidence at all, and stood in the dock with the 'Frome Three' for their final two appearances in front of the magistrates' court. He was then released. Nothing else has been discovered about him except that he was said to live in Butts Square at the time of his arrest. Again, convictions for assault are proof of a violent man, but a rapist and murderer, as well?

Daniel Lusty

Another member of the Maggs-Sparrow gang, Lusty first appeared in the papers at the age of 23 when he was fined £5 for assaulting

William Harrold of Frome. He was another well-known associate of Maggs and it is assumed that he is the one being referred to when Maggs announces that there are more skeleton keys hidden away in Frome. All the rest of his convictions were for theft.

The Final Word

Was it one of those mentioned by name in scenarios A–D, or was it, after all, an anonymous person whose name has been lost in time, never to be revealed? The only problem with the latter solution, as was pointed out earlier, is the clothes. It is a fact they were taken from the farm on the day of the murder, and another fact they were recovered on the day of the second inquest; someone therefore must have taken them from the one place and placed them in the other. Was this the same person, or the murderer and an associate? The fact that the location is so near to Sargeant's house is compelling, if not conclusive, but at the end of the day is just one mystery of several in this case.

We will leave it to you, the reader, to draw your own conclusions as to who carried out the awful killing of Sarah Watts, but would be interested to receive them, or information on any aspect of the case, at the following email address: davidlassman@davidlassman.com.

A Note on Main Sources

The authors were saved much time and effort, in the initial stages of researching this book, through the pioneering endeavour of Lyndon Thomas, whose pamphlet *The Murder of Sarah Watts. West Woodlands 1851* was self-published in 2007 and a copy donated to the Frome Library (where it was 'discovered' by the authors). We are also most grateful to Lyndon for permission to publish two maps from this publication: 'Battle Farm', showing the area on the Ordnance survey map of 1882, and the more general one showing the area of Frome and Woodlands. Finally, we thank him for reading the book in manuscript form and for writing the foreword.

The main source of information on the Watts case comes from contemporary newspapers, both local and national. For prison and certain court records, along with census returns, the Ancestry and Find My Past websites were invaluable, as was Fromesearch regarding baptisms.

Part One: (24 September 1851 – 6 October 1851)

The first report of the murder appeared in the *Bristol Mercury*, on Saturday 27 September 1851, three days after the event in which it was 'surmised that the murderer first committed a capital felony upon her' before killing her with a blow from a stick. The story was picked up two days later by *The Times*, on 29 September 1851, which gave further details and was followed by a good selection of the regional press.

Detailed reports of the inquest and the first arrests are contained in: the *Bath & County Gazette*, 1 October 1851; the *Bath Chronicle*, 2 October 1851; *Bristol Mercury*, 4 October 1851; and *Sherborne Mercury*, 7 October 1851.

The early days of the Metropolitan Detective Branch and Henry Smith's early police career came from four main sources: *The First Detectives* by Belton Cobb, *The Rise of Scotland Yard* by Douglas G. Browne, and *Dreadful Deeds and Awful Murders: Scotland Yard's First Detectives 1829-1878* by Joan Lock, and the Old Bailey online website. A report of the expenses incurred by the use of a London detective appeared in the *Bristol Mercury* (1 January 1852) and the presentation of a watch in the *Salisbury & Winchester Gazette* (24 January 1852)

The early 'careers' of the three suspects – Maggs, Sparrow, and Hurd, – came from various newspapers reports, along with the information from Ancestry and Find My Past Websites.

Part Two (7 October 1851 – 4 April 1852)

The events in the magistrates' court were reported by both the local and national press. The original transcripts no longer survive and the account in the book has been compiled by combining the reports from:

Bath Chronicle: 16 October; 23 October; 30 October; 6 November 1851

Bristol Times: 18 October; 25 October 1851

Sherborne Mercury: 21 October; 28 October; 11 November 1851

Taunton Courier: 22 October; 5 November 1851

Dorset Chronicle: 23 October 1851

Wells Journal: 25 October; 1 November 1851

Part Three: (5 April 1852 – 7 April 1852)

Again there was large coverage in the press of the assize trial, which took place in April 1852. The most useful articles, from which the account in the book was compiled, were:

Bath Chronicle: 8 April 1852

The Times: 9 April 1852

Morning Chronicle: 9 April 1852

Somerset County Gazette: 10 April 1852

Bristol Mercury: 10 April; 17 April 1852

Sherborne Mercury: 12 April 1852

Taunton Courier: 14 April 1852

Police News: 13 April 1889 (includes the article 'Unavenged Murders', which has a review of the case plus the – somewhat bizarre – illustration of Sarah's body being discovered by her parents and which is reproduced within this book.)

Part Four: (8 April 1852 – 16 September 1861)

The careers of the Maggs-Sparrow gang, along with that of the Maggs family, both before and after the Sarah Watts murder trial, seemed to be many and varied; most of the reports coming from various newspapers and periodicals.

Information on various prisons was obtained through the Ancestry and Find My Past Websites. More general background material is listed in the bibliography, although a special mention must be made of Kellow Chesney's *Victorian Underworld*, which remains a classic.

The material on the railway coming to Frome and then beyond, through Battle Farm, came largely from one source: *The Story of the Westbury to Weymouth Line* by Derek Phillips.

Part Five: (16 September 1861 – 20 October 1861)

The main source for this section was the various editions of the *Frome Times* dated 18 September 1861 through to 23 October 1861; also issues of the *Somerset & Wilts Journal* for the same period (mid-September to the end of October 1861).

Selected Bibliography

Crime & Punishment

Browne, Douglas G. *The Rise of Scotland Yard*, Greenwood Press, 1977

Callow, Edward. *Five Years Penal Servitude By One Who Has Endured It*, Bentley, 1878

Chesney, Kellow. *The Victorian Underworld*, Pelican, 1972

Cobb, Belton. *The First Detectives*, Faber & Faber, 1957

Duncan, Major Francis. *The English in Spain*, John Murray, 1877

Higgs, Michelle. *Prison life in Victorian England*, Tempus, 2007

Lock, Joan. *Dreadful Deeds and Awful Murders: Scotland Yard's First Detectives 1829-1878*, Barn Owl Books, 1990

Meyhew & Binney. *The Criminal Prisons of London*, Griffin Bohn & Co., 1862

Sanger, George. *Seventy Years a Showman*, JM Dent & Co., 1926

Summerscale, Kate. *The Suspicions of Mr Whicher*, Bloomsbury, 2008

Swift & Eliot. *The Lost Pubs of Bath*, Akeman Press, 2005

Thomas, Donald. *The Victorian Underworld*, Murray, 1998

Thomas, Lyndon. *The Murder of Sarah Watts, West Woodlands 1851*, booklet, 2007 Frome Library

Histories of Frome

Belham, Peter. *The Making of Frome*, FSLS, 1985

Davis, Mick & Pitt. Valerie *The Historic Inns of Frome*, Akeman Press, 2015

Gill, Derek. *Experiences of a 19th Century Gentleman*, FSLS, 2003

Goodall, Rodney. *The Buildings of Frome*, FSLS, 1985
The Industries of Frome, FSLS, 2009

McGarvie, M. *The King's Peace*, FSLS, 1997
The Book of Frome, FSLS, 2013
Frome Place Names, FSLS, 1983
Crime & Punishment in Regency Frome, FSLS,1984

Maps

Dixon & Maitland, 1838 map of Frome. CD available from Frome Society for Local Study

Ordnance Survey map of Frome 1886. Paper or CD copies available at Frome Museum

Modern town maps are no longer obtainable on paper but can be down loaded from the Mendip District Council site: maps.mendip.gov.uk

Newspapers

Bath Chronicle
Bristol Mercury
Frome Times
Sherborne Mercury
Somerset & Wilts Journal
Somerset County Gazette
Taunton Courier
The Times

Webliography & Contacts

Ancestry: subscription service for census and searching for individuals
   search.ancestry.co.uk
Find my Past: subscription service like Ancestry but with extensive
   newspaper archive **search.findmypast.co.uk**
Frome and District baptisms, marriages and burials **fromeresearch.
   org.uk**
Central Criminal Court (Old Bailey) searchable database of cases
   oldbaileyonline.org
Bath & District Births, Marriages and Deaths, **bathbmd.org.uk**
Lyndon Thomas, **sarahwatts.blogspot.co.uk**
Frome Museum, **1 North Parade, Frome, Somerset BA11 1AT
   fromemuseum.wordpress.com**
Frome Society for Local Study: **fromesociety.wordpress.com**
Frome Library, Justice Lane, Frome, Somerset, BA11 1BE
The Times archive site: http://gale.cengage.co.uk/times.aspx/
Somerset Record Office. Brunel Way, Norton Fitzwarren, Taunton,
   TA2 6SF **somersetarchives@swheritage.org.uk**

Index